DAILY LIFE SERIES

DAILY LIFE IN CARTHAGE

GILBERT AND COLETTE CHARLES-PICARD

DAILY LIFE
IN CARTHAGE

at the time of Hannibal

TRANSLATED FROM THE FRENCH
BY A. E. FOSTER

New York
THE MACMILLAN COMPANY

CONTENTS

ILLUSTRATIONS

MAPS

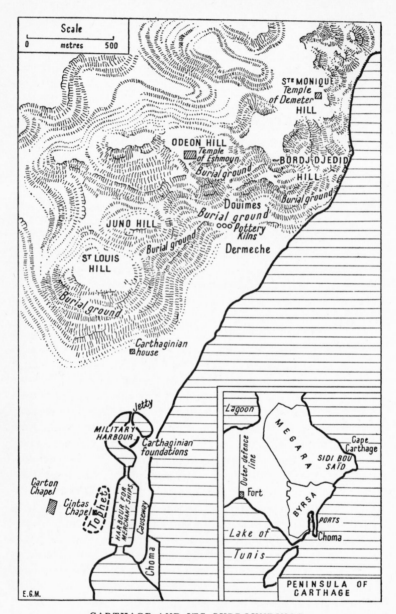

CARTHAGE AND ITS SURROUNDINGS

INTRODUCTION

FLAUBERT gave the title *Salammbô* to the final version of his Carthaginian novel, which was inspired by the excitement and enthusiasm he felt on reading Michelet's account of the War of the Mercenaries. The glamour of Flaubert's romantic style concealed the poverty of the sources on which it was based. When Flaubert, true to his principles of realism, tried to collect precise documentary evidence, he found a void so complete that he almost gave up the undertaking. The skill with which he circumvented this, by drawing generously on Biblical and classical literature, and especially by avoiding all precise details in writing about familiar objects and circumstances, is the least obvious, but by no means the least praiseworthy quality of his masterpiece.

A century has passed since Flaubert wrote *Salammbô*. Do we possess today the documentation which was not available to Flaubert? No further written evidence has been found, and there is little hope that one day the soil of Tunisia will ever yield the equivalent of the clay tablets of Ugarit or the Dead Sea Scrolls. We have Punic inscriptions in abundance, but they are despairingly barren as a source of information. Light is shed on Carthaginian civilization only by foreign writers who were solely interested in the most extraordinary details; it will therefore probably remain in that kind of 'no-man's-land', which separates the realm of the historian who can enter into direct communication with the men of the past by means of written documents, from that of the pre-historian, who can interrogate only things.

Even then, we could easily resign ourselves to this situation if archaeology were able to reconstruct, with some semblance of completeness, the setting in which the Western Phoenicians lived their lives. If we were deprived of all Latin literature and reduced to no other evidence of Roman civilization than the ruins of Pompeii, how well we could reconstruct the daily life of one of Nero's or Vespasian's subjects, from the variety of its buildings and the richness of its decorative art! Since the discovery of the tumulus of Mari, we are much better informed about the customs of the inhabitants of Upper Mesopotamia in the time of King Zimrilim, the enemy of Hammurati, than we are about the contemporaries of Hannibal.

In 1857, the very year in which Flaubert was writing *Salammbô*, Beulé undertook the first systematic excavations in Carthage. He expected to find important remains of the chief Carthaginian buildings which are known to us through texts, namely, the harbour works, the ramparts, the palaces, and the temples. These hopes were soon shattered. With very few exceptions, all the ruins which were revealed then, as well as subsequently, in the Carthaginian peninsula, belonged to the Roman city built there one hundred years after the destruction of Dido's city. Some years after Beulé's attempts, a not too scrupulous architect named Daux published plans of Carthaginian buildings. They were the product solely of his imagination.

Some slight compensation was afforded to archaeologists by the discovery of the Carthaginian burial-grounds on April 7, 1878. It was made by Father Delattre of the Society of White Fathers in Carthage. He had been installed by Cardinal Lavigerie two years before as Priest-in-Charge of the Chapel dedicated to Saint Louis by Louis-Philippe, and for half a century he carried on a tireless exploration of ancient Carthage, paying particular attention to Punic and Christian remains. The fruits of his labours, and of those of two of his successors, Father Lapeyre and Father Féron, are preserved in the Museum of the White Fathers, on the St Louis Hill.

For forty years tombs remained the only material link between Punic Carthage and modern knowledge.

Father Delattre and the Directors of Antiquities, P. Gauckler and then A. Merlin, soon learned to distinguish the surface indications which revealed the presence of a Punic grave. This was often the surface opening of a deep shaft, filled with sand, at the bottom of which, often several yards down, was a funerary chamber. To detect and excavate such a site obviously demanded a certain flair and considerable physical qualifications. Teams of special excavators were formed from the townsfolk of Carthage, many of whom took part in these excavations during the whole of their lifetime. Once the shaft had been cleared the massive stone slab closing the entrance had to be pulled away, revealing the remains of the corpse lying among its jars and other funerary possessions. The most precious articles, like jewels and amulets, were generally found buried in the sand of the tomb. This sand has to be sifted and so a sieve has become an indispensable item of the archaeologist's equipment.

The opening of a Punic tomb is always an exciting moment. Father Delattre and others often made it into a fashionable social occasion, but the archaeologist learns to be chary of inviting too many notable personalities, for very often, when the stone slab is lowered, the funerary chamber is found to be empty, ravaged by earlier searchers, or by Roman builders. In his *De Resurrectione Carnis*, the Christian writer Tertullian describes the opening of Punic tombs at which he had been present, when the Odeon of Carthage was built in the first years of the third century A.D. Some of the corpses still had their hair, and the holy man used this as evidence of the indestructibility of the body, which would rise again at the Resurrection. We ourselves have several times witnessed the macabre spectacle of hair still adhering to a fleshless skull.

However, even the richest Carthaginian tombs never contain the treasures found in Egyptian or Mesopotamian burial-chambers, or even in more modest tombs in Italy or Gaul. The Carthaginian pottery is crude, but sometimes a fine Greek vase is found with it. The terracotta statuettes have none of the grace of the Tanagras. The jewellery is unambitious. An exceptional stroke of luck may reveal a terracotta mask representing the goddess Kore, or a grimacing demon. As for the four great marble sarcophagi with carved statues on their lids, which Father Delattre recovered from shafts in Sainte-Monique, they have remained the only specimens of their kind after fifty years of searching, and will probably always remain so.

In 1921, a Tunisian was seen to be carrying a strange stone; it was a kind of obelisk in grey limestone, over a yard high, decorated on its front face with an engraved design which represented a man dressed in a transparent robe and carrying a child in his arms. This kind of monument had been found before. As early as 1874, a diplomat named Sainte-Marie, working for the

Académie des Inscriptions et Belles-Lettres, had collected more than two thousand stelae. Most of them had some form of crude decoration and dedicatory inscription to the great Carthaginian gods Tanit and Baal Hammon. But the stone found in 1921 put archaeologists on the track of one of the richest archaeological finds in Carthage. Following the indications given by the men who had found it, a complete sanctuary, in which were crowded thousands of stelae, was uncovered some twenty feet below the present surface of the soil. With each stele was a vase containing charred bones. These were carefully examined and analysed by doctors, and nearly all proved to be the remains of very young children. The sanctuary which had been discovered was one in which the monstrous *autos-da-fé* of new-born babies took place, as described by Diodorus of Sicily in a well-known text, which Flaubert faithfully followed in his chapter entitled 'Moloch'.

The first excavations were carried out by the owners of the site, under the supervision of the Director of Antiquities. The sanctuary was given the name of *tophet*, from the name given in the Bible to the sanctuary of Ben Hinnóm, near Jerusalem, which was used for similar sacrifices before it was destroyed by King Josiah. The site was subsequently explored, in rather unusual circumstances, by a Franco-American team in which the most reputed scholars of the two worlds were grouped under a leader who was a kind of impresario, with a gift for publicity which was not always too mindful of historical accuracy. Father Lapeyre continued the investigations in another sector. We ourselves were able to continue them in 1945, and then to entrust them to our collaborator P. Cintas, whose sagacity enabled him to discover, on the very beach trodden by Dido's companions, the most ancient historical monument yet found in North Africa. A description of this will be given later.

The uncovering of the *tophet* proved that the destruction of Carthage by the Romans had not been so thorough that, with one or two exceptions, even the tombs had been destroyed. Already in 1916 Dr L. Carton had investigated a small temple containing ritual articles. A few years later A. Merlin located the remains of a small private chapel in the extreme north of the town. But the most important architectural find of remains of the original Carthage was made quite recently on the St Louis

Hill. A description will be given later of this quarter of the Punic city, which was quite well preserved beneath the Roman buildings later erected upon it.

Traces of the Carthaginian fortifications, for which archaeologists had searched in vain for generations, were finally found in 1949 by General R. Duval, who recently died a premature death while serving as Senior Commander of the troops in Morocco.

To these investigations carried out in Carthage itself must be added those concerned with Punic sites spaced out along the coast and even in the interior of North Africa. A systematic survey was undertaken over a period of about ten years by P. Cintas. In 1947, he was requested by the Director of Antiquities in Algeria, the late L. Leschi, to see whether Punic remains could be found on the site of Tipasa, some forty-five miles west of Algiers. There was not much evidence that the Carthaginians had occupied this site—just a few stelae of the Roman period, bearing the emblem of Tanit, and some Punic-style vaults in a Christian cemetery. Working on observations he had previously made about the location of cemeteries in Punic towns, Cintas was able to excavate, after forty days' work, six tombs which were certainly earlier than the second century B.C. They had been completely hidden by a natural covering of soil and some were covered by a sandstone layer which was obviously not a recent deposit, since Punic articles were found embedded in it.

While the field of research was being extended and discoveries were becoming more and more numerous, stricter methods of excavation were being devised and more exact and broad conclusions were justified. The archaeologist, the 'detective of the past', to use a phrase of Agatha Christie, the wife of the famous English Assyrian scholar Mallowan, must never neglect even the minutest piece of evidence. An insignificant potsherd may provide chronological evidence of the first importance, but half its value may be lost if the most precise indications of the exact spot where it lies are not made. Even the tricks of nature have to be discounted. L. Poinssot, our predecessor as Director of Antiquities in Tunisia, once found an eighteenth-century Russian *kopeck* in a Roman tomb in Dougga! In some mysterious way it had come into the possession of a shepherd who had then lost it. A field-rat which lived in the tomb had then found it and dragged it home with him! Such happenings are well known to experienced archaeologists, and serve to put us on our guard against over-reliance on depth position alone as a means of dating.

We should beware of the modern tendency to praise archaeology as an exact science, and to place it higher than history, on the grounds that the latter is too often little more than fiction. Nobody can deny the interest and the value of physical methods of dating ancient articles. One of these, based on the residual radio-activity of carbon 14, is commonly employed in American laboratories. By this means, organic substances may be dated— within a few centuries. Another method, perfected by P. Thellier, Professor of Terrestrial Physics at the Sorbonne, in collaboration with P. Cintas, is based on the curious property of pottery to fix the earth's magnetic field at the time and place it was fired. These methods have a long way to go before they can compete with the accuracy of results obtained by specialists, who by careful analysis of the style of Greek vases, may be able to date a vase to within twelve years. But they can nevertheless be very helpful in classifying the crude Carthaginian or Libyan pottery which was made for centuries to the same pattern and which is practically devoid of any decoration that could help to date it.

Nor should it be forgotten that the historian of antiquity is interested in inanimate objects, solely in order to learn more about the men who used them. The psychology of the ancients was very different from our own, and we can only hope to understand it by means of written documents, and to some extent by the style of ornamentation on remains. Comparisons with still extant primitive societies can also cast some light, but can also be a dangerous source of error.

It will have been noticed that many of the discoveries we have briefly referred to above, have been made within the last ten years or so. This explains, and to some extent justifies, our attempt to present a fresh picture of daily life in Carthage without reproducing in all respects the masterly synthesis published by Stéphane Gsell in 1920. Nobody could claim to know or interpret the literary evidence better than that master of African history, but the more recent monuments he did not know of, particularly the stelae of the *tophet*, enable us to fill some of the gaps in his picture of Carthaginian civilization. The task we are about to undertake here of gathering together the results of archaeological investigation, and comparing them with documentary evidence, illuminating the one by means of the other, is not unlike that of L. Bréchot, for twenty years Curator of the Bardo Museum, and other expert restorers; by long and patient labour they fit together the myriad pieces of a shattered vase or of a broken statue. Like them, too, we shall often have to fill in missing pieces by informed conjecture, and we can only hope that this will not be too far removed from reality.

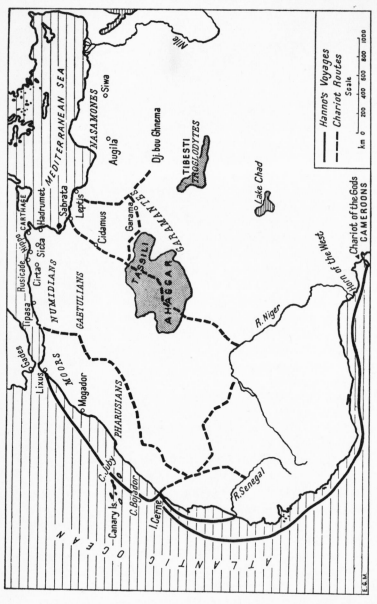

THE GREAT EXPEDITIONS

CHAPTER I

AN OUTLINE HISTORY OF CARTHAGE

CARTHAGE was founded in 814 B.C. by Dido or Elissa, sister of Pygmalion, King of Tyre.[1]

Tyre was at that time the most powerful city of the Phoenicians. This Semitic people, closely related to the Hebrews, came from the Negeb[2] and settled on the Lebanese coast at the beginning of the third millennium. Within a very short time they turned themselves into a sea-faring nation, but for fifteen hundred years their ships rarely ventured beyond Cyprus, or Egypt or the southern shores of Asia Minor. Byblos, the first of their cities,[3] grew prosperous on its trade with the kingdom of the Pharaohs. To the north, opposite Cyprus, in Ugarit (Ras Shamra), a brilliant civilization developed, strongly influenced by Aegean culture;[4] for the early Phoenicians had as their tutors the islanders who were the predecessors of the Greeks in the Aegean archipelago, and especially those in Crete—for the Eastern Mediterranean was dominated by Minoan ships until Cnossos fell to the Achaean invaders in the fourteenth century. Only then did the mariners of Sidon, and later of Tyre, venture to sail through Greek waters to brave the perilous routes across the open sea towards the West.

As will be seen later, pressing economic circumstances finally emboldened the Tyrians to take one prodigious leap to the far end of the Mediterranean and to reach the ocean gateway which, for the ancients, marked the limits of the habitable earth. It was probably in the twelfth century B.C. that direct relations were established between the Levant and Tarshish, or Tartessus, in Andalusia, which by virtue of its mines had become the most important industrial centre of the Western World.

It then became necessary to set up intermediate stations along this two-thousand-mile route. According to Pliny, the foundation of Utica, the first Phoenician colony in Africa, dates from the year 1100 B.C. Tyre was then reaching the height of its power, as was also Israel. The friendly alliance between Hiram and

Solomon (*c.* 970–935 B.C.) is typical of the flourishing development of the small Syrian States which found themselves temporarily freed from the oppression of the Mesopotamian and Egyptian giants.

But from the beginning of the ninth century B.C. the wealth accumulating in the great port of Tyre through its Mediterranean and Red Sea trade, attracted the attention of that most redoubtable of marauding tribes, the Assyrians. Threatened, held to ransom, and besieged, Tyre sought to remove to the safety of a new capital (for such is the meaning of the words Kart Hadasht, the origin of the word Carthage). The first move was to Cyprus and then, very shortly afterwards, as far away as possible, to a semi-desert African land. Myths explaining the origin of the chief cults of the young city were subsequently adapted by the Greeks and Romans and transformed by them into the touching legend of Dido.

The first two centuries of the history of Carthage are veiled in obscurity. No chronicle has come down to us and such remains as have been discovered by archaeologists on the site of Dido's city date from almost a hundred years after its foundation.

No doubt its beginnings were difficult and humble: in the ninth century B.C. and the first half of the seventh, the power of Tyre, which was ceaselessly harried by Sargon, Sennacherib, and Esarhaddon, declined long before the colony in Africa had grown strong enough to provide relief. The Greeks took advantage of this eclipse and from 750 to 500 B.C., against little opposition, they drove out the Phoenicians and poured thousands of their own emigrants into Eastern Sicily, into the south of Italy, into Southern Provence and even into Andalusia and Cyrenaica, thus completely encircling the Carthaginian territory.

The Carthaginians, however, knew that they must stand alone. They had already been reinforced on several occasions by refugees from the besieged metropolis of Tyre and now rallied all the colonists driven from Lixus and Gades, beyond the Pillars of Hercules, to Malta, by way of Sardinia and Western Sicily, in organized resistance to the common enemy.

In return for the protection which the city of Carthage offered against the Greeks and the African barbarians, the new colonists were required to renounce in her favour all claims to political or economic independence. In this way an empire was built up with a rigidly centralized economic system which concentrated within the African port all the wealth of the West and especially of the silver- and tin-mines of Tartessus. Herodotus, in the fifth century, collecting traditions going back with few gaps as far as 650 B.C., was able to show a rich and powerful Carthage which had already attained adult status. Archaeologists have supported the evidence of history by unearthing well-built tombs whose abundant contents came mostly from Greece, Egypt, and Etruria. But if the Carthaginians made their purchases in many different places, their indigenous art was at this time predominantly inspired by that of Egypt. This was in keeping with the national tradition. Dating from the beginning of the third millennium, the close relations between Byblos and the kingdom of the Pharaohs led the Phoenicians to adopt many customs and practices originating in the Nile valley. Just how great this dependence was in the second and third millennia is shown by the excavations made by Montet and Dunand at Byblos and by Schaeffer at Ugarit. The only competing influence was that of the Mesopotamian and Aegean cultures. This reached Carthage by way of Hellenic influences which by the sixth century were fairly extensive, in spite of the bitter conflicts between the Greeks and the Carthaginians.

Historical tradition dedicates this period to the memory of the kings of Carthage, warrior-kings who led their armies against Sicily. We do not know how they were chosen, but their authority, if not absolute, was at least much more real than that of the magistrates in the succeeding period.

The struggle went on all through the sixth century. Carthage formed an alliance with Etruscans against the Greeks. She also profited from the unification of Asia under the Persians, though this meant accepting the theoretical sovereignty of the Great King. With such backing she was able to win two great victories: in 525 the destruction of the Phocaean colony in Corsica and in 510 the expulsion of the Spartan prince, Dorieus, from Tripolitania. It was probably at about this time, too, that the Greeks found their way barred to Tartessus, where they had been competing with Phoenician traders since 630 B.C. Henceforth Carthage was, and remained, the Queen of the Western Seas. In competition with her sister Tyrian colonies whom she now treated with brutal authority, she set up her own trading-posts. Already in the seventh century her colonists had occupied Ibiza in the Balearic archipelago. In the sixth century towns took the place of these trading-posts which were spread along the coast of Africa at frequent intervals (on an average of roughly twenty miles) to meet the demands of coastal traffic. Archaeologists have found traces of this colonization at Tipasa in Algeria, at Hadrumetum (Sousse) in Byzacium and at Leptis on the Gulf of Sidra.

These efforts prepared the way for a decisive offensive. It seems certain that an agreement was arrived at with the Persians to destroy the Greeks simultaneously in the East and in the West. This undertaking met failure in 480 at Salamis and at Himera in Sicily.

The defeat at Himera is perhaps the most important date in the history of Carthage. Beaten, and cut off from Asia by the Athenian fleet which henceforth dominated the Eastern Mediterranean, Carthage was obliged to resort to desperate measures. A political revolution overthrew the Mago dynasty and placed at the helm the aristocracy which for two centuries, by means of the Court of a Hundred Magistrates, exercised a dubious tyranny over citizens and subjects. The importation of manufactured articles was forbidden and austerity was imposed on all. The cult was reformed and pride of place in the Carthaginian Pantheon was given to Tanit, the divine personification of Carthage as Pallas was of Athens. Finally, every effort was made to increase the supply of food and metals by naval and military expeditions. Up till this time the city had only a small outer suburb which was threatened by the Libyans, who demanded tribute. The armies of Carthage now conquered territory which at its greatest embraced most of Tunisia and which was systematically developed. Hanno's great expeditions against the coasts of Morocco and Senegal, and those of Himilco in the Atlantic, tightened her grip on the gold and tin trade.

After a long period of withdrawal the Punic government felt strong enough in 409 B.C. to attempt to take advantage of the downfall of Athenian supremacy following an unsuccessful attempt to conquer Sicily. A century of savage warfare followed with scarcely a break. The Carthaginian armies devastated the Greek settlements in Southern Sicily, but the indomitable resistance of

Dionysius of Syracuse saved Greek influence in the island from extinction. At the end of the fourth century, Agathocles, one of his successors, even succeeded in leading a counter-offensive into Africa itself, and at one moment the destruction of Carthage seemed imminent.

This long and ferocious duel, however, did not prevent Carthage from accepting, from the beginning of the fourth century, the civilization of the very Greeks against whom she was at war. The year 396 B.C., from which dates the introduction of the cult of Demeter and of Persephone, the Greek goddesses of corn and of the dead, marks a vital turning-point in its cultural history.

Moreover, the creation by Alexander, between 334 and 323 B.C., of a great empire which dominated the Eastern World forced the Phoenicians to make a radical change in their policy. To remain isolated and hostile would have meant, in the not far distant future, complete political and economic ruin. Agathocles' expedition, in which Macedonian mercenaries took part, brought home to them their danger. The Carthaginian government therefore resigned itself to a *rapprochement* with the Hellenistic empire and especially with the Lagos monarchy in Egypt. The Carthaginian merchants welcomed this opportune source of profit at a time when their hold over Spain and the Far West was weakening.

Further, the rapid decline of Greater Greece and Etruria allowed Carthage to maintain its position as the leading Western power. This was soon disputed by Rome, with whom she had preserved good relations so long as the Latin city had remained strictly agricultural and landbound. But in the second half of the fourth century and the first third of the third, Rome had conquered by force of arms the great industrial centre of Campania and the Greek ports in Southern Italy. These fresh acquisitions compelled Rome, almost against her will, to intervene in Sicily at the very time when Carthage was gaining complete control of the island. The result was the First Punic War (263–241 B.C.), which, although Regulus failed to emulate the exploit of Agathocles, ended in disaster for Carthage. The loss of Sicily was less serious than the destruction of the fleet and financial ruin.

Far graver, however, was the social crisis which followed

defeat: the mercenaries revolted and stirred up the poverty-stricken peasants of Libya, thus provoking the 'truceless war' which provided Flaubert with the subject of *Salammbô*.[5] The failure of the régime was complete in every sphere.

Carthage was saved by a fresh revolution headed by Hamilcar Barca. This inspired leader realized that the only hope of salvation was to reconquer the mineral wealth of the West. But the old Punic colonial methods, which consisted in gaining economic control of a country by occupying a few ports, were no longer adequate. Following the example of Alexander, Hamilcar created a military empire in Spain, with himself as absolute ruler (228–219 B.C.). After his death, Hasdrubal and Hannibal conquered the entire peninsula as far as the River Ebro. Carthage, where the Barcid faction sought the support of the democratic party, seemed bound, under their leadership, to become the capital of a Western empire whose civilization and organization would have resembled closely those of the Hellenic kingdoms. Rome only awoke to her danger when the Greeks in Marseilles and Ampurias found the Punic invaders at their gates. Hannibal then conceived the two-fold plan of crushing the enemy of Carthage beneath the vast manpower of the Celtic lands, which he was confident he could control; and of splitting the Confederation of Italian States from the Latin empire. He then planned to incorporate them into the Punic empire (218 B.C.). He was partially successful in his first objective, but failed completely in the second, in spite of the victories of Lake Trasimene and Cannae (217–216 B.C.). Two Greek sovereigns, Philip V of Macedonia and Hierod of Syracuse, joined with Carthage, but without committing themselves very deeply in the struggle. Seeing that her enemies' forces were widely dispersed, Rome seized the initiative. While Hannibal was pinned down in Italy, Scipio conquered Spain (210–206 B.C.).

Scipio defeated Carthage by her own methods—by harnessing the nascent patriotism of the Libyans (205 B.C.). Several of the Tell tribes: Moors from Morocco, Massaesylians from Constantina, and Massylians from the Tell Atlas—the last two united under the name of Numidians—had formed small kingdoms in the fourth century but were kept in subjection by the Carthaginians. Scipio made use of the ambition and talent of one of these semi-barbarian princes, Masinissa, whose kingdom was the strategic key to the whole of Tunisia. The fate of the Mediterranean world thus turned on the outcome of the rivalry between Masinissa and Syphax. Hannibal and Scipio, as their respective champions, met in battle under the walls of the Massylian capital, Zama, in 202 B.C. When Carthage was defeated, she lay at the mercy of Rome. The last half-century of her existence was a long-drawn-out death-agony. Unable to rise again by her own strength, she might, however, by joining forces under Masinissa, have become the capital of a united African kingdom powerful enough to cause anxiety in Rome. But Rome thought it best to destroy Carthage, though this was not accomplished easily. Her territory became a Roman province, in which Punic civilization survived under the indifferent and greedy proconsuls of the Republic. In addition refugees planted the seeds of Phoenician culture in the Numidian kingdoms. When the beneficent rule of the emperors ended the oppression of the Senate, the descendants of Carthage were given the opportunity of playing their part in the spectacular rise of Roman Africa, keeping their own language and religion, until the great upheaval which in the course of the fourth and fifth centuries A.D. was to change the face of the world.

REFERENCES

NOTE. *The contractions BAC, CRAI, HAAN, MAO and MC are explained on p. 256.*

1. Cf. Chap. I, n. 2.
2. According to R. Dussaud, *Les Découvertes de Ras Shamra*, pp. 73 sqq. His view has been contested by other scholars. Cf. G. Contenau, MAO, IV, pp. 1791–2.
3. The most important excavations in Byblos have been carried out by the French archaeologists P. Montet and M. Dunand. Published results are summarized in G. Contenau, *op. cit.*
4. The excavation of Ras Shamra was begun in 1929 and continued until 1939. It has been resumed in recent years, under the direction of C. Schaeffer, yielding the most important discoveries yet made on a Phoenician site. Above two Neolithic layers, Phoenician influence begins to show itself towards the end of the third millennium. After being destroyed by an earthquake in the nineteenth century B.C., the town reached the height of its prosperity in the second millennium. To this period belong the

Temples of Dagon and of Baal, a number of very comfortable private houses, and a palace. A whole library of terracotta tablets has been found: they are inscribed with religious poems in proto-Phoenician in an alphabet of cuneiform characters of Babylonian origin. The Egyptians and Hittites were rival contestants for possession of the town of Ugarit. It was strongly influenced by the Mycenaeans and was finally destroyed at the end of the twelfth century B.C., during the invasion by the 'Sea Peoples'.

5. Flaubert's novel follows fairly closely, and amplifies, the narrative of the Greek historian Polybius, who was a friend of the Scipios and an eye-witness of the Third Punic War. His work was a general history of the Mediterranean world from 220 to 167 B.C., but in order to underline the importance of events in the West, which the Greeks tended to neglect, he wrote two introductory books on the First Punic War and its consequences. Chapters LXV to LXXXVIII are devoted to the War of the Mercenaries. Polybius' purpose was quite the opposite of Flaubert's. He wrote as a politician seeking to deduce principles of government from history; and he only deals with the War of the Mercenaries to emphasize the disadvantages of using professional soldiers—a normal procedure with his Greek compatriots. The atrocities of that war were, for him, pathological facts which he studied clinically, without any particular emotion. In any case, Flaubert was inspired to write his novel after reading Michelet's romantic version of Polybius' narrative.

CHAPTER II

THE CITY OF CARTHAGE

THE traveller who makes the sea crossing from Marseilles to Tunis generally catches his first glimpse of the African coastline in the early hours of the morning. Leaving the mountains of Cape Bon well away to the east, the ship skirts a succession of long inhospitable beaches, at first flat and bare, then rising to high sand-dunes and finally to sheer red cliffs, on which stands the white village of Sidi Bou Said. This village serves also as a landmark for travellers coming from the east who have made the sometimes difficult passage against violent currents, round the wind-swept promontory of Cape Bon. Beyond Sidi Bou Said the coast becomes low and sandy again and the hills retreat inland. On the southernmost of these hills rises the elaborate silhouette of Cardinal Lavigerie's neo-Byzantine cathedral. This is Byrsa, the acropolis of Punic and Roman Carthage. The last promontory which juts out from the beach is now covered with gardens: it marks the entrance to the Punic harbours; and the reefs which fringe this little headland are the remains of the *Choma*, the artificially constructed mound on which Scipio's soldiers established their first bridgehead. Beyond this point the coast is little more than a thin strip of sand between the sea and the Lake of Tunis and pierced by the narrow channel which the ship will soon enter after passing through the Straits of La Goulette.

The traveller who arrives by air, however, sees as his plane circles to land on the airfield of El Aouina (situated midway between the ancient and the modern capital) a bird's-eye view of the whole Carthaginian promontory. The airfield stands in the centre of an isthmus separating the Lake of Tunis from the Ariana Lagoon. This lagoon is all that remains of a gulf which since ancient times has been silted up by the River Medjerda.[1] The hills which were seen from the ship now appear as the head of the peninsula and fringing the coast; others block the western horizon and cut off the peninsula from the hinterland. Surrounded as it is by the sea, two lakes, and a succession of hills, the peninsula forms a small independent natural unit, belonging more to the Mediterranean than to the continent; Carthage, in the words of Appian, is a ship riding at anchor. This configuration is rare on the inhospitable shores of Africa. It is not surprising, therefore, that the Phoenicians made use of it when they were seeking to establish in Libya something more than a mere port of call, but when they were not yet in a position to secure control of a large area.

According to a time-honoured tradition, this occupation took place in 814 B.C.[2] In spite of the unanimity of classical sources this date has recently been challenged by modern critics.[3] The only valid reason put forward by the champions of a later date is the scarcity of eighth-century finds on the site. But in archaeology, negative arguments have even less weight than in other disciplines. Some of the most ancient objects brought by the Phoenicians to Carthage were unearthed only in 1947 and much remains to be explored, particularly in the lower strata. The very conditions of life in Carthage in those first centuries explain why its founders and their immediate descendants left only few and insignificant traces of their presence, and even these were soon obliterated by the rapid development of the city.

All the available information about the Phoenician method of colonization shows that it differed radically from that of the Greeks.[4] By the Greek method, numerous groups of emigrants left their overcrowded motherland far behind them and settled in a new country with no thought of return. Then they set to work at once to re-create the image of their native Greece. The Phoenicians on the other hand sought merely to establish trading-posts providing a safe port of call for their ships, food and rest for their crews[5] (if necessary, through the winter), and warehouses for such merchandise as was needed for bargaining with the natives. The shores of Africa, less than any others, invited them to settle permanently. In this barren land, occupied by poverty-stricken barbarians, there was nothing to tempt an Oriental people. Prehistorians now believe that the Ibero-Maurusians, close relatives of the Cro-Magnon man, still occupied most of the coast where the Tyrians first landed.[6] But the shores controlled by these

savages were on the route to the Eldorado of the ancient world—
that fabulous kingdom of Tartessus[7] which possessed the agricultural resources of the rich Andalusian plains, the copper- and
silver-mines of Castile and, above all, the tin-mines. Tin was an
essential ingredient of bronze, a metal rare in the East, whither
it had to be brought from the misty Cassiterides by sailors from
Atlantic shores.

The Phoenicians therefore sought first of all to occupy islands
or peninsulas which could be easily defended. On these they
established rest and repair stations on as small a scale as possible,
manned by personnel who were probably only too anxious to get
back home at the first opportunity. Deep in the gulf into which
flows the River Medjerda and adjoining its estuary is the small
island of Utica, which became the first station of this kind.[8] By
the end of the twelfth century a small town was built there under
the aegis of a temple dedicated to a sun god. Political reasons
connected with Tyre itself led to the founding of a larger settlement at the end of the ninth century.[9]

Tyre was at that time in the throes of a serious crisis. It was
threatened from outside by the Assyrians, whose armies arrived
almost every year to demand an exorbitant tribute, and who, if
resistance was offered, pillaged the countryside and besieged the
city. It was also rent from within by the struggle for power that
was going on between the aristocracy on the one hand, and the
king and people on the other. This is the source of the romantic
story which tells how the High Priest Acherbas was murdered by
his brother-in-law Pygmalion, and how the victim's widow Elissa
sought safety in flight. The unsettled condition of the metropolis
called for the foundation of a 'new city'—Kart Hadasht—in
which the wealth from the Western World could be kept safe
from covetous hands.

The island of Utica could not accommodate or feed a numerous
population, but it was an easy matter, by blocking off the
Carthaginian isthmus, to isolate a domain of some 12,000 acres
which would be large and productive enough to satisfy the needs
of a well-populated colony. Even today the fields of La Marsa
and Gammarth are rich in olive and fruit trees, vegetables and
cereals. The Lake of Tunis provides abundant supplies of fish.
These advantages were enhanced by a climate which remained

healthy even during the hottest days of summer. Finally, the inlets along the shore and the protective coastal strips made it easy to construct harbours. All these merits of the site must have been well known to the colonists in Utica who could act as guides to the newcomers and offer them effective protection while they settled in. Moreover, Carthage was only a few hours' safe sailing distance from Utica.

The 'new town' was thus conceived at the very outset as a self-contained whole, made up of three distinct parts: an upper town or citadel, to be the centre of religious and economic life, and to which the name of Byrsa was given; a lower town grouped round the harbours; and finally, a rural suburb called Megara where dwellings would stand amid gardens and fields. The main living-quarter was at first very small—so small, indeed, that a vast open space separated it from the upper citadel. Its limits are marked by the resting-places of the dead. These, according to the usual custom of the peoples of antiquity, encircled the cities of the living.[10] Its limits were also marked by the shrines which, by Phoenician custom, were relegated to the outskirts of the town.[11] As the town grew, the newer quarters were built over the former cemeteries, and thus the realm of the dead was gradually forced backwards to scale the rim of the plateaux which overlooks the city of Carthage.[12]

THE HARBOURS

The heart of Kart Hadasht was the harbour.[13] Today, from the top of St Louis Hill, two adjacent lagoons are visible towards the south-west. One is circular with a round island in the middle; the other is oval, and until fairly recently stretched almost as far as the Salammbô promontory. References made by various authors (Appian,[14] Strabo,[15] and Diodorus of Sicily[16]) show that at the time of the Punic wars Carthage possessed an inland harbour with two basins: a rectangular one for merchant ships, and a circular one for naval vessels; in the centre of the latter was an island dominated by a small building which was the Admiral's headquarters. In spite of serious objections, which will be referred to later, it seems likely that these two lagoons are the remains of the *Cothon*, a word derived from a root meaning to cut or hew. It designates a harbour that has been excavated rather than a

basin formed by jetties.[16a] The sanctuary or *tophet* of Tanit and
of Baal stretched along the western shore of the rectangular
lagoon. At the lowest level of his excavations, P. Cintas discovered
a chapel of the eighth century B.C.—the most ancient Phoenician
building yet found in Africa.[17] It was built on a sandy beach with
a substratum of rock; from this it may be supposed that behind
Salammbô Point there existed a natural lagoon of the kind often
formed on low-lying and alluvial shores. The Tyrian ships must
have sheltered in this pool, which was enlarged and equipped
as a harbour by later generations. As was their custom, the
Tyrians consecrated the site where they first landed, dedicating
it to the gods who had protected their voyage and who therefore
became the guardian deities of the new city.

This first anchorage had one serious disadvantage: it lacked
a supply of fresh water. All the wells on Carthaginian soil are
brackish—the only freshwater spring is by the shore, some
distance from the lagoons. From the foot of the cliffs of Bordj
Djedid it is possible to see the entrance to an underground
passage leading deep into the hill behind. This is the 'Spring of
the Thousand Amphorae',[18] which was discovered by chance at
the beginning of the nineteenth century, together with a rich
haul of gold coins. The architecture of the entrance is Roman,
but farther in the stonework and the water-channels are of Punic
workmanship. These and other remains reveal the interest the
Carthaginians took in this part of the shore: from Point Bordj
Djedid huge blocks of half-submerged stone form a rectangle
130 by 160 feet.[19] They are the base of a fort, probably of Punic
construction. Some 250 feet to the south the rainwater from a
small valley pours down in a torrent. At the time of the
foundation of Carthage this *wadi* formed a small estuary which
could be used as an anchorage.[20] It was well sheltered from
the winds, but not from the flood-waters, which must have
been both torrential and destructive, to judge by the quantity
of liquid mud which even today pours over the road running
along the bottom of the valley. Moreover, these alluvial deposits
very rapidly silted up the inlet. The rainwater was captured in
tanks, and from the third century B.C. houses were built along
the dried-up valley.[21] But when Carthage became the seat of
a great maritime power, the modest pool which had received

Dido's ships was enlarged and transformed by a vast building programme.

Appian, writing in the second century B.C., borrowed from Polybius, an eye-witness of the fall of Carthage, a description of the harbours as they were at that time:[22] 'The harbours were so arranged that ships could pass from one to the other. The entrance from the sea was 70 feet wide and could be closed by iron chains. The first harbour, reserved for merchant ships, had a large selection of berths. In the centre of the inner harbour was an island which, like the harbour, was lined with quays, along the whole length of which were boat-houses providing accommodation for 220 ships; above these were lofts for storing the rigging. In front of each boat-house stood two Ionic columns, so that the perimeter of the harbour and of the island looked like a portico. On the island itself stood a small building used as a headquarters for the Admiral and as a post for the trumpeters and heralds. The island was just opposite the entrance of the harbour and rose steeply from the water, so that while the Admiral could see what was happening outside, little could be seen of the interior of the harbour from the open sea. Even from incoming merchant ships, the arsenals remained hidden, for they were surrounded by a double wall and merchant vessels passed from the first harbour into the town without going through the arsenals.' Appian adds elsewhere[23] that this *Cothon* consisted of two parts—one rectangular, the other round. Strabo,[24] who wrote a little more than a century after the destruction of Carthage, specifies that the island was round, and mentions covered berths running all along the circumference of the island as well as along the outer bank of the channel. The similarity between these descriptions and the shape and disposition of the Salammbô lagoons would seem more than fortuitous, even if archaeological evidence were not available. But excavations have uncovered, if not the harbour works described by historians, at least a quantity of remains, all the more impressive in size and number because a special effort at systematic demolition must have been made to destroy installations which were so essential to Carthaginian sea-power. Even more destructive to the Punic installations were the reconstructions of later periods.

Beulé was the first to explore the circular harbour[25] but

unfortunately, in his enthusiasm, he gave an over-confident and often inaccurate reconstruction. However, many of his statements have been confirmed by dredging operations carried out between 1954 and 1955. It is certain that the bottom of the circular lagoon is paved, which proves that it was not dug out in the Middle Ages for a salt-mine, as some have hastened to suggest. In fact the paving seems to be in two layers, the older Carthaginian, and the more recent Roman. The most recent searches have revealed blocks of stone which, on the north side, formed the foundation of a wooden bridge linking the island to the mainland. They are bonded together by lead dovetails, which is a pre-Roman technique.

Of the quays surrounding the island and lining the outer side of the basin, no remains belonging to the original city of Carthage have been found. The two circular walls now surrounding the island probably date from the later Roman Empire. The remains of walls and other buildings discovered by Beulé are not extensive enough to justify his suggested reconstruction of the covered berths surrounding the island and the basin. A. Merlin has found Punic remains on the island itself:[26] rows of rectangular sandstone pillars running from east to west were probably part of a large building, of which nothing is known. Along the coast, level with the basin, traces of a sea-wall running the whole length of the Carthaginian shore are still visible. Saumagne has shown that the line of this wall coincides with the limits of the Roman property tax survey. It cannot be disputed, however, that it continued as far as Salammbô Point, and therefore beyond the limits of the Roman administrative boundaries. Moreover, its foundations are pre-Roman. This wall had been destroyed down to the level of the circular basin. The accounts of the siege of Carthage relate that because the Romans had blocked the exit from the basins, the Carthaginians made another way out for the fleet they had constructed overnight, by suddenly breaching the walls protecting the military harbour. In the course of recent works undertaken by the Ministry of Public Works to make the lagoons more healthy, a channel was cut between the circular lagoon and the sea at the narrowest point. This revealed the existence at this very spot of an ancient channel and also revealed that submerged blocks of stone at the entrance to the channel had once formed the supports of an ancient quay which had been demolished.

Finally, further works undertaken in the last few years by the Army on the eastern bank of the rectangular lagoon have revealed a stonework, or rather the levelled foundations of huge walls. But the most remarkable remains of this first harbour are to be found at Salammbô Point, near the residence of the General in Command of the troops in Tunisia. This promontory is protected by a pile of submerged stones which formed part of a structure similar to the one in the rectangular lagoon of Bordj Djedid, but on a much larger scale. It is generally agreed that these were the remains of an artificial mound, called by the Greeks a *choma*, which served as a landing-stage. Scipio reached it by a causeway which he built from La Goulette, and established a bridgehead there. It does indeed seem certain that the canal which linked the *Cothon* with the sea ran into the Bay of Kram: ships entering it were sheltered from the sea-winds by the *Choma*.

The harbours were put back into use by the Romans, who, even if they did not enlarge the basins themselves, built, on the western side of the merchant harbour, vast arched constructions covering most of the sanctuary of Tanit and Baal.[27] These gigantic walls, which are up to twenty-six feet thick and which were razed to the foundations at the beginning of the fourth century, doubtless when Maxence was sacked, give no clue as to their purpose. But it is possible to hazard a guess that they were the foundations of the granaries in which was stored wheat from Africa destined to supply Rome. Thus it seems reasonable to conclude, as did S. Gsell as far back as 1918, that the Salammbô lagoons are the remains of the harbours of Carthage. Subsequent discoveries, far from adding fresh difficulties to those cleared up by Beulé, the master of African archaeology, have confirmed the main outlines of his theories and have revealed fresh architectural remains which appear to have been part of the harbours. It is not therefore necessary to consider in detail the theses of Dr Carton and Charles Saumagne,[28] which admit that the outlet from the harbour was near Salammbô Point, but refuse to admit that the ancient harbour basins coincided with the two lagoons.

Other scholars[29] have thought that there existed a harbour formed by jetties built out into the sea. Naval officers who had sounded the Bay of Kram at the beginning of the century believed they had located under the sea the ruins of the walls of such a harbour. But the methodical explorations carried out in 1947 by divers from the *Elie-Monnier* proved that they were nothing more than natural reefs.[30] More recently, Colonel Baradez[31] has resurrected a theory formerly put forward by Roquefeuil and Oehler. According to this, the Falbe quadrilateral is not the *Choma*, but an artificial basin which served as a merchant harbour. Gsell had already shown that this cannot be reconciled with any of the descriptions found in antiquity.

The small size of the Carthaginian ports (ten acres for the first, and a little more than twenty for the second) have come as a surprise to all historians, and this explains the efforts which have been made to find a solution other than that demanded by the facts. Rome and Alexandria had much larger harbours; but as P. Cintas[32] has very judiciously shown by studying the dimensions of Tipasa, the Carthaginians remained faithful to an archaic conception of a harbour: that of a simple expanse of water providing for the arrival and departure of ships which, when out of service, were stored out of the water in enclosed berths radiating from the perimeter of the circular basin. This logical and convincing explanation should discourage any further attempts to find a deep-water harbour at Carthage, and make us sceptical of the existence of any such harbours before the Hellenistic Age, in any Phoenician towns in Asia.

THE RAMPARTS

The problem of the walls of Carthage is as difficult as that of the harbours. The contrast between the grandiloquent descriptions transmitted by tradition and the remains discovered by archaeologists is even more striking. At the time of the Punic wars, the peninsula formed an immense entrenched camp,[33] defended on the side of the mainland by an impregnable triple line: on the outside, a moat backed by a palisade, and then two ramparts. The rampart nearest the town, about fifty-seven feet high and twenty-eight feet wide at the base, was also used as an arsenal. Rows of casemates, one above the other, and cut into the inner face, could shelter 300 elephants, 4,000 horses, 20,000 infantrymen, and 4,000 horsemen. Towers projected from the wall at every 200 feet or so.

Nothing remains of the two ramparts. Gsell has rightly remarked that the large hewn stones which composed them and which were knocked down in 146 B.C. by Scipio's soldiers, have certainly been used again since—in the first instance by the builders of Roman Carthage. But the great exterior moat is still visible from the air[34] as a light-coloured streak cutting straight across the isthmus for over a mile. General Duval discovered it from the air in 1949 and ordered digging to be started. The moat, sixty-five feet wide, is lined on the east by a band of rock, scarred in numerous places. Round holes arranged in alternate rows, and which sometimes contained the bottoms of amphorae, must have housed wooden posts. These last doubtless supported look-out posts raised above the mound which formed the first rampart, beyond the moat. Other long narrow slits at right-angles to the ditch perhaps held planks or hurdles which protected the flat top. This work has been identified beyond all doubt. It runs about one league to the west of St Louis Hill, roughly coinciding with the line suggested by Carton and Gsell; it corresponds with the narrowest part of the isthmus. The remains which have survived at the western end prove clearly that this is a Carthaginian defence work, and not the entrenchment which Scipio had dug at an arrow's flight to the east.

Just at the spot where the moat reaches the Lake of Tunis is a stone construction, with a rubble core, which doubtless formed part of the masonry rampart defending Carthage on the lake-side. This fortification reached the sea south of the harbours at the site of the modern village of Kram.

Fragments of a sea-wall are certainly to be found lying among the ruins which line the beach of Carthage between the quadrilaterals of Falbe and of Bordj Djedid. But a detailed study of them would be necessary to distinguish them from subsequent Roman constructions. The builders of the Caesarian colony certainly used the remains of the Punic rampart which they gave as the boundary of their tax survey of landed property.

We know nothing at all about the lay-out of the northern rampart which defended Megara. It was just a simple wall situated some distance from the shore—since Mancinus' soldiers, as well as Scipio's, were able on two occasions to advance up to the wall on foot. Perhaps that part of the peninsula to the north of La Marsa, called Gammarth today, remained outside the enclosure. General Duval was unable to find any trace of its moat beyond a point just over half a mile from the Lake of Tunis. One may suppose that the north-eastern corner of the rampart was in this direction. In this region the ground is very sandy and very wet when it rains. Doubtless it was even more so in ancient times, when the Ariana Lagoon communicated with the sea. The Carthaginians probably considered that it was not worth while, in order to deny access to a zone so unsuited to military operations, to extend their fortifications as far as Djebel Khaoni; it would have been an expensive operation and would have dispersed the troops required to man the rampart. The perimeter they had to defend was already, according to Livy, some twenty miles in length.

The citadel of Byrsa had its own fortifications forming a stronghold inside the entrenchments of the camp. We have seen that it embraced the Juno and Odeon Hills as well as the Hill of St Louis. Father Lapeyre thought he had discovered its outline along the southern edge of the Byrsa plateau,[35] but what he found was in reality the remains of later buildings occupying an earlier Carthaginian site. They had no connexion with the Punic buildings and have never been identified.

THE TEMPLES

Shrines in Carthage were numerous and famous. We know that they were of many different architectural styles and that their appearance changed a great deal with the passage of time.

The Canaanites' very austere conception of the divinity had at first deterred them from building shrines and from making graven images.[36] The spot where supernatural forces were believed to manifest themselves was kept bare, or at the most marked by small monuments which were at first just plain stones. Often these stelae covered the ashes of sacrifices which had been offered to regenerate the divine power. The Phoenicians in Africa remained faithful throughout their civilization to this kind of holy place or *tophet*, to use the Biblical term.

Nevertheless, the influence of the Egyptians, and probably of other nations too, encouraged the belief that the gods needed a dwelling-place. One of the Ugarit poems describes the building of a temple dedicated to Baal, and Schaeffer actually discovered its ruins.[37] There does not in fact seem to be any radical contradiction between the idea of a temple and that of the *tophet*, for the house of god appears to be an architectural development of the sacred stone or of the stele in which the god was embodied.

The Carthaginian *tophet*, as we have seen, ran along the full length of the merchant harbour. There must have been compelling reasons why the Carthaginians did not put to practical use a site which would have been so convenient for warehouses or stores. The Romans did not fail to do so, leaving for Saturn, Baal Hammon's successor, only a minute sanctuary hemmed in on all sides by the towering walls of quayside installations. There is every reason to accept Cintas's suggestion that this part of the beach was held sacred by the Carthaginians as the spot where Dido's galleys had put ashore, and which was doubtless also considered to be the site of the funeral pyre on which the founder-Queen voluntarily sacrificed herself to obtain the protection of the gods for the young city. The Queen's tomb has not been found; perhaps it was little more than a modest mound of earth. But on the virgin soil of this first landing beach, Cintas has brought to light[38] a tiny building which was doubtless used in the ceremonies commemorating the royal sacrifice described by Justin. The bas-relief on the stele shows that these ceremonies closely resemble the rites practised by the Greeks in honour of their heroes who, like Dido, were in their turn often the founders of cities. A woman, half-reclining on a small hillock, is about to pour upon it a libation for the ever-thirsty dead.[39] The 'Cintas chapel' has all the characteristic features of a miniature Oriental temple: a small chamber, barely a yard square, contains a small vault, a holy of holies hewn out of the rock, in which had been placed a number of terracotta jars made at the end of the eighth century.[40] A courtyard, scarcely any larger, and enclosing a tiny altar, precedes this chamber and in front of the courtyard three concentric curved walls form a kind of maze through which the faithful had to pass to lay their offerings on the altar. The whole construction was built of crude stones held together by mud, and whitewashed, like the white sepulchres of the Gospels and the *marabouts* of Moslem saints.

The recent excavations in St Peter's revealed a roughly hewn niche under the high altar, which for the Christians of the second century enshrined the memory of the Prince of the Apostles: this serves to remind us that frequently a modest monument may become a focal-point for piety, solely by virtue of its simplicity and great antiquity. In other parts of the excavations round the Cintas chapel, traces of walls have been found which suggest that during the first centuries of the city's existence several chapels like the one discovered by Cintas were built round Dido's tomb. These shrines may have been the scene of human sacrifices, although no victims' remains have been exhumed in the Cintas chapel. In any case, in about 700 B.C. at the latest, the practice began of burying, over the whole area of the *tophet*, jars containing the ashes of children who had been 'passed through the fire', i.e. burnt in the arms of the bronze statue as described by Flaubert (plagiarizing Diodorus); and whose throats were perhaps previously cut to release the blood containing the divine force. At first, these jars were merely hidden beneath miniature dolmens of dry stones. Later, small stonework altars covered with stucco were built to house the urns.[41] By the sixth century B.C. such funerary monuments very often reached massive proportions and the urns were interred beside or in front of them. Instead of being in the form of an altar, this type of funeral monument was shaped like a tiny temple, with a symbol carved on its façade to indicate that a god dwelt within.[42]

There is every reason to think that these *naiskoi* are miniature reproductions of shrines which stood in other quarters of Carthage. Their décor showed that Punic architects, like those of Phoenicia, remained under Egyptian influence, but that they drastically simplified or impoverished their models. The façade is almost entirely occupied by a rectangular door framed in massive columns. Above runs a concave cornice, called an 'Egyptian throat'; the Punic architects continued to use this motif even on buildings in the Greek style, so that it became one of the characteristics of their art. Above the cornice, a frieze bears the symbol of the god: sometimes the sun-disc, either plain or winged, an emblem which Baal Hammon adopted from Amen Ra, and sometimes the rearing *uraei,* or hooded cobras, whose awe-inspiring power was also held to proceed from the sun. Within the false doorway was depicted the interior of the temple, where another divine symbol was shown— generally a simple column or an oval or lozenge-shaped stone,[43] but sometimes also a human figure apparently swathed like a mummy.[44] Some of these funeral monuments, instead of representing a temple, have the form of a throne.[45] This by itself was enough to evoke the majesty of the god and therefore it was sometimes worshipped vacant. More often, however, the divine column rests upon it. Lastly, some funeral monuments took the form of a miniature altar,[46] supported by a kind of pylon or truncated pyramid surmounted by an Egyptian-style lintel. In front, steps were hewn to give access to the urn cavity of the altar. Two incense-burners stood one on either side of these steps. These recall the most likely derivation of Baal Hammon (the god whose surname was El), namely 'Lord of the Altars where Incense burns'.

All these funerary monuments soon covered the entire area of the *tophet,* which was fairly long, but very narrow. At a very early date the decision was taken to raise the level of the ground. No scruples were felt about burying the earlier monuments. The Cintas chapel disappeared in this way very soon after it was built, since by the end of the eighth century B.C. it was partially destroyed and covered over by other shrines, which in turn were soon buried in the same way.

The untidiness of the *tophet,* the meagre offerings and the crudity of its funeral monuments emphasize the aesthetic indifference of the Carthaginians, and their artistic insensibility, and are out of keeping with the atrocious nature of the sacrifices they felt called upon to make. These people who stood so much in awe of God that they suppressed their most natural and human impulses, were never capable of giving expression to their religion through the plastic arts. If, therefore, we judge solely by their monuments, we can imagine them as hostile to any transcendental notions. In fact, as with other Semitic peoples, the absolute nature of their religious devotion killed all other spiritual activities, so that the *tophet,* the most ancient and venerable of holy places, was also the spot where any departures from the primitive austerity were rigorously excluded. The other sanctuaries were doubtless richer, and certainly included real buildings which, like the *naiskoi*, were probably decorated in the Egyptian manner.

Oriental influence persisted until the fourth century and was even more strongly marked during the period of withdrawal and isolation which followed the capture of Himera in 408. Fresh waves of Phoenician settlers doubtless arrived from the mother country, anxious to preserve the national traditions which were in jeopardy there. In Sousse, a stele dating from the end of the fifth century[47] B.C. shows Baal Hammon enthroned in a temple whose architecture preserves all the typical Egyptian characteristics, including the massive doorway with straight columns and the lintel decorated with the winged disc.

However, in the fifth century, a great change occurred in the *tophet*: the massive sandstone monuments were replaced by pointed limestone obelisks,[48] which were situated farther away from the temples. Certain architectural details still survived, nevertheless: for example, representations of columns are carved on either side of the front face of the obelisk, above which runs a frieze; and the top of the stele forms a triangular pediment which is surmounted and flanked by statues.

All these motifs are borrowed from Greek architecture and there is every reason to think that the main edifices in Carthage came to resemble more and more those that the Carthaginians had every opportunity of seeing in Sicily during the almost continuous wars of the fourth century. We are no longer reduced to the necessity of reconstructing this Greco-Carthaginian architecture from simplified representations on monuments; fairly extensive documentary evidence is available on the methods of construction and the shape of both public and private buildings.

Like their Egyptian masters, the Phoenician architects could, on occasion, build massive and extensive structures able to withstand the ravages of time. But as a rule they contented themselves with materials that were light, cheap, and plentiful, and which, in view of the low cost of labour, could be frequently renewed. Their Carthaginian counterparts, however, did not hesitate to use, even for their ambitious constructions, a soft and friable sandstone which was easy to work. At first, adequate supplies were found in the hills of the peninsula. When these early quarries gave out, they were replaced by others on the far side of the bay at the tip of Cape Bon, near the present village of El Haouaria.[49] At this wild spot, almost inaccessible from the land, deep galleries were driven from the beach into the heart of the limestone cliffs. These intricate workings, lit here and there by shafts or openings left by accidental falls of rock, are just as impressive and even wilder than the stone-quarries of Syracuse, with which the ancients themselves compared them. The only access is from the beach, and doubtless these quarries served as jails for the wretched prisoners of war, convicts, or slaves, who were condemned to labour in them. Standing alone in the centre of one of these caves is a block of stone vaguely resembling a squatting camel. It may owe its strange shape to a freak of nature, but perhaps also to the patient ingenuity of one of these outcasts. The main reason why the only outlet from these galleries was towards the sea was the convenience of transporting the stone by barge across the bay directly to Carthage. Stone cubes, whose sides measured several yards, could be brought to the building site without having to be cut into smaller pieces first. But because of their poor quality, it was impossible to use these enormous stones in buildings intended to last. They were particularly unsuitable for use on the outer surface of a building where decoration was required. The lime-stone was then covered with a stucco layer to hide its irregu-larities and to receive shallow ornamentations. When large stones were laid together, metal clamps were used, generally made from molten lead poured into dovetails hewn in the stone. The wall joining the island in the harbour to the shore was of this con-struction.

The only buildings earlier than the Hellenistic period are in fact built of El Haouaria limestone. These are the tombs dating from the seventh and sixth centuries. The walls were made of large rectangular blocks of stone carefully laid without mortar;[50] two niches cut in the wall contained the chattels of the dead person, and the sarcophagi lay beneath a paved floor. The walls of the chamber were covered with stucco. The ceiling was lined with cedar and surmounted by a roof made of steeply pitched blocks of stone which propped each other up. Their weight thus acted downwards and prevented the structure from collapsing in the middle. In Utica, Cintas has recently discovered such a structure which probably dates from the eighth century B.C.[51]

These sepulchres are closely related to Phoenician tombs of the thirteenth century B.C.[52] The prolonged survival in Carthage of this type of building illustrates the partiality of the Tyrian colonists for Oriental traditions which were beginning to go out of fashion in Phoenicia itself.

However, less expensive building methods which later became general must have been commonly used from the earliest times. The unbaked bricks and puddled clay used by the inhabitants of Egypt and Mesopotamia must have served for most of the houses. Even in the seventh century, tombs were built in Utica of unbaked brick surmounted by a huge sandstone slab.[53] Doubt-less, at this time, walls were being built whose base was of stone, but the upper part of which was made of brick or clay piled up inside an outer casing. To make them waterproof they were apparently given a coating of pitch, but this use of pitch, which surprised the Greeks, has not been verified by archaeologists. Perhaps it was mainly used in the building of flat roofs. On St Louis Hill in Carthage,[54] several fragments of walls belonging to houses built before the third century B.C. were constructed of brick-filled casings; this method was still in use in Roman times[55] and survives even today in the Tunisian Sahel. These brick-filled walls were later strengthened by a facing of vertical stones. Then the inner brick was replaced by stone rubble, still keeping the stone facing. All these methods were used in the St Louis houses. The latter method is common in Roman-African buildings. This inferior masonry was often hidden beneath layers of stucco which gave an effect of marble. The use of concrete casing was intro-duced later by the Romans, and enabled huge walls and arches to be built which were virtually indestructible. The Kbor Klib, a monumental altar built a century after the destruction of Car-thage, has a core of large stone slabs set in the ground. And yet, during the Punic wars, the Carthaginians had borrowed from the Greeks the practice of using a layer of cement to cover their floors, or to waterproof reservoirs and public baths. Such modest building techniques reveal the need for economy and speed, rather than for care, but they suited the local resources and the inhabitants. It is surprising to discover that they were used later in Moslem architecture in the Middle Ages and even today they are still in use.

From the fourth century, the increasing influence of Greece is even more evident in the decoration of buildings. Egyptian motifs were replaced by or mixed with the Greek orders—especially the Ionic, or rather its variant the Aeolian, which is characterized by the V-shaped bend in the channel connecting the volutes. An elegant little stucco-covered colonnade, discovered at Carthage in the ruins of one of the St Louis houses,[56] proves that the Carthaginian artists at the time of the Punic wars could hold their own with those of the great cities of Greece, Alexandria, or Delos. This did not prevent them, however, from remaining faithful to traditional motifs, such as the 'Egyptian throat', which appears on the mausoleum at Dougga and at Medrassen. The evolution of religious architecture between the fourth and second centuries B.C. illustrates both the fondness of the Carthaginians for Greek fashions and their loyalty to national traditions which they felt it would be impious to abandon.

In Carthage itself, in the southern quarter of the town, just over a mile west of the *tophet*, where Salammbô railway station stands today, stood a chapel dating from the later centuries of independence. It was discovered in 1916, but was destroyed almost immediately during the construction of the railway, and Dr Carton was just able to draw a plan of it, and to collect the contents.[57] He found a very simple rectangular *cella*, divided lengthways by a partition wall of beaten earth. In the centre of the end wall was a seat framed between two small Doric columns fixed against a wall of puddled clay; votive statues stood on corbels, and along the top of the wall ran a frieze heavily decorated with rows of heart- and egg-shaped ornaments, pearls, palm leaves, and rosettes of polished stones, all of which were painted vermilion. The floor was paved with small tiles inlaid with pieces of white marble. This truly Greek decoration is in striking contrast with the architecture, which is of pre-Hellenic Aegean origin and which resembles that of the Etruscans, who, like the Carthaginians, remained faithful to Pelasgian traditions long after they had been abandoned by the Greeks, but which had survived among the peoples on the periphery of the Greek empire. The Salammbô chapel was very probably surrounded by sacred precincts bounded by walls which the Greeks called *temenos*. This lay-out must have been not unlike the sancturies in the Punic tradition, subsequent to the conquest, which have been unearthed at Thinissut on Cape Bon[58] or at El Kenissia[59] near Sousse. Their untidy plan shows how little these African country-folk knew of the Greek love of harmonious proportions, even though they were influenced by details of decoration drawn from classical art. Minute chapels, and open-air altars, were scattered in haphazard fashion over enclosed courtyards; the faithful had constantly added to their number to house barbaric statues, intended to illustrate the numerous incarnations of the sovereign deity and of his supernatural agents.

At a later date, when the African religion came under the discipline of Rome, attempts were made to subordinate such fantasies to the rules of classical architecture. The most typical example of such a Roman-African temple is the shrine of Saturn at Dougga.[60] All the essential elements of a Punic temple are there: monumental porch, open-air courtyard, and diminutive chapels housing the gods. But instead of the open space in front there is a columned *propylaeum*; the porches round the rectangular square give it the appearance of a forum; and the chapels of the great god and of his companions are lined up at one end in hierarchical order like the triple sanctuary or *cella* of a capitol. Countless variations were introduced into this lay-out. In Carthage, the Temple of Caelestis, the Latin successor to Tanit, consisted of a vast open space surrounded by chapels dedicated to all the local gods. At Dougga, this same Caelestis was honoured with a completely classical Corinthian temple, surrounded by a semicircular wall or *temenos*. In the Bardo Museum is a delightful miniature chapel, discovered at Thuburbo Majus, which is no doubt an exact replica of a Hellenistic temple in Hannibal's Carthage.[61] It was dedicated to Demeter, a Greek goddess who became very popular with the Carthaginians from the fourth century B.C. On a high stone base, decorated with mouldings, stands a porch, supported by two Ionic columns exactly like those dug up at Carthage on St Louis Hill. The doorway of the sanctuary, framed between two pilasters decorated with rosettes, is surmounted by a rectangular tympanum carved with dolphins facing each other on either side of a flower-shaped ornament. On the threshold is the image of a pig, the goddess's favourite sacrifice. But this little monument is surmounted by something which defies the rules of classical architecture, although these inspire the decoration. A rectangular entablature, whose disproportionate height crushes the building—it is as high as the columns—is formed by four smooth lintels one on top of the other, separated by fillets, decorated, respectively, with denticulations. The sculptor, or the architect whom he copied, seems to have tried to preserve in his work the massive rectangular shape of the Egyptian shrines, instead of lightening the upper part by using the double pitched roof and the triangular pediment of the Greek temples.

DOMESTIC ARCHITECTURE

If Carthaginian religious architecture, conservative by nature, was susceptible to Greek influences, domestic architecture could hardly resist them either. The Carthaginians were sometimes capable of ambitious building schemes. For example, as we have seen, the naval harbour had covered berths flanked by an outer row of Ionic columns, which gave the appearance of a circular portico. Not far from the harbour was the central meeting-place (or *agora*) where the people assembled. Such meeting-places were never found in Oriental towns, which were generally ruled by dictators, but the Greeks regarded them as the very symbol of their liberty. In Moslem towns the promenades and other open spaces essential to business were situated on the outskirts of the town near the harbours, as they still are today. However, it is possible that in early times the Phoenicians constructed open spaces of this kind, through their close contact with the Aegeans whose cities contained *agorai*. The *agora* in Carthage was situated half-way between the harbour and the citadel of Byrsa, which seems to indicate that, like its Greek counterpart, it fulfilled both a commercial and a political function. It must not be imagined as an open space of regular proportions surrounded by magnificent buildings. Pre-Roman meeting-places, perhaps modelled on that of Carthage, have been discovered in two other African towns which had a Phoenician civilization, Leptis Magna in Tripolitania and Mactar in Central Tunisia. These meeting-places, with their irregular proportions, were very different from the Roman *fora*, which were straight-sided and surrounded by a portico. However, at a later date these same cities built such *fora* in the Roman manner. The Greek *agorai*, and in particular that of

Athens, were at first fairly irregular also, and were not made regular until the fifth century, when they were surrounded with porticos.[62] Towards the middle of the fourth century an ambitious Carthaginian general named Hanno sought to win over the people by offering them a sumptuous banquet served under the public porticos. Gsell supposes that these must have been part of an *agora*. But Hanno could equally well have installed his guests under the colonnade which surrounded the temple courtyards. These vast courtyards, like those of present-day mosques, were indeed an obvious meeting-place for idlers, as well as for the devout. They were probably also a centre of intellectual activity, where the *Kohanim* gave instruction in theology.

No Punic or neo-Punic public building has been preserved, though we know from texts that there existed in Carthage an assembly-hall for the Senate and Law Courts for the magistrates, probably copied from the Greek *bouleuteria* and basilicas. However, we are fairly well informed about the Punic house of the third and second centuries. Even in recent years it was thought that in 146 the Roman army destroyed even the foundations of the humblest Carthaginian building, and then ploughed up the 'accursed' soil and sprinkled it with salt. Yet in the new Carthage which was built a hundred years later in accordance with the terms of Caesar's will temples were erected to the native gods on the very same sites they had occupied in Dido's city.

The discovery of the sanctuary at the Salammbô railway station set a fresh problem. The building was in ruins, but not completely obliterated. However, a Roman burial-site, dating from the first century A.D., which covered it, proved beyond doubt that the building dated from Punic times. Dr Carton located other remains anterior to the siege, but most of them cannot be accurately dated. Charles Saumagne, on the slopes of St Louis Hill, and recently M. Vézat, in the plain of Douar Chott, brought to light floors of houses which had been covered over by a layer of ashes from the fire of 146. On these floors were found coins and ceramics which were indisputably Carthaginian. Nevertheless it came as a great surprise when a whole sector of the original Carthage was discovered beneath the southern part of the St Louis plateau. Father Lapeyre, who was the first to start excavations in this district, found in the upper layer a jumble of Roman remains of different periods which he considered, without adequate reason, to be parts of the Proconsul's palace. He also found Punic remains, which he thought were either tombs or parts of the Byrsa rampart. As early as 1952, Mme Picard[63] was able to demonstrate that they were in fact the fairly well-preserved remains of a residential quarter dating from the Hellenistic period. These excavations have since been continued by Father Féron, who succeeded Father Lapeyre.[64] The whole of this quarter of the town is now clearly revealed, ten to thirteen feet below the Roman level, with its streets, and its walls preserved to a height of about three feet. These recent excavations show that Carthage, during the later centuries of its independence, had adopted the main improvements introduced into town planning by the Greeks. Its streets were straight, if not wide. The streets in the whole of this sector of the city ran along axes which were nearly the same as those subsequently chosen by the first Roman surveyors when they made their fiscal survey of this sector and the surrounding district. Whether this was pure coincidence, or intentional on the part of the Romans, it does prove that the Carthaginians had worked to an overall plan. The streets had sewers constructed in the same way as those found in the Greek towns in Sicily. Access to the steeper slopes was provided by flights of steps, like the sixty steps which led up to the Temple of Eshmoun. This stood at the top of the hill in which the Romans later hewed the tiered seats of their amphitheatre.

The plan of these Byrsa houses is very simple; square or rectangular rooms were placed side by side with little regard for architectural effect. The houses discovered in the little town of Dar Essafi,[65] which caused a stir in the Press a few years ago, were similar. They belonged to fishermen and workers who extracted purple dye from sea-shells. These dwellings grew up round a little harbour on the east coast of Cape Bon, about halfway between the quarries of El Haouaria and the acropolis of Kelibia, the name of which recalls its resemblance to the round shields of the Greek hoplites.

Diodorus, in his account of Agathocles' expedition right at the end of the fourth century,[66] tells us that this district was inhabited and prosperous, but that there were no large towns; the population was scattered in settlements or small towns of some thousand inhabitants. This explains why the first discoveries were of burial-places only, the size and wealth of which made the complete absence of habitations all the more remarkable. In 1953, Cintas, who for some ten years had been excavating a large number of cemeteries in this district, conceived the idea of investigating some remains of walls hidden under a dense growth of dwarf palm trees, and designated in the Archaeological Atlas[67] by the intials R.R. (Roman Remains). On his very first survey, he found the ground strewn with potsherds dating from between the fourth and second centuries B.C. Excavation soon confirmed that the site had been abandoned in the second century B.C. There were, for example, no traces of the mosaics which are nearly always found on the site of the humblest Roman village. Instead there were a large number of pink cement floors, studded with frag-ments of white marble. These are typical of Hellenistic architec-ture. It proved possible to explore two or three houses. One was distinguished by a large pointed block of stone which Cintas thinks is the tympanum of a rounded arch or *ghorfa*, similar to those which are found in Tunisia today. Following an ancient tradition such arches were used in the Sahara market-town of Medenina, south of Gabes, and they have spread recently to the whole district, on account of their cheapness and ease of con-struction.

If our reconstruction of Punic towns is correct, they must have looked very like those of Tunisia today, with their houses covered by vaulted or flat whitewashed roofs. The Punic houses, like those in Asia, Egypt, or even Greece, had very few openings on to the street. In this they were quite different from the Roman houses, whose façades, with their broad windows, look singularly modern. A little light and air penetrated from the courtyards; but whereas in the typical Roman-African dwelling (as in the palaces of the Arab parts of Tunisia) the square *patio* surrounded by a portico was the central feature, the Carthaginian house had only a modest courtyard tucked in a corner away from the centre. A Roman villa in Acholla dating probably from the first century A.D. does not follow the regular classical plan.[68] While the houses of rich merchants in the same town were able to afford the luxury of an interior courtyard with a bathing-pool in the middle and surrounded by a portico, the less wealthy owner of this villa could only take the air in a long narrow courtyard, on either side of which was an ambulatory with red painted stucco columns or with pillars. The living-rooms are grouped along one long and one short side; the other long side is taken up by a large water-tank. This is a very ancient type of dwelling. As early as the second millennium, and particularly in Cyprus, L-shaped houses were built in this way, along the sides of a courtyard. In Hellenistic Delos, this lay-out is still found, side by side with square houses built round a *patio*.

However, in Carthage there also existed buildings of quite a different kind, built upwards and divided into apartments like modern flats. Scipio's soldiers found themselves confronted with a difficult task when they reached the *agora*; they had to make their way up to Byrsa by three steep streets lined with six-storied houses, each one of which had been converted into a fortress. What did these sky-scrapers look like? An ingenuous sketch on the wall of a funeral-vault at Cape Bon[69] probably illustrates them; it shows a town protected by a wall surmounted by towers; an inside view of the walls shows that the towers of the rampart are in fact houses. A closer look reveals a massively built ground-floor supporting a kind of columned *loggia*. Above rises a row of round arches, or perhaps cupolas, like those which exist today in El Oued. This scene might easily be the product of the childish imagination of the artist, but for the fact that it bears a striking resemblance to the lordly manors so crudely depicted by the African mosaic-workers at the time of the Byzantine Empire.

This type of manor-house, totally unrelated to anything Italian, may be African in origin. And yet it seems to belong to a rural environment; the solidly built ground-floor, devoid of openings, would protect its inmates from surprise raids, and the *loggia* would provide the fresh air so necessary in the African climate. *A priori* it would be more feasible to imagine the Carthaginian houses as similar to the tall *insulae* of Pompeii and Ostia,[70] whose basic structure has been so skilfully reconstructed by V. Spinazzola and G. Calya. But the history of the tall house, the *insula* of the Latins, as opposed to the *domus* which extended horizontally, is still very uncertain. In particular, we know very little about its Hellenistic antecedents. The Romans were led to develop it by

1. Gate and street of a Carthaginian city (Kerkouane, at the point of Cape Bon):
Mission archéologique française en Tunisie

Remains of a Carthaginian house in the same town (third to second century
B.C.): *Mission archéologique française en Tunisie*

2. Carthaginian priest in the presence of Baal Hammon. Stele from Hadrumetum
(fifth to fourth century B.C.)

the density of the population in the Imperial cities, but earlier examples must have existed in the East. Only at Delos have a few modest multi-storied buildings been found. It is noteworthy that in these, the upper floors are lit and ventilated by a *loggia* very similar to that shown in the Cape Bon sketch. It was evidently from Greece that the Carthaginians borrowed this architectural solution, a profitable one in view of the restricted building area available, even though it involved the sacrifice of comfort and of hygiene.

Anyone who has walked through the stifling streets of the *Hara* of Tunis, where a thoughtless architect was responsible for a monstrous accumulation of very tall buildings, will be able to imagine that the central quarter of Hannibal's Carthage must have been far from pleasant. And yet the Carthaginians were not unacquainted with comfort and hygiene. Here again, progress came by way of Greek technique. It is surprising to find, in one of the houses of a modest little town like Kerkouane, an admirably equipped bathroom, complete with slipper-bath and a wash-basin which allowed its owner to wash his face while sitting in the bath.[71] The bathroom is lined with fine waterproof cement and is just like one found in a house in Corinth of the same period. In Carthage the waste water was led away by sewers, but these were not of the same grandiose proportions as those built by the Romans. No adequate solution was found to the problem of providing a water-supply. Flaubert committed a deliberate anachronism when he attributed to the original city of Carthage the magnificent fifteen-mile-long aqueduct which brings water from Mount Zaghouan; for part of its length it ran underground (a section still used today), and for another part high up on lofty arches across the valley of the Oued Miliane. This work of art dates from the Antonines, in the second century A.D. The supply of water from the 'Spring of a Thousand Amphorae' and from wells was inadequate and usually brackish so that Carthage had to rely mainly on water-tanks. The remains of several of these have been found which, because their orientation does not accord with the Roman fiscal survey, can be dated earlier than 146. They were usually shaped like an elongated bath, rounded at each end, or, less commonly, shaped like a decanter.

The later Carthaginians owed to the Greeks not only their domestic decorations, but also their household installations. They had always concealed the poor quality of their building materials beneath thick layers of lime on the outer walls and roofs, and of stucco on the internal walls. The latter were often decorated with paintings or reliefs. The naïve frescoes of Djebel Mlezza give some idea of the type of decoration found in a modest dwelling. They are childish drawings, not without life or colour, which recall the pottery or the designs drawn on ostrich eggs, or other forms of popular art still to be found in Tunisia at the present time. The main themes are stylized drawings of houses, of ships, or even of human figures, arranged very much as they are nowadays in the designs of carpet-weavers and tattoo-artists in the South. But this popular art, which owed more to Libyan tradition than to Phoenician taste, was absent from the dwellings of the nobles, who were careful to follow the Greek fashion. From the third century B.C. onwards, this fashion brought within the reach of the middle classes, from one end of the Mediterranean to the other, a remarkably uniform degree of comfort and luxury. Not being able to use stone and marble, which were precious building materials reserved for kings and rich magnates, the Greek or Greek-influenced citizens in both East and West copied them in cheap materials like stucco, that providential resort of humbler builders. The lower parts of walls were divided into large panels in imitation of marble facings. In the ruins of the Salammbô chapel, Dr Carton has pointed out the remains of *orthostates*, which are large imitation marble panels of this kind. They have also been found in the oldest houses of Pompeii and in Delos, where some remarkably fine examples have been discovered.

In Alexandria, stucco-workers excelled in decorating friezes, uprights, and ceilings with light winged figures in relief, which stood out from a plain background, or with tiny landscapes depicting the life of the countryside. The thrones of the divinities discovered in the Salammbô chapel and in the private shrine of a villa belonging to Hamilcar,[72] have their uprights decorated with 'winged victories' in full panoply, which stem directly from this form of Alexandrine art.

It is surprising to find them in Carthage before 146, since they were not adopted by the Romans until a hundred years later.

For example, on the walls of the Farnese villa, which belonged to a contemporary of Caesar and Augustus (perhaps to the famous Clodia, who was Tibullus' Lesbia, and the sworn enemy of Cicero), there soared these same *Nikai* which so delighted Hannibal's friends. But the scrupulous devotion of the artists of antiquity to orthodox tradition adequately explains why these motifs, which are later found on the tombs of the time of the Antonines and of Marcus Aurelius, lasted so long. Carthage, at any rate, adopted them at their birth; this confirms both the fondness of its upper classes for Greco-Egyptian fashions, and the close economic and cultural ties which existed between the new Tyre and the capital of the Ptolemys.

From Greece also came the custom of covering the floors with a layer of very fine cement, tinted red by the crushed brick from which it was made, and into which small fragments of white marble were inset. These *lithostrota* are found from one end of the Mediterranean to the other, for example at Delos, Pompeii, and in the former Gallo-Greek colony at Glanum, whose ruins have been found under the Roman town at Saint-Rémy-de-Provence. In Africa, the presence of a floor of this type is the most obvious sign of a recent Punic settlement. Such floors have been found in Utica; over them had been laid the black and white mosaics of a Roman villa dating from the first century A.D. and over these again, more mosaics with an elegant flowered pattern, laid by one of Hadrian's subjects. It is possible that Cato was referring to these floors in a speech of 152, where he mentions that Punic paving had been introduced into Rome.[73] The grammarian Festus, through whom this text has survived, thought that this referred to paving made of Numidian marble, such as that recently excavated in a house of the first century A.D. in Utica. But the technique of cutting marble was still not known in the second century B.C. The only contribution of Le Chemtou, the *Numidicum* of the Ancient World, to the *lithostrota* was the marble fragments mixed in with the cement. In Carthage, the Carton chapel and the houses of Byrsa and Dermech were paved in this way.

When they emerged from the narrow, noisy, plague-ridden streets of the lower city, the Carthaginians found a semblance of peace, and perhaps a little verdure (even before they reached the gardens and fields of Megara) in the cemeteries which fringed the city on the north and west. Doubtless these were very like Moslem cemeteries. Like them, they contained no imposing tombstones. Instead, the presence of the dead, often buried in deep tombs or graves, was usually indicated only by a plain stone. Not until the last two centuries did the custom grow up of shaping these stones into stelae, on which was crudely carved a figure with upraised arm, representing the deceased in the attitude of prayer, or perhaps the god who watched over him in death.[74] The rich, however, could afford the luxury of an almost life-size figure, frozen in an archaic and stylized attitude, derived from sixth-century Sicilian craftsmen. However, the monotonous appearance of the Carthaginian burial-ground was sometimes broken by lofty towers in the shape of death-lanterns; similarly, in Moslem cemeteries, a *marabout* with its cupola sometimes breaks the monotony of the sea of stelae or heaps of stones which mark the last resting-place of the faithful.

A few important personages erected above ground an 'everlasting resting-place', either to perpetuate their memory, or to flatter themselves with the hope that thus they would escape the common lot of lowlier souls, relegated to underground *sheols*. They hoped in this way to enjoy divine bliss in heaven, and to spare their mortal remains the indignity of lying underground in close proximity to those of the less privileged classes. Mausoleums existed in Phoenicia; for example, the Meghazils of Amrith,[75] multi-storied towers, one of which is supported by four lions and surmounted by a pyramid, have survived to this day. It was thus in their country of origin that the Carthaginians had become acquainted with this kind of monument, which they introduced into Africa, where it remained popular throughout antiquity. Archaeologists have not yet succeeded in discovering where these tower-like tombs first originated. However, two classes of mausoleums are found in Africa, the first massive like the Egyptian pyramids, the second tall and slender, like gigantic stelae. To the first belong the great Libyan tombs, today known as the Medrassen,[76] and the 'Tomb of the Christian Woman'.[77] Their decorative scheme includes the 'Egyptian throat' (a kind of hollow moulding), and the Aeolian capital, and was thus obviously influenced by Punic art. But up to the present, no building of this size has been found on Carthaginian soil, and it is possible that these mausoleums are only tumuli similar to the *bazinas* which were native to Libya, but decorated in the Punic manner. On the other hand, when a Numidian prince of Dougga ordered his tomb in the second century B.C., his Phoenician architect kept strictly to the fashion of his own native land.[78] A tall three-storied tower, surmounted by a pyramid, is portrayed in a fresco on the side of a Cape Bon burial-vault.[79] The ruins of two mausoleums in the Punic style, which unfortunately have never been the subject of detailed study,[80] still exist in the extensive plains from which Carthage drew much of its agricultural wealth. We shall have occasion later to refer to the symbolic decorations of the Dougga mausoleum. These make use of Anatolian motifs borrowed from fifth-century artists to illustrate the soul's journey in the after-life. The great Masinissa himself had just such a tomb built at Kroubs, on the outskirts of Cirta.[81] This type of monument was very much in the fashion at this time in all the countries which had adopted the Hellenistic civilization. The Romanized Africans remained faithfully attached to it, and as their wealth increased, there was soon scarcely a man of any importance even in the smallest town who could not boast that the dead members of his family were housed in one of these towers, formerly the preserve of kings and magistrates. Even the caravan traders of Ghadames, and the chief of the Garamantes of Fezzan built them on the outskirts of their oases, as if to mark out the astonishing advance of Mediterranean civilization across the desert.

Thus, in their choice of tombs, as well as in the style and decoration of their houses, the Carthaginians accepted in an ever-increasing degree the fashions that came from Greece. Hamilcar and Hannibal would indeed have been surprised at the weird architectural fantasies, such as twisted columns, copper domes, and inverted obelisks, which Flaubert's imagination delighted in collecting from a mass of Oriental bric à brac to adorn Salammbô's native land. With its simple whitewashed houses, covered with flat roofs or cupolas, and its narrow twisting streets, Carthage must have looked very much like a modern Tunisian town. If a Carthaginian could be brought back to life again today, he would find that the mosques, with their large courtyards and colonnades, were very like the temples he had known so well. It has always been characteristic of the Tunisians that they readily adopt foreign fashions in their decorative schemes; on the other hand they have always remained equally attached to artistic procedures long out of date in their country of origin. Today, in the suburbs of Tunisian towns, the façades of the houses are still embellished with stylized floral patterns which enjoyed a great vogue in France just after the 1925 Exhibition of Decorative Arts. Future archaeologists will no doubt be led by this into attractive but mistaken conclusions about their date of origin. In the ordinary environment of his daily life, the Carthaginian was a Mediterranean in no way very different from his contemporaries on the Mediterranean shores, nor indeed from any of those who came after him.

REFERENCES

1. By the third century B.C., the gulf was almost completely enclosed by a littoral belt. When the east wind held back the sea, it was possible to walk on foot from Carthage to Utica. Hamilcar took advantage of this fact during the War of the Mercenaries. S. Gsell, HAAN, III, p. 110; Bernand, *Bull. Géog. Hist.*, 1911, p. 113.

2. S. Gsell, *op. cit.*, I, pp. 374 sqq. and pp. 397 sqq.

3. E. Forrer, 'Karthago wurde erst 673–663 von Christ gegrundet', *Festschrift Franz Dornseiff*, Leipzig, 1953, pp. 85–93. Cf. E. Frezouls, B.C.H., 1955, pp. 153 sqq.

4. See J. Bérard, *La Colonisation grecque de l'Italie méridionale et de la Sicile dans l'Antiquité, l'histoire et la légende*, Paris, 1930.

5. On the subject of Phoenician navigation, see Bérard, *Les Phéniciens et l'Odyssée* is still useful. P. Cintas, *Céramique punique*, pp. 504–5; *Fouilles puniques à Tipasa*, p. 270.

6. L. Balout, *Préhistoire de l'Afrique du Nord*, p. 489.

7. On the subject of Tartessus and the quest for tin, see below, Chap. V and VII.

8. The foundation of Utica was given as 287 years before that of Carthage (Pseudo-Aristotle, *De mirabilibus auscultationibus*, 134). Pliny the Elder confirms this date (*N.H.* XVI, 216).

9. For bibliography, see E. Frezouls, quoted in n. 3 above.

10. The upper city covered the St Louis and Juno Hills. In the seventh century B.C., the lower city occupied that part of the shore bounded by the harbour lagoons to the south, and by the *wadi* which flowed along the site of the present Antonine Baths Avenue, to the north; on the east it was bounded by the sea, and on the west by the depression which skirts the St Louis and Juno Hills (Douimes sector). A vast necropolis separated the lower city from the upper city, which was built on the hills. The sides of these hills are full of tombs, the oldest of which go back to the beginning of the seventh century B.C., while the most recent date from the fourth century B.C.

11. The sanctuary of Tanit and Baal, or *tophet*, extended immediately to the west of the lagoon which corresponds with the commercial harbour. A small temple dating from the final years of Carthage was discovered in 1916 under the Tramway depot, Tunis-Marsa, which has been given the name Salammbô, just over a mile from the *tophet*. Above Byrsa rose the famous Temple of Eshmoun. In our view it was on the Odeon Hill above the slopes in which the Roman amphitheatre was constructed. The Demeter shrine, built in 396, dominated the town to the north, on the Sainte-Monique Hill. No trace of it has been found apart from a *favissa*, a hidden store of incense-burners made in the image of the goddess.

12. The fourth-century cemeteries occupied the slopes of the plateaux of Bordj Djedid, and of the amphitheatre, dominating Carthage to the north-west. After the fall of Carthage, the dead were buried on the Sainte-Monique, the Odeon and the amphitheatre hills. Farther south, a few tombs of the same period have been discovered under the village of El Kram. In this direction, the city never extended beyond the harbours: the Romans had no difficulty in occupying the base of the ridge on which La Goulette and Kherreddine stand today. Thus, at the time of the siege of 149, the lower town extended from the Bay of El Kram, in the south, to the foot of Bordj Djedid in the north. To the west it merged into the upper town, thus forming one single built-up area.

13. C. Picard, *Carthage*, pp. 27–9 and bibliography, p. 91.

14. Appian, *Pun.*, 95.

15. Strabo, XVII, 3, 14.

16. Diodorus, III, 44, 8.

16a. On the meaning of the word *Cothon*, consult E. Kursten's article in *Charités* (Bonn, 1957, pp. 110 sqq.), entitled 'Kothon in Sparta und Karthago'.

17. P. Cintas, 'Un Sanctuaire précarthaginois sur la grève de Salammbô', *Revue tunisienne*, 1948. MC, pl. 7 and 8.

18. C. Picard, *op. cit.*, p. 60. MC, pl. 5.

19. C. Picard, *op. cit.*, p. 60 and bibliography, p. 98.

20. Dr Carton situates the inner harbour of Carthage in this estuary. (See below, n. 28.)

21. The whole of this quarter was destroyed; in the course of an exploratory dig in 1952, directed by the Office of Antiquities, only a few featureless fragments were brought to light (details not yet published).

22. Appian, *op. cit.*, 96.

23. *Ibid.*, 121, 123, 124, 134.

24. Quoted above, n. 15.

25. M. Beulé, *Fouilles à Carthage*, pp. 112 sqq.

26. A. Merlin, CRAI 1912, pp. 277 sqq.; 1918, pp. 145 sqq.; BAC, 1909, pp. 51-3, pl. VI; 1911, pp. 157-9, pl. X; 1915, pp. CCXLIV–CCXLVI.

27. C. Picard, *op. cit.*, p. 27.

28. L. Carton, *Revue archéologique*, 1911, 2, pp. 234 sqq.; *Documents pour servir à l'histoire des ports de Carthage*, pp. 24 sqq.; *Topographie carthaginoise*, pp. 11 sqq., situates the naval harbour in a vast bay which he imagines once occupied the site of the present plain of Dermech. As we have seen, there certainly was a small creek there into which a *wadi* ran, but which has been filled in since Punic times. Charles Saumagne, *Historia*, V, 1931, pp. 173 sqq., considered that the *Cothon* extended at right-angles to the shore, starting from Salammbô Point, thus bringing within the commercial harbour, the southern part of the rectangular lagoon. This bold theory, which has never had any archaeological support, is now quite untenable in view of the later discovery that the Tanit sanctuary extended parallel to the shore of the southern lagoon, on the very spot where Saumagne had wanted to site his harbour basin.

29. Cecil Torr, *Classical Review*, V, 1891, pp. 280-4; VII, 1893, pp. 374-7; VIII, 1894, pp. 271-6; *Rev. Arch.*, 1894, I, pp. 34-7 and 294-307, and Oehler, *Neue Jahrbücher für Philologie*, CXLII, 1893, pp. 321-32.

30. Ph. Tailliez, *Plongées sans câble*, p. 108.

31. J. Baradez, CRAI, 1955, p. 1.

32. P. Cintas, *Fouilles puniques à Tipasa*, p. 14.

33. C. Picard, *op. cit.*, pp. 19 sqq. and bibliography, p. 90.
34. General R. Duval, *L'enceinte de Carthage*, CRAI, 1950, p. 53; MC, pl. 73.
35. G. G. Lapeyre, *Revue africaine*, 1934, pp. 334 sqq.
36. G. Ch.-Picard, *Les Religions de l'Afrique antique*, Paris 1954, pp. 74–5.
37. C. Schaeffer, *Ugaritica*, II, p. 128.
38. P. Cintas, 'Un sanctuaire précarthaginois sur la grève de Salammbô', *Revue tunisienne*, 1948, and *Céramique punique*, pp. 490 sqq. MC, pl. 8.
39. MC, pl. 11.
40. *Ibid.*, pl. 9.
41. G. G. Lapeyre and A. Pellegrin, *Carthage punique*, p. 149.
42. C. Picard, *Catalogue Mus. Alaoui, Nlle série*, I, Cb 101–Cb 159; Cb 255–Cb 336; Cb 479–Cb 503.
43. *Ibid.*, Cb 492; Cb 500.
44. *Ibid.*, Cb 489. MC, pl. 13.
45. C. Picard, *Catalogue Mus. Alaoui, Nlle série*, I, Cb 504–Cb 514. MC, pl. 16.
46. C. Picard, *Catalogue Mus. Alaoui, Nlle série*, I, Cb 342–Cb 355.
47. MC, pl. 34.
48. *Ibid.*, pl. 32 and 60.
49. P. Gauckler, *Nécropoles puniques*, II, pp. 383–4.
50. MC, pl. 14, 15 and 33.
51. P. Cintas, *Karthago*, V, 1955, pp. 117 sqq. MC, pl. 1–2.
52. C. Schaeffer, *op. cit.*, I, p. 87.
53. P. Cintas, *Karthago*, II, 1951, fig. 15.
54. J. Féron and M. Pinard, *Cahiers de Byrsa*, V, 1955, pp. 31 sqq. For the question of date, cf. our communication submitted to the Commission for North Africa, BAC, 1957, session of February 11 and 'Maisons puniques à Carthage', *Revue archéologique*, 1909.
55. We have found it in particular in Acholla: cf. *Karthago*, IV, 1954, p. 123. It was also used in Punic buildings of the fifth century B.C. in Sabratha in Tripolitania: J. H. Reynolds and J. B. Ward Perkins, *Inscriptions of Roman Tripolitania*, p. 273. Also in Cyprus as early as the eighth century: E. Gjerstad, *Cyprus Swedish Expedition*, pp. 2 sqq.
56. C. Picard, *Karthago*, III, 1953, pp. 121 sqq. J. Féron and M. Pinard, *op. cit.*, pp. 55–6.
57. L. Carton, *Un sanctuaire punique découvert à Carthage*.
58. A. Merlin, *Le sanctuaire de Ba'al et de Tanit près de Siagu*, *Notes et Documents*, IV, 1910.

59. L. Carton, *Mémoires presentées par divers savants à l'Académie des Inscriptions*, XII, Part I, pl. 1 sqq.

60. L. Carton, *Nouv. Archives des Missions*, VII, *Le Temple de Ba'al Saturne à Dougga*, and G. Ch.-Picard, *op. cit.*, pp. 153 sqq.

61. C. Picard, *Catalogue Mus. Alaoui, Nlle série*, I, p. 300, Cb 1082. MC, pl. 51.

62. R. Martin, *Recherches sur l'Agora hellénique*.

63. C. Picard, *Karthago*, III, 1953, pp. 117 sqq.

64. See above, n. 54.

65. P. Cintas, *Contribution à l'étude de l'expansion carthaginoise au Maroc*, pl. 13 and fig. 2.

66. *Diodorus*, XIX, 102 sqq.

67. *Atlas archéologique de la Tunisie*, sheet 17, Kelibia, position 14.

68. Results of excavation not yet published. Cf. BAC, 1946–9, p. 380.

69. MC, pl. 52–3.

70. V. Spinazzola, *Pompei alla luce dei scavi nuovi della via dell' Abbondanza*; G. Calza, *Ostia*, pp. 18–19.

71. MC, pl. 50.

72. A. Merlin, BAC, 1919, pp. 178–96.

73. Festus, *De Verborum significatu s.v. pavimenta punica*.

74. C. Picard, *Catalogue Mus. Alaoui, Nlle série*, I, Cb 1–Cb 94.

75. C. Contenau, MAO, III, p. 1465.

76. S. Gsell, HAAN, VI, pp. 262–5.

77. M. Christofle, *Le Tombeau de la Chrétienne*, Algiers + Paris, 1951.

78. L. Poinssot, CRAI, 1910, pp. 780–7 and MC, pl. 82–3.

79. E. Gobert and P. Cintas, *Revue tunisienne*, 1939, pp. 190 sqq. MC, pl. 52.

80. These are the two mausoleums of the region of Hedil, North Tunisia; that of Ksar Chenan, Saladin, BAC, 1900, pp. 126–7; and that of Ksar Rouhaha, Saladin, *ibid.*, pp. 127–8.

81. Ballu, BAC, 1917, pp. 226–9.

CHAPTER III

CARTHAGINIAN SOCIETY: THE RULING CLASSES

THE CITY AND THE NATION

WHEN we come to study Carthaginian society, one thing stands out above all others: the fact that we are dealing with a city-state. This may seem obvious, but it is nevertheless important. The *polis* is such an integral part of the classical civilization from which our cultural environment is derived that it seems natural to us to regard it as a necessary stage in human development. And yet it was really a novel conception which, although it originated on the plains of Mesopotamia and India, only found the human and economic conditions which allowed it to flourish, on the shores of the Mediterranean. Because they were citizens, the Carthaginians belonged, in spite of many differences, to the same type of society as the Greeks and the Romans. The normal distinction between the Indo-European and the Semitic worlds does not hold for the *polis*; in this context, the line of separation was in Asia Minor, between Phoenicia on the one hand, and on the other Egypt, Israel, and Persia. In these latter countries, the *polis* never developed, and even in Mesopotamia, the Sumerian towns soon lost their originality within the framework of the Semitic kingdoms. In Europe there is a similar gulf between the Greeks and the Italians on the one hand, and the Celtic, Germanic, and Slav peoples on the other. This fundamental distinction between the two types of society was clearly perceived by the Greek sociologists. Eratosthenes confidently maintained that men who possessed so good a political constitution as did the Carthaginians could not be regarded as barbarians.[1] The cause of the similarity between the Greek and Punic societies seems to be due neither to the influence of Greek institutions on Carthage, for that could only have been felt very late, nor to the influence of the Phoenicians on the early Greek civilization. It is much more probably due to the fact that both the Hellenes and the Phoenicians derived their civilization from the Aegeans. The same mould shaped the minds of men whose forms of thought were diametrically opposed on such fundamental issues as the general conception of the universe, the relationship between man and nature, and man and the supernatural, or even his relationships with his fellow-beings. (As G. Dumesnil has shown, traces of the old social order reappeared within the framework of the city-state.) Thus, while the Carthaginians adopted the same system of government as the Greeks, they spoke the same language as the Hebrews, regulated their religion on principles very similar to those of the Bible, and showed an almost complete lack of ability in the plastic arts. However, owing to the similarity between the economic conditions in Greece and Carthage, a similar political system grew and flourished; had it been the result of outside influences, it would soon have declined and perished.

At first, the Carthaginian settlement was essentially an urban one, even though its economy was largely agricultural. Most of the population, and in particular the wealthier classes, lived in the town, where even the poorer classes, including the slaves, generally enjoyed a standard of living well above that of their rural counterparts. The town, in fact, was not merely a storehouse for the wealth of the community; it was above all the only centre of political life. This meant that both the size and the population of the town were bound to be restricted. A city might extend its hegemony fairly widely, but the inhabitants of the conquered territory outside the relatively restricted suburbs could never be anything more than inferior beings, serfs, tributaries or, in the most favourable circumstances, semi-citizens or subordinate allies.

These characteristics were more sharply defined in Carthage than in many of the Greek cities, or in Rome. During the first three centuries of its existence, the Punic community's only living-space was the thirty or so square miles of the peninsula. Its economy was based entirely on maritime trade or on piracy. In the sixth century B.C. it conquered territory in Africa which, for a city-state, was very extensive, nearly 20,000 square miles, or perhaps 30,000 or 40,000. But this 'empire' was divided, politically and economically, into two parts: first, the city territory proper, the *chora*, within which the soil belonged to the citizens, who cultivated it mainly with the help of rural slave-labour, and whose resources were normally devoted to the maintenance of the urban community, and second, a province inhabited by tributary peoples, within whose borders were a number of isolated independent allied towns; the revenues of this province were used by the State for political ends. Later on we shall attempt to define the approximate extent of this territory; it appears to have made up about a quarter of Punic Africa.

We have very little information about the size of the population. However, Strabo, who was a contemporary of Augustus, and consequently lived a hundred years after the destruction of Carthage, maintains that the town alone had a population of 700,000 inhabitants.[2] This estimate cannot be sustained, as the town proper only covered about 700 acres. Even allowing for a very high density, the population could not in fact have exceeded 100,000. The suburbs extended for about seven or eight square miles within the city walls; even supposing a density of population similar to that of present-day towns in the Sahel valley, whose mixture of dwellings and gardens resembles the countryside of Megara, there could not have been room for more than another 100,000. The estimates made by ancient historians of the size of armies are generally suspect, and in any case the armies were mostly composed of mercenaries. We can, however, accept the fact that during the 'truceless war', in which they were cut off from all outside help, the Carthaginians were unable to make available more than 10,000 men to Hamilcar and roughly another 10,000 to Hanno. During the siege of Carthage in 149, the city was defended by 30,000 men. Another force, probably smaller, operated in the surrounding country. And yet all fit men, capable of bearing arms, including slaves, had been mobilized. The total population at that time, therefore, must have been about 200,000.[3] At the end of the siege, a mere 50,000 people were left in the Byrsa stronghold.

The figure of 700,000 mentioned by Strabo is probably that of the population of the *chora*, within which the Carthaginians alone enjoyed civil and political rights. This territory probably covered some 7,000 or 8,000 square miles, thus giving an average of 100 inhabitants to the square mile, which seems reasonable.

The preponderance of the town in the city-state led to a strong sense of moral solidarity. We shall see that in spite of all the political conflicts which divided them, the Carthaginians preserved a common front, not only against foreigners, but also against allies or subject peoples who were part of the same body politic. This solidarity was founded not only on the city's institutions and a patriotism which revealed its true strength at moments of crisis, but also on religious feeling. Each city chose from the pantheon which belonged to the whole nation one or two deities to become its patron god, and whom it honoured above all others. From the fifth century B.C. onwards, it was Tanit who won this privileged position, at the expense of Astarte, and even of Baal Hammon, who was relegated to second place. It is probable that before this religious revolution, the new Tyre remained under the protection of the patron god of the metropolis, namely Melkart. Every year emissaries were sent to him, bearing a substantial tribute. This custom died out in the fourth century B.C. The revolution of the third century therefore brought about the final emancipation of Carthage in religious matters. But Melkart remained in high esteem, and his aid was sought in particularly difficult times, as, for example, when a foreign army, led by Agathocles, appeared before the walls of the city. Doubtless there were internal political reasons for the relative subordination of the Tyrian god; it seems that this 'King of the City', as his name means in Phoenician, was more particularly regarded as the protector of the monarchy. His replacement by Tanit was confirmation in the religious sphere of the foundation of a republican oligarchy. This hypothesis is strengthened by the fact that the Barcids were devoted followers of Melkart, and no doubt were planning to restore him in their own interests.

This civic solidarity was capable of inspiring sublime devotion, but it weighed heavily upon the individual and, in particular, on the lower classes. In Carthage, political restrictions became a tyranny all the more cruel because they were not tempered, as in Greece, by a growing respect for the value of the human personality, or, as in Rome, by an extreme regard for the law. This tyranny, however, had this much in common with Greece: it mistrusted any individual who stood out from the common run of men, whether for good or for evil.

Another defect of the city-state was its inability to expand and its exclusive attitude to those who wanted to become its citizens. Carthage suffered particularly from this defect, which also led to the downfall of Athens. These two towns were both equally unfair in their treatment of their allies, even those of the same race, to whom they persistently refused to grant political or economic equality. In these respects, and to their grave detriment, the Greeks and the Carthaginians were much less generous and far-sighted than the Romans. This contrast is all the more striking as far as Carthage is concerned, because she had to face this problem at the same time as did her Italian rival. The crisis in the city-state, which in Greece occurred in the fourth century, was in the West delayed until later. It must be remembered too that at least one Carthaginian politician, Hannibal, appears to have understood the gravity of the problem and to have seen how to solve it; only military defeat prevented him from doing so.

Although Carthage was politically autonomous, it remained morally and spiritually part of the Phoenician nation.

The Carthaginian language was essentially Phoenician, and therefore Semitic in origin. This language survived in Africa and Sardinia many centuries after it was no longer spoken in Asia. It is known to us chiefly through inscriptions. Thousands of ex-votos and epitaphs have survived, though unfortunately they are only commonplace and stereotyped formulae. Thus all the stelae of the *tophet*, with one or two exceptions earlier than the reform of the fifth century, bear the phrase: 'To the Lady Tanit, Face of Baal, and to the Lord Baal Hammon, this is dedicated by so and so, son of so and so'. The rare texts which manage to avoid this uniform banality consist of a few religious inscriptions, tariffs which lay down the share due to the priests for every class of sacrifice, and also dedicatory temple inscriptions. But the neo-Punic inscriptions of later date than the destruction of Carthage are often more interesting, especially dedications of civil or religious buildings, in the towns of Tripolitania or Central Tunisia. Many are bilingual, Latin-Punic, or, as in Dougga, Libyan-Punic. The only literary fragments which have survived are the passages from the *Poenulus* of Plautus translated into Punic. The longest of these is a prayer offered by the merchant Hanno to the gods of the port where he has just landed, asking them to allow him to find his daughters and his nephew again.

These texts are written in a language very like Hebrew. This resemblance was strong enough to have been noticed in the fourth century, not only by cultivated people like St Augustine and St Jerome, who often drew attention to it, but also by the African peasants themselves. And yet Phoenician was, by that time, little more than a patois which was no longer written and which had been extensively mutilated. The Greeks and Romans, on the other hand, were never conscious of the relationship between their languages, or between them and other Indo-European tongues like Celtic.

The twenty-two-letter written alphabet was invented by the Phoenicians in about the twelfth century B.C., after numerous attempts to use cuneiform or Egyptian characters. From this system, adopted first by the Greeks, and later by the Romans, are derived all the alphabets used in the world today, excepting, of course, those of the Far East. The Phoenician alphabet was written from right to left; it had no vowel signs, but did have semi-vowels, the gutturals *aleph* and *he*, the *wav* (w), and the *yod* (y). When it began to spread in the fifth century—we shall try to explain later why it was so late—the Carthaginian script was very like that of the motherland. At about the time of the fall of Carthage it was modified by the adoption of the cursive forms which led to the neo-Punic alphabet.

The Carthaginians not only kept the language and the writing of their native land, but helped to spread it among the peoples under their rule. Foreigners living in Carthage, especially the mercenaries, adopted Punic as their common speech. Among the Libyans, Punic became the language of culture. The script, which was invented in the second century B.C. to transcribe their various dialects, and which still survives today under the name of *tifinagh* among the Touaregs, was doubtless derived from the Phoenician alphabet.

The Carthaginians also kept the calendar and the system of weights and measures they had brought with them from Phoenicia.

Both language and methods of measuring time and space reflect a philosophic conception of the universe. It was in their metaphysical outlook that the Carthaginians differed most radically from the Greeks, and therefore from classical ways of

3. Lion-shaped gargoyle from a building in Carthage: *Musée du Bardo*

Carthaginian jewellery, toilet articles, amulets and religious objects from the period of the Punic Wars. In the centre a mirror; above it, left, a razor

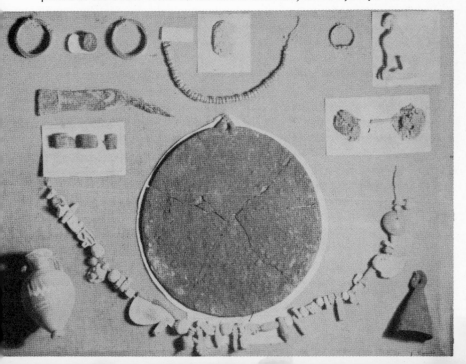

(*Below*) Statuette from a *tophet* in Cartha[ge] doubtlessly representing Baal (sixth century B.[C.])

4. (*Above*) Carthaginian female clothing depicted on a stele from Carthage (fourth to third century B.C.)

thinking. The Phoenicians never accepted the principle of rational causality. The world never appeared to them as a machine, governed by definite laws which man was capable of understanding and which would then enable him to master nature. The fundamental principle of Protagoras, 'man is the measure of all things', was profoundly repugnant to them. Instead of this physical causality they adopted a mystic causality. This is expressed in the poems of Ugarit, which are the most ancient manifestation we have of Phoenician thought; and also on the neo-Punic stelae carved in the second century A.D., just when this Phoenician culture was on the point of disappearing. Already in the fourteenth century B.C., the poets of Ugarit[4] described the growth of vegetation, the ripening of the harvest and its transformation into food which can be assimilated by man, as a continually repeated conflict between two divine beings, who are themselves ultimately dependent on El, the supreme father: Aleyan Baal, representing the principle of moisture (or the growth of plants), and Moth, the incarnation of summer drought and of the ripening grain.

The stelae of La Ghorfa[5] illustrate very clearly the cycle of operations by which Providence animates the cosmos. It reveals a conception of the world very similar to that expressed in Psalm cxlviii. At the summit of the stele sits the lord enthroned in highest heaven, surrounded by the sun, the moon, and the stars. Corresponding to the angels in the Psalm is a mysterious figure represented by the sign of Tanit, who proceeds from the lord and transmits his beneficent force to nature. Then come 'the waters under the heavens' (v. 4), the ocean above, from which fall the rains, with its fish; the atmosphere with its winds, symbolized by birds (v. 8); and then, the earth with its men, animals, and plants; and finally at the base of the pyramid, the abyss with its monsters and dragons. The providence of the lord, moved by the sacrifice in the temple, comes down on earth through the ministration of the 'angel', represented by the sign of Tanit, and of the subordinate gods, ministers of the all-highest who assure human, animal, and vegetable fertility. We shall see later that the Greek mystic sects, like that of Pythagoras, which found some resemblance between these notions and their own doctrine, certainly succeeded in rationalizing them. But fundamentally they are related to the old Canaanite naturalism which was adopted in part by the Hebrew *Yahwism*.

Mythological symbolism came so naturally to the Carthaginians, that the most Romanized among them used it in the decoration of classical monuments commemorating historical events, in place of the narrative or allegorical devices of Imperial art. Thus at Mactar, reliefs carved in A.D. 170 show the transformation of the town into a Roman colony: first is shown a violent struggle between a centaur and a griffin, the servants of the patron gods of the native city, Apollo and Bacchus; then these two monstrous adversaries are pacified and reconciled by the intervention of the capitoline trio. In Tripoli, on the triumphal arch dedicated to Marcus Aurelius, the patron divinities of the town, Apollo and Minerva, hasten to the rescue of Roman armies, in chariots drawn by griffins. In this hierarchy of natural forces, man is not without means of action—and these belong to the realm of magic. The most potent is sacrifice, for this regenerates the divine power itself. But a mere offering to the gods will not do: in principle, the offerer sacrifices himself and the victim must never be a substitute. And so the efficacy of the sacrifice is proportional to the value of the victim. This explains the continued persistence of human sacrifices. The *mol'k*, a holocaust of children, was thus the perfect form of Punic sacrifice. There is no better proof of the unwavering loyalty of the African Phoenicians to their traditions than their obstinate refusal to abandon this practice even under pressure or compulsion.

The ethical and aesthetic notions of the Carthaginians are the logical outcome of their metaphysics.

We have no direct knowledge of their ethical system. The uncomplimentary views held by the Greeks and Romans can easily be explained: they were due either to political hostility, or to the fact that the Greeks and Romans came into contact only with the least scrupulous elements of Carthaginian society, namely, merchants or soldiers. However, the Carthaginians certainly treated human life, whether their own or other people's, with even less respect than did the Greeks. Their readiness to sacrifice themselves, the cruel tortures they inflicted for trivial reasons, not only on the lower classes, but even on important personages, are ample proof of this. There is nothing surprising in this contempt for the human person in a nation which considered that the most deserving act of all was mystic suicide. Until Greek influence became too strong, the only beings whom they regarded as worthy of divine status, like Dido, the brothers Philenes and Hamilcar the Magonid, all perished in this way. Did the Carthaginians believe that such deaths really redeemed the sins of the victims or of the community? Like the Hebrews, the Carthaginians practised expiatory sacrifices. Human sacrifice could have this property. Thus when the Carthaginians were threatened by Agathocles, they imputed their misfortunes to their own negligence towards the gods and in one ritual holocaust sacrificed to Tanit and Baal Hammon 500 children chosen from among the most noble families. Like the ancient Phoenicians and the Hebrews, they believed that public misfortunes were the result of the wrath of the gods. But the sins of which they accused themselves were ritual and not moral. For example, the noble families upon whom fell the obligation to sacrifice their first-born had substituted young slaves, thus depriving the gods of their consecrated victims, and drawing down upon the city the fate to which these victims had been dedicated. Or they had neglected to pay the tributes due to Melkart of Tyre. As early as 396 B.C., a defeat in Sicily was attributed to the wrath of the gods: in this case, of foreign gods, Demeter and Kore, who were appeased by a temple built in Carthage. But the divine anger was provoked not by the atrocities committed by the Punic army against the worshippers of these gods, the Greeks, but by the destruction of one of their shrines in the suburbs of Syracuse.

The gods could also punish certain wrong-doings of the individual: they chastised all those who violated any building or tomb which had been placed under their protection, or who broke an oath which they had been called upon to witness. Their intervention was not due to their indignation at the crime thus committed but to the personal affront done to them. It was provoked only when they had become personally involved in the matter by the act of imprecation.

Similarly the blessing of the divine favour was a matter of the greatest importance, as can be seen from the concluding formula on many stelae: 'Because he heard his voice and blessed him.' It was to be won, not by moral conduct, but by the scrupulous performance of ritualistic practices, notably sacrifices, or by a contract of dedication. In such transactions with their gods, the Carthaginians resorted to the same sharp practices as they employed in human affairs and were delighted when they could manage to get the better of the dreaded Baal.

The great religious revival which the prophets brought to the Hebrews and the philosophers to the Greeks, by which the Divinity became the guarantor of an absolute morality, perfect beyond that of human society, never happened with the Carthaginians.

The reforms of the fifth century B.C., which were part of a spiritual evolution in that direction, did purge ritual of the grosser sexual practices and gave the faithful a more respectable picture of their gods. But the Carthaginians never discovered the virtues of love, unselfishness, and charity. For this reason, unlike Buddhism and Christianity, which had both sprung from a very similar theology of sacrifice, their religion never attained the mystical idea of renunciation which enriches, instead of crushing, the personality.

The refusal to admit any harmony between man and his world was an insurmountable obstacle to the development of a naturalistic art. The Carthaginians, therefore, strove to copy Greek or Egyptian monuments, but as they were incapable of understanding the inspiration behind them, the results were worthless. Their work in relief was particularly mediocre and shows that this form of art must have been held in scant esteem. The statue of a winged goddess, reconstucted for the Lavigerie Museum by P. Cintas, is not merely crude, but vulgar and commonplace, and without any appeal to the emotions.[6] And yet it is a ritualistic image of the Lady of Carthage herself.

Apart from a few buildings like the sarcophagi of Sainte-Monique,[7] which are obviously the work of foreign craftsmen, the stelae of the *tophet* are the only monuments of any aesthetic interest. Unlike the *cippi* which preceded them, the stelae have decoration only on the front face, i.e. in two dimensions. The technique consists of incisions in the stone of low relief. There was thus a conscious effort to ban, as far as possible, the third dimension, whereas the Greeks made every effort to give the illusion of solidity. This prejudice must certainly be attributed to the fact that both Judaism and Islam condemned graven images which represented living beings and in particular those which cast a shadow. Such an attitude might be explained by fear of the magic powers inherent in the statue. But the Egyptians and the Greeks thought that this power could be controlled by the use of the image itself. The attitude of the Semites therefore reveals a feeling of terror and of hostility in the presence of the world as revealed through the senses. They sought to make it harmless by mutilating it and by suppressing all signs of movement and life.

This denial of reality did not completely banish all forms of art. Islam was able to create a decorative style by utilizing certain natural shapes, borrowed in particular from the vegetable world, which were combined with purely abstract motifs, geometrical figures, or written characters. Punic art could have taken a similar road. It did sometimes succeed in producing a feeling of austere grandeur by the use of very simple geometrical elements such as the crescent, the sign of Tanit, and the roundel.[8] But this severity is broken by plant decorations such as palm leaves and curved branches,[9] which herald the fantasies of arabesque. On the wader-bird stele,[10] the image of a bird, repeated identically four times like Darius' archers on the Palace of Susa, takes the place of abstract designs. On such monuments, which are the best and most original products of Punic art, the play of light and shade, and the opposition of striated and flat surfaces, produce a rather attractive decorative effect. But these modest masterpieces are rare. More often, the stone is mutilated by a completely inartistic hand and with no idea of composition. The figures are scattered at random, as in a child's drawings. This complete inability to compose, which was certainly due to lack of feeling for, and indifference to, harmony, was the fundamental reason for the artistic impotence of the Carthaginians. This deficiency explains how skilful draughtsmen capable of copying from a Greek model a head full of life and feeling,[11] or of engraving on the bronze blade of a ritualistic razor[12] the figure of Hercules throttling the Cretan bull, or the coils of the monster Scylla, were nevertheless quite incapable of creating a style of their own.

The Carthaginian architects never succeeded in doing more

than placing next to each other at random the courtyards and the chapels of their sanctuaries. Doubtless, like the worthy Tunisian mason in George Duhamel's story, they drew up the plan after they had finished the building. In their decorative art, they collected motifs borrowed from the most diverse orders, without in the least understanding the harmony of relationships which should have bound them into a coherent whole. Their scribes never wrote more than 'tiny fidgety letters scrambling hurriedly across tiny stones'. Calligraphy, which the Egyptians, the Romans and the Jews and the Arabs put to such varied and decorative uses, and from which the Arabs derived the most original motifs for ornamenting buildings, remained a closed book to the inventors of the alphabet.

We are forced to conclude that there was a veritable atrophy of certain intellectual faculties and of certain forms of feeling in a people otherwise gifted, and we must look for the cause in their warped religious feelings. But these in turn were undoubtedly the result of the abnormal conditions in which Punic society developed after its brutal separation from the human environment in which it was born, and from its isolation in a hostile world whose forces seemed in league to crush it. If the Carthaginians remained loyal to their incomplete and almost pathological vision of the world, it was because the Punic community itself was never perfect. An examination of its various component parts, and their relationship with each other, will make this clearer.

PRIESTS AND NOBLES

For four or five centuries, the tiny nucleus of Dido's colonists and their early descendants lived primarily from the sea. The subsequent political and economic development of the State naturally brought about a considerable diversification of Punic society. One of the most useful facts revealed by Carthaginian inscriptions is the trade of the deceased; they represent all the social classes, from the civil and religious aristocracy to the humblest citizens— the kind of poverty-stricken proletariat which swarms in all Mediterranean ports at all periods of history. To them must be added the slaves, foreign residents, and Libyan peasants who flocked into the town.

Obviously the way of life of all these people varied according to their position on the social ladder. We shall ignore for the moment those who lived and worked in the areas outside the city and its immediate surroundings: merchants, adventurers, Sahara caravaneers; and also the military leaders who founded distant empires—the *condottieri* of Spain and Italy.

THE PRIESTHOOD[13]

In the city, pride of place must certainly be given to the priests (*Kohanim*). They, the servants of Tanit, of Baal Hammon, of Melkart, Eshmoun, Reshef, Shadapra, Istart, Jam, Dagon, and many other gods,[14] secured for the city the indispensable protection of their dreaded masters. If the Carthaginians neglected to renew the supernatural strength of the gods by sacrifice, these gods would degenerate and would lose their power to promote the harvest, to ensure the fertility of man and beast, to inspire prudence in magistrates and might in warriors. Therefore, when political or economic disaster came, the priests denounced the lack of piety on the part of the worshippers, unleashing those surges of mysticism which ended in dreadful holocausts, such as Flaubert legitimately described from his own personal experience of the Aissaouas brotherhoods.[15]

The honour of being a *Kohen* was certainly fraught with danger. The man who dedicated himself to a god placed himself entirely at his disposition, and the dread lord could, if need be, instantly claim his very life. Sometimes, indeed, this sacrifice was made. King Malthus, annoyed with his son, a priest of Melkart, who refused to aid him in an attempted *coup d'état*, had the unfortunate man crucified in his priestly garments: and doubtless this barbaric form of torture was really a human sacrifice. Even in the third century A.D., in Roman Carthage, those who were condemned to face the wild beasts in the arena were made to dress as priests: the men, as priests of Saturn (the Latin equivalent of Baal Hammon), and the women as initiates of Ceres. By this subterfuge the gods were offered their ration of human blood which, because human sacrifices were forbidden under the Romans, would otherwise have been denied them. Even if the priest escaped death, he had to relinquish his human personality; in the shrine of Saturn Sobareusis, near the town of Nepheris, a

priest wore the yoke like a conquered warrior. At every moment
of the day, his contact with the dread divine presence exposed
him to dangers from which he could be saved only by that perfect
purity which came from the strict observance of endless taboos.
According to Silius Italicus,[16] Melkart was served in his temple
at Gades by priests dedicated to celibacy, shaved of beard and
hair, clothed in ungirdled linen robes, decorated with a broad
embroidered stole; they had to walk barefoot in his temple.
Women and pigs were banned from the shrine. There is a curious
resemblance between these prohibitions and those prescribed by
an inscription from Thuburbo Majus[17] for the faithful wishing
to enter the Temple of Aesculapius-Eshmoun. For three days
they were forbidden to know a woman, they had to banish beans
and pork from their diet, and had to keep away from the
barber and the public baths; the last two obligations were doubtless necessary preliminaries to the sacred toilet before initiation.
In other sanctuaries the priest or priestess had to abstain from
wine.

Permanent chastity was not demanded of all Punic priests,
since many of them were married and even handed on their
ministry to their heirs. Nevertheless, Tertullian[18] tells us that it
was still the custom in his time (end of the second and beginning
of the third centuries A.D.) to forbid the priestesses of the African
Ceres to consort with men or even to see their nearest relatives:
to mitigate the rigours of this obligation, elderly ladies only were
chosen, who were willing to leave their husbands, and, anxious
for their welfare, to provide them with a younger substitute.
Apparently the husbands were entirely satisfied with this arrange-
ment. The Carthaginians borrowed the cult of Demeter and
Ceres from the Greeks in Sicily, but they must have greatly
modified it, since a distinction was always made between the
African and the Punic cults. In the Hellenic countries men were
excluded only from certain ceremonies in the cult of these two
goddesses; but it seems likely that the Phoenicians, following their
rules for other cults, had transformed into a permanent obligation
what was originally only a temporary taboo. Nevertheless, this
same cult included a number of very licentious rites. Carcopino's[19]
ingenious interpretation of a text of Sallust shows that the chief
rite, celebrated on December 13th, throughout the whole of

Africa, was the occasion for feasts, games, and frolics which were certainly not without obscenity.

These are illustrated by a curious relief, carved on the funeral-stone of a priestess of the African Ceres, and preserved in Bardo Museum.[20] In childish perspective, it depicts a banqueting scene. Two persons are lying on beds separated by a small table, on which are dishes and wine-bowls containing drinks. The only intact figure is that of a woman, whose sole attire is a brassière and a pair of ear-rings. A sacred feast at which such exiguous attire was correct wear for the lady guest can hardly have been very austere. There is, however, nothing surprising in the fact that one and the same cult should impose upon its followers a rigorous continence at one moment, and allow the utmost licence at another. For it was not because of any moral preoccupation that chastity was imposed. This came later, under the influence of philosophy. But in the earliest times, sexual taboos, like sexual licence, were part of magical procedure. They were part of the cult of those gods on whom depended natural fertility, and were therefore intended to further this fertility by bringing about a magical partnership between man and the reproductive forces of nature.

This brings us to the very controversial subject of the sacred prostitutes. There is no doubt whatever that in the temples of Astarte, especially those in Cyprus, there lived a number of female attendants who were at the disposal of visitors. This has often been regarded as a typical characteristic of the Phoenician religion, to be found in all Tyrian colonies. Many authors have thought that Tanit, whom they considered to be a form of Astarte, admitted courtesans to her temples. In the neo-Punic shrine of this goddess, which he excavated in El Kenissia, near Sousse, Dr Carton thinks he can identify the sacred brothel attached to the temple.

This is almost certainly a mistake: Tanit is not the same as Astarte. Only one author has mentioned the existence of sacred prostitutes in Africa: the Roman moralist Valerius Maximus, a contemporary of Tiberius, scourges the immorality of the Punic matrons, who, he alleges, came to the Temple of Venus in Sicca to sacrifice their virginity.[21] But Sicca was not really a Punic town at all—it was a colony in which Carthage had settled a group of Elymaei from Eastern Sicily. These people, probably of Oriental origin, worshipped the great goddess of fertility, identified by the Phoenicians with Astarte, by the Greeks with Aphrodite, and by the Romans with Venus. The chief temple on Mount Eryx, of which the Sicca shrine is a copy, was indeed famous for its women attendants. If certain Punic women chose to come and offer sacrifices at this one place in the whole of Africa, in a shrine of foreign origin at Sicca, it was probably because they could not do so in their home towns. Sacred prostitution, then, so far from being a common characteristic of the Punic religion, seems rather to have been restricted to a few temples where immigrant deities were worshipped.

It is very likely that the naturalistic and licentious character of the Phoenician religion was modified by the religious reformation of the fifth century which led to the triumph of Tanit. In the levels of the *tophet* which are earlier in date than this reformation, crudely realistic terracotta statuettes have been found, representing men and women whose sexual attributes have been deliberately exaggerated. Other sexual symbols appear on funerary stones. All this disappeared in the fifth century. As we have already seen, this craving for austerity as a reaction against naturalism is essentially similar to the reforms urged by the Hebrew prophets and the Greek philosophers.

Silius Italicus, who has given us a fairly satisfactory idea of the obligations imposed on the Punic priesthood, was also very well informed on the subject of their costume, the simplicity of which symbolized this ideal of purity. The essential garment, Egyptian in origin, was a long transparent linen robe worn over a loincloth. This is the kind of garment which is worn by the priest sacrificing a child, depicted on the famous stele, from the *tophet*, preserved in Bardo Museum.[22] This priest is beardless like the priests of Gades and Egypt. On his shaven head is a round hat very like a fez. The same costume is worn by a priest called Baalyaton, who appears on a stele discovered in Phoenicia and preserved in the Ny Carlsberg Museum.[23] The Carthaginians had not, therefore, adopted the Egyptian priests' robes direct, but by way of Phoenicia. Similarly, many other legacies of the Nile civilization came by the same route to Africa. Another of the *tophet* stelae[24] depicts a priest with his shaven head uncovered, whose appearance is even more strikingly Egyptian. His robe is adorned with the emblem of Tanit, doubtless embroidered upon it. On the Hadrumetum stele, which shows Baal Hammon enthroned,[25] there stands, in front of the god, a tiny hairless figure who appears crushed by the divine majesty.

Not all priests, however, were obliged to shave their heads and chins. In the *tophet*[26] we sometimes come across a figure identifiable by the long transparent linen robe worn over a short tunic, as well as by the wine-pourer (*oenochoe*) and the bowl which he offers for a libation; on his chin he wears a pointed beard, and his hair, which is visible over his forehead, is covered by a veil falling down over the shoulders like an Egyptian *klaft*. Another bearded man appears on another ex-voto. Clothed in a long robe, he is making a gesture of adoration before an altar on which lies the head of a sacrificial bull.

The sole ornament worn on the white robe by the priests of Gades was a coloured band. Since Silius used the term *laticlave*, it must have resembled the purple stripe worn by Roman senators. The bearded priest from the *tophet* does indeed wear a long, narrow, rectangular band of material over the left shoulder. On the Sainte-Monique sarcophagi, the male statues of priests, or, as we prefer to think, of gods, wear a kind of fringed outer toga over a long robe.[27]

On a stele of the Imperial period from Mactar, is a figure wearing a cloak with an embroidered band. This is probably some kind of civil decoration rather than a sacred emblem; Latin inscriptions from Leptis[28] in fact say that the Senate and the people of that town accorded the right to wear the laticlave to the city notables as a supreme honour, either for their personal merits or because of their noble lineage.

Another sacred emblem, reminiscent of the ornament worn by the Hebrew priests, was a band of metal across the forehead. There are several specimens of these in our museums, all apparently dating from the Roman period, but they must also have been used in the neo-Punic cults. They bear the sign of Tanit, the bust of the goddess, and also of Baal Hammon, represented by Zeus Ammon, with whom he was often confused.

These garments remained relatively simple. The gods themselves, whose servants must have been dressed like them, wear no elaborate accoutrements on any of the Carthaginian monuments. The Baal Hammon on the Sousse stele was copied from a famous temple statue and is shown in numerous documents. He wears a long robe, and a tall pointed hat, which in other statues is replaced by a crown of feathers rather like a Red Indian's head-dress. This barbaric-looking adornment originated in Mesopotamia. Punic razors have been found, on the blade of which this same god is depicted wearing an Egyptian loin-cloth, pleated in front, and a tall hat. The goddesses were sometimes more richly attired; a well-known sarcophagus from Sainte-Monique[29] is surmounted by the recumbent figure of a young woman draped in the feathers of a gigantic dove: the head and beak form a kind of helmet, while the wings, folded over her legs, cover a kind of under-skirt. When this effigy was discovered, it was thought to represent the priestess buried there, clothed in her sacred robes. Unfortunately the urn contained nothing more exciting than the bones of an aged Negress! We think it represents the goddess Tanit, watching over the last resting-place of her servant.

From what has been said earlier, it is fair to suppose that the ranks of the Punic clergy included some who were under the most rigorous discipline, which allowed them hardly any lay activities, while others, chosen from the political aristocracy, were exempt from perpetual observance of those taboos which, in principle, their office entailed. In the same way, in Rome, side by side with the *flamines* and vestal virgins, who were burdened with a host of obligations, the pontiffs and the augurers lived a normal life, when not performing their religious functions.

Nevertheless, the Phoenician clergy possessed a most powerful *esprit de corps*. Inscriptions prove that the chief priestly offices were in the patronage of a few families, who enjoyed a monopoly very like that which the tribe of Aaron had established for itself in Israel. To keep an eye on the priestly caste, and also, perhaps, to settle their differences, the Republic decided to institute magistrates called by the Latins 'Prefects of Matters Holy'; in Carthage they formed a *collegium* of ten members.

There was a strict hierarchy within the clergy. Each temple came under the authority of a High Priest (*Rab Kohanim*) who exercised authority over the priests proper, the subordinate priests, and a multitude of lower ministers. Of these, the first were the scribes. We shall show their importance later. Then came the assistants to the cult; butchers to cut up the sacrificial animals, lighters of the sanctuary-lamps, sacred barbers whose office was to attend to the tonsures of the priests as well as those of the faithful who sought initiation into some minor order. And finally a host of non-specialist assistants, including pious men and sometimes temple slaves. There were also the serfs who tilled the temple estates and the craftsmen who worked in their workshops. In Egypt, and throughout Asia Minor, temples wielded great economic power; it would have been very surprising if they did not do so in Carthage too.

The priests had first of all to see that the ceremonies of the cult were properly conducted, by keeping meticulously to a body of sacred law. What has been preserved of this law bears a very significant resemblance to the Book of Leviticus. The priests' most vital function was to organize sacrifices. These were an essential part of the Punic religion, regenerating and releasing the beneficial power of the god and forming a mystic binding link between the offerer of the sacrifice and the divinity. Libations and offerings of incense were also of considerable importance, as is proved by the fact that the great god El was invoked exclusively under the name of Baal Hammon, which means 'The Lord of the Altars where Incense burns'. Blood sacrifices were classified according to their purpose, and the various categories correspond exactly to those of the Hebrews: holocaust, expiatory sacrifice (to atone for a misdeed), and the sacrifice of communion. To these must naturally be added human sacrifices. For each god, the kind of sacrificial victim—bull, calf, ram, sheep, goat, feathered fowl —and its sex, were minutely prescribed. The main purpose of the inscriptions in which these regulations have survived was to fix the fee to which the priests were entitled. This usually consisted of a cash payment according to a tariff and a share of the victim's flesh.[30]

But the Carthaginian priests, unlike those in Rome, did more than merely ensure the mechanical observance of ritual. The Phoenician priesthood had always been the centre of a very active intellectual life. They discussed the nature of the gods, and, in addition to writing the standard liturgical texts, they composed sacred poems. The latter were veritable epics, recounting the adventures of the gods and explaining in mythical terms the decrees of the ritual and the symbolism of the ceremonies.

The discoveries in Ugarit (Ras Shamra)[31] which have brought to light the temple libraries of a North Phoenician town of about the fourteenth century B.C., have revealed the amazing richness of this literature which had been lost for so many thousands of years. Certain passages are obviously related to the story of Genesis, though they have none of the unity of inspiration which dominates the Bible. Like Hesiod's *Theogony*, the Ugarit poems portray a crowded pantheon of gods, often at grips in bloody combat. Indeed every Phoenician city had its own particular pantheon in which the immortals enjoyed a different order of precedence from that of neighbouring towns. Moreover, within each town the priests elaborated their own particular cosmogony, which was naturally to the advantage of the god they served. This accounts for the violent theological quarrels, which in some cases have survived (as, for example, in the names of the two most famous leaders of schools, Sanchoniaton and Thabion).

We can be sure that the Carthaginian clergy did not allow the intellectual traditions they had inherited from the motherland to fade away. The story of Dido, as it has come down to us through Latin historians and poets, is a rationalized recasting of one of the Carthaginians' sacred poems. Unfortunately, although many of these works survived the siege of 146 in the libraries that Scipio donated to the Numidian kings, they subsequently disappeared when the Punic tongue was no longer read and its manuscripts were no longer copied.

This cultural role of the Carthaginian *Kohanim* was similar to that of the Egyptian and Mesopotamian priests and was of considerable historical importance. Indeed it was thanks to the priests that the Phoenician language and civilization did not disappear from Africa even when they were dying out in Phoenicia itself, but still survived for many centuries after the Roman conquest, until the process of absorption had finally wiped out the differences between the African cults of Tyrian origin and the other mystic religions which had spread throughout the Roman Empire.

In spite of the shortage of documentary evidence, there are occasional indications of the way the priests defended the nation's

spiritual heritage. Their chief activity in this respect must have
been in the fifth century when Carthage, defeated in Sicily and
deprived of all contact with the East by the Greek victory in
the wars against the Medes, found itself isolated and directly
threatened with destruction by Hellenism. The political, economic,
and social revolution imposed upon Carthage an aristocratic and
totalitarian régime, which suppressed all relations with Greece
and cut down expenditure on everything not concerned with the
survival of the community. This revolution had as its counterpart
a religious reformation which set Tanit above all other gods, even
above Baal Hammon himself. Like the action taken at about the
same time by the Hebrew prophets and by the first Greek philosophers, the reforms arose from the desire to purge and simplify
their religion, by reacting against the incoherence and moral
scandals of naturalism. At the same time it marks a return to very
ancient conceptions; indeed Tanit resembles very closely the
'Great Mother', the all-powerful mistress of heaven, earth and
hell, who was worshipped by the pre-Hellenic peoples of the
Aegean Sea, from whom the Phoenicians, like the Greeks, inherited the basic features of their civilization.

The famous 'emblem of Tanit', a triangle surmounted by a bar
with upturned ends and a circle above, preserves the form of an
idol with outstretched arms, which is the exact representation of
the 'Great Goddess', in Cretan palaces of the second millennium.
Nevertheless, much remains to be explained: the name Tanit
appears to be of Libyan origin, and yet no trace of a female cult
exists among the very early Berbers, who never even gave precedence in their sanctuaries to the female partner of a male god.
However, it is historically important that this spiritual revolution
in Carthage resulted in an even more tenacious affection for
Phoenician traditions. Whereas before, inscriptions had been rare,
they suddenly multiplied in their thousands, at the very moment
when the Phoenician tongue was losing ground in Asia to Aramaic
and, a little later, to Greek.

It is probable that the scribes' schools had to leave Tyre at this
time and take refuge in Carthage, which thus became the only
centre of Phoenician culture in the world. Henceforth the united
efforts of the priesthood seem to have been concentrated on
resisting Hellenism, even though they themselves failed to remain

immune from its influence. The official adoption in 396 B.C. of the cult of Demeter and Kore, and the speed with which its popularity spread, showed how dangerous to Punic culture was this contact with less narrow, more humane ideas, which were much more concerned with the fate of the individual. The priests managed to counter this influence with great skill, both by 'Punicizing' the foreign cult, whose ministry had at first been restricted to Greek priests, and by bringing within their own theology domains previously foreign to it. The symbolic decorations carved on the neo-Punic stelae in the first two centuries of the Roman occupation express a general conception of the world adopted by most of the mystic religions which sprang up in the Hellenistic world, as the result of the rejuvenation of ancient Oriental rites by contact with Greek thought.

The supernatural world appeared as a hierarchy of divine beings, subordinated to a supreme lord. The performance of a certain number of rites, bringing increasing revelation, earned for the faithful initiate not merely prosperity in this world, but also eternal salvation. The latter was conceived as a state of bliss in which the soul dwelt in the upper regions of the atmosphere, enjoying the company of the gods. The introduction of such ideas into Africa does not seem to be due to the influence of Rome, which itself absorbed them passively, nor to propaganda from the East, for that would have brought with it new gods. It must be admitted that the Punic clergy, who had remained in contact with Egypt and Syria, were able through those countries to familiarize themselves with a fundamental theology which was then accepted by the initiates of all the sects, and which was adapted by them as far as possible to the tradition which they represented. We shall also see that Greek philosophers who had settled in Carthage contributed their share towards this reconciliation.

Thus the expression of mysticism remained Phoenician even in Africa, and this helped to prolong the life of Carthaginian culture long after the destruction of the city itself. The Roman annexation broke down the political framework of Punic society, but the religious framework survived in the circles of worshippers which were tolerated by the Roman authorities. The interior organization of these circles was based on the former hierarchy of the Punic clergy and also on that of the *thiasi*, or Dionysian sects, which proliferated throughout the Hellenistic world. Thus the Phoenician tradition continued to direct a most important sector of African spiritual life, although civil and non-religious life had long been Romanized. Gradually, however, the Romans came to accept a religion which they had at first despised. Under the Severi, who were of African origin, Saturn and Caelestis, the heirs of Baal Hammon and Tanit, were accorded the same honours as Jupiter and Juno, whom they came to resemble more and more closely. This marked the end of the Phoenician culture, for Latin had by now become the liturgical language in the classical temples in which a Romanized clergy officiated.[32]

In their role of preservers and defenders of traditional civilization, the priests of Carthage were also responsible for the persistence of customs which filled even the ancients with horror and which shock our feelings and morals so much that we can scarcely believe that they really existed, in spite of the irrefutable evidence of texts and of archaeological discoveries; customs such as human sacrifice, and, especially, the holocaust of thousands of very young children, whose ashes have been discovered in the Salammbô *tophet*.

It is certainly no part of the historian's role to condemn what he discovers, in the light of our own moral code, which necessarily differs from that of the ancients. This is especially true in regard to religious practices, particularly when these are inspired by mysticism, which at all times and in all places modifies the normal scale of values. But the historian must mention, and must attempt to explain the persistence among certain peoples of practices abandoned by their neighbours, and which, by this very fact, must have been condemned by them as immoral and repulsive. It is clear that the Carthaginians did incur censure as a result of their religious aberrations.

THE LANDED ARISTOCRACY

From its origins to its fall, Carthage was dominated by an aristocracy based on birth and wealth. In the early legends, Dido was surrounded by Tyrian nobles who had supported her against the tyranny of Pygmalion. According to Justin,[33] it was they who forced her, by a crude trick, to commit suicide. In the sixth century, the nobles struggled against the personal power of the kings (Malchus and then the Magonids). When the latter dynasty fell in the fifth century, an oligarchic régime was established which lasted until the First Punic War. Then the Barcids, with the support of the people, obtained the powers of a *princeps*, but they still had to reckon with the Senate, where their enemies remained numerous.

After the defeat of Zama, Hannibal induced the people to pass laws which severely restricted the power of the aristocracy, by removing their control of the administration of justice and by compelling the corrupt magistrates to disgorge their ill-gotten gains. The nobles did not hesitate to provoke the intervention of the Romans in order to get rid of Hannibal. Nevertheless, the popular party still remained faithful to the memory of Hannibal and managed for a while to regain power. The Greek historian Polybius, who was by nature conservative, sees in the relative predominance of the popular party in Carthage during the wars against Rome one of the causes of the downfall of their city.

In any event, it is certain that the intransigence of the popular party favoured the designs of Cato and of the inveterate enemies of Carthage and that it brought about rejection of the only solution—advanced by a third party, which would perhaps have enabled Carthage to survive—namely, an alliance with Masinissa. But the last senators of Carthage had lost that intransigent pride, that fierce patriotism, which had been the strength of their ancestors. They were more preoccupied with saving their own social position than with saving the State, and they exasperated their compatriots by their cowardice, without succeeding in weakening the implacable enemy who was resolved on their downfall.

In a colonial State with a very mixed population, the aristocracy prided itself on belonging to the dominant race. Evidence of this is found on the stelae, where genealogies were set out with the greatest care, together with the offices held by the family ancestors; Phoenician names were fondly handed down from one generation to the next, the grandson usually taking his grandfather's name.

The Carthaginians, like most Orientals, considered only the male line of descent to be important. The greatest families willingly accepted marriages with foreigners. As early as the fifth century, the Magonid Hamilcar was the son of a woman of Syracuse, although this in no way prevented him from remaining the inveterate enemy of her compatriots. Of the Barcids, Hasdrubal and Hannibal married Spanish women. Marriages were common between Carthaginian nobles and Libyan princesses. Moreover the example of Sophonisbe, the daughter of a Carthaginian general who became Queen of Numidia, and whose touching story inspired one of Corneille's tragedies, shows that such exchanges were by no means confined to one sex. It is even possible that the Carthaginian aristocracy admitted within their social circle the noble houses of other countries. According to tradition, Dido's companions included a number of Cypriot families, among them that of the High Priest of a goddess whom Justin calls Juno, and who was perhaps Tanit, for the office of High Priest remained hereditary within his family.

The prestige of the Carthaginian nobility was based above all on wealth. All the ancient writers agree on the importance of money in Carthage. In the first centuries, when the Punic settlement consisted only of the town and its suburbs, their wealth could only come from over the seas. It was already so in Tyre. In the words of R. Dussaud, 'in Egypt, the King was deified in view of his power and of ancient theological traditions: in Tyre, the King was deified because of the wealth which came to him through foreign trade. It was no mere metaphor which Ezekiel employed, when he put into the mouth of the King of Tyre the words: "I am a god, I sit in the seat of God, in the midst of the seas. . . ." It is obvious how closely the Phoenician cult was linked, in the prophet's eyes, with foreign trade.'[34] In the colony, the régime did not differ much from that of Tyre: it is probable that the kings of the early centuries, the Magonids for example, exercised almost a monopoly over sea communications with the distant West, and over the vast profits derived from them. Moreover, one of the last representatives of the family, Hanno the Navigator, played in person the role of merchant adventurer and explorer of distant shores. We shall refer again to his activities in a later chapter.

The fifth-century revolution profoundly changed the whole social and political basis of the Carthaginian State; thanks to conquests of territory on the mainland, a landed nobility was able to develop alongside the aristocracy of trade and commerce; or rather the power of the ruling families was based on the twin supports of foreign trade and agriculture. One has only to think of the highly unpredictable conditions of overseas trade in ancient times, to realize how greatly this transformation must have increased the stability of the Punic State, whose rulers were henceforth able to compensate for the fickleness of fortune on the seas by the relative regularity of agricultural returns.

A vital passage in Polybius,[35] which has apparently not received the attention it deserves, provides information about the organization of agricultural revenues in Carthage in the middle of the third century. The historian speaks of the consternation among the Carthaginians when the mercenaries revolted. 'In truth', he writes, 'the Carthaginians needed only their land [chora] for the necessities of life, but the preparations for war and the amassing of provisions were only possible by virtue of the revenues they drew from Libya.' The Punic domain in Africa, therefore, consisted of two distinct parts, of which one was enough to feed the capital. But what was this territory? It cannot have been merely the immediate suburbs in the peninsula, for this area would certainly not have sufficed to feed the population of the city. Polybius was probably referring to the fairly extensive district where the land belonged to Carthaginians. He makes a distinction between this and the peripheral regions where the Libyans retained possession of the land, on condition that they paid heavy tribute.

From this it is easy to understand how dangerous to Carthage were the expeditions of Agathocles and Regulus: both had as their objective, not the capital itself, which they could not have captured permanently, but the rich and fertile lands of Cape Bon, where the Carthaginian aristocracy had their principal estates. Diodorus and Polybius[36] agree that both the Greek and the Roman armies had as their main objective the rich domains of the Punic senators, which were surrounded with vineyards, olive groves, orchards, and pastures rich in cattle. Although not all the results of the excavations of the Cape Bon burial-grounds have been published, those that have confirm entirely the evidence of these historians that there were scarcely any large towns in this

region, although it supported a very dense and wealthy population. During the Roman era, Africa remained one of the leading
agricultural powers in the Mediterranean. But the stability of its
prosperity depended principally on the cereal crops of the plains
of the Medjerda, of the interior valleys of the High Tell, and of
the well-watered vales of Byzacium. This gave rise to quite a
different economic and social organization from that which
existed under the Carthaginians, whose agricultural system, under
the influence of particular circumstances, developed in a remarkably original way.

The *chora*, or agricultural region of Carthage, was not very
extensive: it included the western part of the Tunisian Tell, the
lower valley of the Medjerda, Cape Bon, and the northern part
of the Sahel. Generally speaking, this was a hilly area with marl
and clay soils, fairly well watered, and originally covered nearly
everywhere with a *maquis* so dense as to form almost a forest,
which consisted mainly of wild olives and mastic trees. The
Carthaginians soon realized that this natural vegetation could
easily be replaced by productive trees (olives, vines, almonds, and
pomegranates), which would give valuable food and, in particular, oil which was the only kind of fat used throughout the
Mediterranean basin for food and for domestic or manufacturing
purposes, and which was, in consequence, extremely precious.
In the areas where the *maquis* remained, the sweet and fragrant
flowers supported bees, which produced excellent honey, used
instead of sugar, and wax, which was used for many more purposes than it is today. The smaller domestic animals found plenty
of food in the undergrowth, while oxen and horses could graze
in the marshy valleys of the *wadis*.

The richer plains of the Medjerda and the *wadi* of Miliana,
on the other hand, were better suited to the production of cereals,
which also grew well in the Sahel valleys. The cultivation of
trees did not extend to these regions until the period of the
Roman Empire, although even then wheat remained the staple
crop.

For political and social reasons, the two areas remained sharply
separated. Naturally, the Carthaginians at first took over the land
nearest to the town, installed themselves there as masters and
drove out the native population, or reduced them to the status

of farm-hands, or even serfs. On the other hand, in the wheat-bearing plains, which were conquered later, the land remained in the hands of native farmers who were not personally sub-servient to the lords of Carthage. But the State exacted from them tribute in kind—in principle, one tenth of their crops, although at times it rose to a quarter or even a half.

However, exploitation based on servitude is not a good basis for cereal production. Cato, in Italy, writing for the instruction of landed proprietors, firmly opposed it. Mago doubtless reaches the same conclusion, since nearly all the passages of his book which have survived deal with the cultivation of trees, or the rearing of herds. These valuable estates, near to the city, were, except in some serious emergency, safe from the incursion of Libyans who had remained independent. But the latter were able to trickle back into the outer zone, occupied by their fellows who remained settled there, and in time of need provided useful seasonal labour, particularly at harvest-time.

The Carthaginian nobles, who were anxious to preserve the monopoly of the valuable products grown on their estates, appear to have forbidden their cultivation, not only by the Libyans, whom it was important in any event to keep as specialists in the production of wheat for the city, but also by the Sardinians, who were called upon to fulfil the same function. Regulations imposed in African territories at the end of the first century A.D. by the Roman emperors, still forbade the cultivation of crops other than cereals. It was not until the more liberal policies of Hadrian and his successors, that these restrictions were repealed, and special advantages offered as an inducement to encourage the cultivation of olive trees and vines right up to the confines of the Sahara.

Thus the rural economy of Carthage was based on a rigid system of expert specialization in a fairly limited zone. The Carthaginian landed proprietor was therefore quite different from the Roman *latifundiary* (owner of vast estates built up by buying out small peasants in debt), who monopolized the best land of the province, at the end of the Republic and the beginning of the Empire. He was much more like Cato's *agricola*—the master of a relatively modest estate, from which, by great personal exertion, he extracted the maximum yield. He was no absentee landlord. In the words of Mago,[37] 'The man who acquires an estate must sell his house, lest he prefer to live in the town rather than in the country. Anyone who prefers to live in a town has no need of an estate in the country.' There was nothing onerous in such an obligation. The Carthaginians were the first to discover the delights which are enjoyed today by the inhabitants of Hammamet and Soukra, and which have attracted in recent times men like Gide and Bernanos, and many others. Vast orchards on sandy soil, watered like the oases with innumerable cool water-courses, extend right down to the sea. The elegant design and refined comforts of the houses complete the lavish work of nature.

Doubtless these 'Punic paradises' did not glow as they do today, with the bright colours of oranges and lemons. They were more like the ancient Arabian gardens where age-old olive trees grew side by side with pomegranates and fig trees. Decorative flowers were also grown. Flowers and fruits were regarded as the manifestations of divine beneficence, and therefore found a place on the stelae, although unfortunately, they are too stylized to be recognizable. As for the dwellings of the masters, they enjoyed the Mediterranean conception of comfort, which aimed above all at bringing everywhere the refreshing coolness of running water.

We have seen already that a modest house in a fishing village at the tip of Cape Bon possessed a bathroom equipped according to the latest Greek technique. Tombs from this region contained more *objets d'art* from Greece, and more jewellery, than burial-places of the same period in Carthage itself. Often the villas had towers where the owner could sit in the shade, and on the first floor there were *loggias* with wide openings overlooking the sea. Farther south, these towers assumed a more austere appearance, like the one owned by Hannibal in Byzacium, not far from Thapsus. These were real miniature fortresses (*bordjs*), able to resist an attack from bands of nomads.

The master lorded it at the head of his slaves. Many of the latter came from abroad as prisoners of war, or were bought in the slave-market. But the exploration of burial-places has shown that a Libyan population did survive in Cape Bon. They used crude pottery, shaped by hand, like that still used by the

Bedouins, and they practised rites (like painting red the bodies of the dead and burying them in a squatting position), which go back to prehistoric times. Did these natives retain some land of their own, side by side with the Carthaginian colonists, or did they work for the latter as mere labourers? It is impossible to give a definite answer. But the existence of a discontented rural proletariat presented a serious menace which Carthage had to face at moments of political crisis.

In normal times, however, the efficiency of the system depended on the overseers. A passage from Mago refers to these foremen, who were slaves themselves, and from whom both authority and technical competence were demanded. It was essential to keep them interested in their work. He therefore recommended that they should be allowed some privileges, such as the right to found a family, a privilege not allowed to other workers, and the chance to put aside savings with which they could eventually buy their freedom. He also advised the removal of those who treated their subordinates with brutality. This he did not from humane motives, but because men who are brutalized with blows soon become indifferent workers and because human live-stock was expensive.[38]

The main achievement of the Carthaginian colonists was to introduce into Africa the agricultural practices of the most ancient Mediterranean civilizations, to adapt them to the climate, and to perfect agricultural science to the point of becoming acknowledged masters. The famous agricultural expert was Mago, a retired general, who condensed the whole science of the agriculture of his time into twenty-eight books. This treatise became so famous that the Roman Senate, which included Cato, himself the author of a similar work, had it translated into Latin, after the Roman conquest. It was, in fact, the only Punic work that the Romans regarded as of any interest. As late as the first century A.D., Columella was still praising Mago as the father of agricultural knowledge. Unfortunately the fame his treatise enjoyed did not preserve it for posterity. A few brief fragments only survive through being quoted by Pliny, Varro, Columella, and other lesser authors. These same authors also mention a compatriot who emulated Mago, named Hamilcar.

This development of scientific agriculture deserves special

mention, for in ancient times techniques made very slow progress, even when they were of vital interest to the community. Moreover, the Carthaginians do not appear to have been of a very inventive turn of mind. We shall see that their industry, even in the essential sphere of ship-building, was not noticeably superior to that of their neighbours. The progress they made in agriculture, which soon became part of the heritage of Mediterranean civilization, is therefore a remarkable and happy exception.

Mago apparently lived at the time of the Punic wars, that is to say when Carthage was emerging from isolationism and was becoming increasingly ready to adopt Hellenistic civilization. Greek was widely known and the work of Greek specialists often utilized. Mago was one of the enlightened Carthaginians of whom Hannibal is the best known, who made themselves familiar with Greek ideas and were able to contribute some of their own. One of the characteristics of the Greek mind was the urge to rationalize techniques. Throughout antiquity very little was contributed to man's material lot until the last three centuries B.C. and the first century A.D. But this practical utilization of knowledge lapsed without achieving any definite results. It did not reappear until a thousand years later at the end of the Dark Ages.

As most of Mago's work has been lost, it is not possible to estimate exactly the extent of the progress made by Punic agriculture. The cultivation of cereals which was, as we have already seen, left almost entirely to the Libyans, profited little from these advances. Nevertheless, the stelae of the *tophet* often show a simple wooden plough without wheels, similar to those still used today by the Tunisian *fellahs*.[39] The Carthaginians must have invented a fairly advanced threshing-machine—a kind of sledge fitted with small toothed wheels which the Romans called the 'Punic Cart' (*plostellum punicum*).[40]

The Tyrians' greatest effort was devoted to cultivating vines and olives, which they were undoubtedly the first to grow in Africa. Mago enumerated a whole set of instructions for dealing with the excessive heat and dryness of the African climate: vineyards should be planted facing north; plants should be placed in trenches with stones at the bottom to protect their roots from winter rains and summer heat, trenches should only be filled in gradually, to encourage the roots to go down deep, and dung mixed with grape-pressings should be used as a fertilizer. Finally, the vines were to be pruned in spring, and not in the autumn, as the Italians preferred to do.[41]

The mastic tree grows naturally in the Tunisian *maquis*. The Carthaginians soon learnt to graft on to the wild stock, but they also planted olive groves of new trees, regularly spaced seventy-five feet apart, the trees of one row placed opposite the gaps in the other as is still done today around Sfax. Some trees bore up to a thousand pounds of olives.

Fruit farming lacked the variety it has today. The citrus fruits which were introduced by the Arabs in the Middle Ages, and which now constitute the chief crops of Tunisian orchards, were unknown to the Carthaginians. Many modern authors have thought that the golden apples which Hercules stole from the vigilant Hesperides and their dragon, in the farthest limits of the Western World, were in fact oranges, and the Greek hero may indeed have borrowed this exploit, like others, from the Melkart of Tyre. But it seems probable that these miraculous fruits, like the precious jewels on Aladdin's tree, were entirely due to the imagination of Oriental story-tellers.

The humble Barbary fig, which often satisfies the hunger of the Bedouin, and the cacti which throw an impenetrable hedge round many modern gardens, were unknown to the ancients, and were imported from America only in the sixteenth century. But the Carthaginians were proud of their own figs and of their pomegranates. The former were so fine that Cato is said to have held some up in the Senate to arouse the envy of the Roman peasants against a rich defenceless land not far away. The same Romans called the pomegranate *mala punica* more often than *granata*, and imported them from Africa for Italian markets. Moreover, this fruit was the emblem of Tanit, and is often found in the place of honour on stelae, perched on top of a column.[42] The goddess shared this emblem with Kore. A well-known story, invented by some ingenious Alexandrian, explained how Pluto had regularized the abduction of Persephone by giving her a pomegranate-seed to eat. Indeed, this brightly coloured fruit, whose peel encases thousands of seeds, seemed to be the very symbol of fertility. It was doubtless the Aegeans who chose it as an emblem for the goddesses of the earth, those queens of the mysterious treasures held within its bosom, and of the sources of all life.

The date palm is probably the tree most frequently seen on stelae.[43] An amusing drawing shows two men with a long lead clinging like monkeys to the trunk of a date palm. This kind of gymnastic feat was necessary in order to fertilize the stamens of the female tree with pollen. The date palm also appears, together with the war-horse, on Carthaginian coinage. The Phoenicians, like all Orientals, regarded the tree as symbolical of Providence and its blessings. Thus in Greek the word *phoinix* means both a date palm and a Phoenician. However, it is by no means certain that Carthaginian domination extended as far as the Jerid, which produces the best dates in Tunisia, or if it did, it was only for a short while. The date palms round Gabes and in Tripolitania are too near the sea, and produce only inferior fruit.

In the zone of sub-desert steppeland stretching between the mountains and the east coast of Tunisia, the cultivation of almonds, often grown in conjunction with olives, can be very remunerative. Mago says that almond trees were grown in nurseries with infinite care, and then planted out in the same manner as olive trees.[44]

Cattle-breeding was the chief, and often the sole, resource of the Libyans, but they practised it with the same lack of care as their present-day descendants. The Carthaginians, on the other hand, were most careful and methodical.

While the soil of Tunisia is very suitable for fruit trees, it provides poor pasturage today for herds: hard, dry alpha grass on the steppes, or thorny plants with small stiff leaves in the *maquis*. Only in the depths of a few marshy *wadis* is any lush grass to be found. In ancient times, things were probably better. We know that elephants lived in Barbary, which implies the existence of grassy plains. These were perhaps the plains of the Tell, which were later ploughed up for grain-crops.

The nomad Libyans (the word nomad was originally the same as Numidian) grazed their goats and long-tailed Barbary sheep there, while in winter, they came down to the pre-Sahara steppes, where the alpha grass grew. This kind of life, which, like all shepherds, they combined with hunting and brigandage, was made possible by the speed and endurance of their native Barbary horses.

The Carthaginians took over the native sheep and horses, and the former often appear on stelae as sacrificial victims.[45] The ram was also one of the animals dedicated to Baal Hammon, who was identified with Ammon at an early date. The horse represented the god of war, probably Hadad, and often appears on coins. But it was no longer possible to rear animals by moving them from one pasture to another.

Meadows were soon developed round the estates, especially in Cape Bon. The fodder they provided allowed cattle to be reared in conditions far superior to those found by the nómad Libyans. So fine was the stock that the description of market animals, given by Mago, was reproduced word for word in all the treatises on stock-breeding used in ancient times. 'The animals should be young and stocky, with good limbs, and long robust and blackish horns; the forehead should be broad and wrinkled, the ears velvety, and the eyes and the chops black; the nostrils should be large and rolled back, the neck long and muscular, the dewlap generous, hanging almost to the knees, the chest well developed, the shoulders broad, the belly large and full like that of an animal replete, the flanks long, the loins broad, the back straight and flat, or even slightly hollow, the buttocks round, the legs thick and straight, short rather than long, the knees firm, the hooves large, the tail very long and hairy, the coat stiff and short, but soft to the touch, and reddish or brown in colour.'[46]

Everyone knows that the Carthaginians captured and reared elephants, but these were only used for military purposes, as they were by all the ancient Mediterranean peoples. Unlike the Phoenicians, the Carthaginians made no use of camels. The Gaetulians, or desert Libyans, however, began to use dromedaries, in imitation of their brothers in Egypt. But the Sahara was still crossed by oxen or horses.

Punic farms were well supplied with poultry. Cocks appear on various monuments and as victims named in the sacrificial tariffs. Doves, dedicated to Astarte and to Tanit, fluttered in thousands in the precincts of their temples. Sometimes, apparently, they arrived in great droves, which gave rise to a story that the goddess of Mount Eryx (in Sicily) paid a yearly visit of nine days to

Carthage, accompanied by her doves. Water-birds, Carthaginian hens and pink flamingoes, haunted the Lake of Tunis in their thousands, as they still do today. They also appear frequently on stelae. A frieze of walking, long-legged water-birds, on a stele in Lavigerie Museum, is one of the best achievements of Punic sculpture, and is all the more praiseworthy because the artist apparently did not copy it slavishly from a model.[47] In addition to poultry, the Carthaginian farm sometimes had tame gazelles and even ostriches.[48]

The Mediterranean *maquis* is rich in flowers, and provides plenty of food for bees. Mago believed that these insects were produced by spontaneous generation in the flanks of a slaughtered bull. The Carthaginians may have been poor entomologists, but bee-keeping was much more important for them than for us, since honey was the only form of sugar available to them. The wax of their bees was reputed to outclass that from all other bees. It was used in medicine and in encaustic painting.

It is evident, therefore, that the Carthaginian farmer was neither an ignorant rustic, nor a grand lord who cared little for what his estates produced. He was like the English gentlemen-farmers in the eighteenth century, who also lived in a country that was primarily devoted to maritime trade, and who sought to extract from their estates, by rational methods and unremitting care, an income equivalent to what business or industry would have brought them. In one respect, however, the Carthaginian farmer differed fundamentally from the sceptical and enlightened English gentleman-farmer; all his labour and even his knowledge would have seemed to him useless, without the help of the gods. It must be remembered in this connexion, that in Africa, more than anywhere else, changes in meteorological conditions could turn the same soil from a paradise into a desert.

The ancient Phoenicians of Ugarit, who were highland peasants before they turned to the sea, had developed their mythology and ritual round their notions of those supernatural beings whose violently changing relationships controlled the growth of all vegetation.[49] Two gods especially worked in opposition: Aleyan Baal, the fertilizing spirit of rains, springs, and rivers, who revealed himself in the growth of meadow grass and trees: he prevailed during the rainy season, but was brutally displaced by Moth, the divine son, the spirit of the corn, who triumphed over him in the warm season. Moth was identified with the seed of the wheat, and suffered death at the hands of the goddess Anat: he was cut down with the sickle and burned, finally returning once more to the underworld, when Aleyan regained the throne.

Later, the *Kohanim* reconciled these two enemies and even fused them into a single deity, who was worshipped in some places as Eshmoun, and in others as Adonis. Nevertheless, Aleyan, Moth, Eshmoun, and Adonis were definitely subject to the superior gods El or Hadad, of whom they sometimes appear to be merely the ministering agents. Carthaginian theology preserved this kind of division of labour between the supreme providence and its ministering deities, who alone came into contact with human beings. But, as the learned theologians became more particular about divine transcendence, they tended to transfer their piety to the superior gods, the rulers of heaven, Baal Hammon (or El) and especially to Tanit, at the expense of their lesser minions.

This explains why the fertility of nature is represented on the Carthaginian stelae as the gift of the superior god and goddess: to them are dedicated the food-giving plants, date palms, pomegranates, and ears of corn, the cattle and the implements of the fields. Nevertheless, the idea of the existence of intermediary divine beings persisted. It appears very clearly on neo-Punic stelae, perhaps because the influence of classical religions had made the idea of polytheism familiar. These ministering gods appear in the shape of the inhabitants of Olympus, while the supreme god was still represented by more or less abstract symbols. On ex-votos found in La Ghorfa,[50] Bacchus naturally presides over the growth of the vine, while his nude companion, who can be identified with Venus, reigns over fruit trees; the sculptor has succeeded in expressing most happily, by the exuberance and riotous intertwining of their reliefs, the joyous abundance of nature made fertile by divine intervention.

Some Carthaginian theologians considered wheat to be under the direct protection of Baal Hammon; a ritual statue of the god, found at Hadrumetum, shows him holding a bunch of corn-ears, and he was often invoked under the title of *Frugifer*, a term associated with Saturn. This linking of the vital corn and the king of the gods was already accepted in the Phoenician town of Hadrumetum; a fine burial throne preserved in the Museum at Sousse, and which dates back to the fourth century,[51] shows an ovoid sacred stone garlanded with ears of corn. But in most parts of Africa, the corn goddesses were the *Cereres*, Demeter and Kore, who had been naturalized 'Punic' since the fourth century B.C. On the stelae found in or near Althiburos[52] they appear as the subordinates of the supreme sun god, represented by Baal Hammon. They therefore fulfil the same role as do Bacchus and Venus in the neighbouring shrine at La Ghorfa. Their companion Pluto, moreover, vies with Saturn for the title of *Frugifer*. In spite of these theological differences which are evidence of the wealth and variety of Carthaginian religious thought, there was complete agreement on the vital importance of sacrifices as a means of promoting universal fertility. This principle, the very basis of Phoenician religion, still persisted at the end of ancient times, on the eve of the triumph of Christianity. It is the inspiration behind one of the last monuments of African paganism, the stele of Cuttinus, a contemporary of the Diocletian tetrarchy (284–305).[53] This man, with a Punic name, was a rich landowner in the fertile plains of the High Tell and had obtained the blessing of Saturn by sacrificing an enormous ox and a fat ram. His ex-voto shows, one above the other, the god himself guarded by genii clad in Roman uniforms, but seated on a bull, like the ancient Phoenician god El; then, the sacrifice being offered by Cuttinus and his family; and finally the last two scenes, with all the naïve grace of a Roman relief, show Cuttinus' men first ploughing, and then reaping and gathering into their carts, a really providential harvest.

The evolution of the religious attitude of the Phoenician to the earth and its fruits is clearly the result of the relative importance of agriculture and sea-faring in their economy. In the second millennium, the 'red' people who had recently emigrated from the Negeb to Libya were just beginning to find ways of exploiting their new home. They were therefore primarily interested in the gods who presided over, and were even identified with, the growth of food-producing plants. Round about the year 1000 B.C., the protecting deities of the great ports figure as the lords of sea and

heaven, and their worshippers forget their close relationship with
the cycle of the seasons. When the Phoenicians in Africa became
interested in agriculture again, they revived their faith in the
divinities of the earth, who brought fertility to fields and herds;
and when they still kept as their most important gods the lords
of heaven and of the stars, it was because of their powers to
dispense warmth and rain, the supreme factors in the growth of
vegetation.

This 'return to the soil' on the part of some at least of the
Carthaginian aristocracy in the fifth century B.C. was vital to
the evolution of Carthaginian civilization. It was certainly the
prime factor in the relative stability of the Republic in its last
centuries.

This was because the preponderance of the ruling classes
depended above all on their economic power. We know that their
wealth allowed the great to keep a considerable number of people
personally dependent on them. Besides their domestic or rural
slaves, and the free workers in their trading enterprises, they
secured the services of a number of indigent citizens by various
acts of prodigality. These might take the form of provisions in
kind. In the fourth century, the ambitious Hanno the Great hoped
to obtain the people's suffrage by offering them banquets on the
occasion of his daughter's wedding. Killing, so to speak, two
birds with one stone, he also hoped to use the occasion to poison
the members of the Senate.[54]

Sumptuous banquets of this kind were doubtless staged under
the porticos of the temples and may be survivals of an institution
common among primitive peoples, which is known to sociologists
as 'potlatch'. In the course of such feasts, the chief personages
rivalled each other in a prodigal display of wealth; the winner
of this form of tournament emerged with his authority enhanced.
In Roman Africa municipal office, though elective in principle,
was in fact bought by the notables at the price of costly acts of
generosity. These were enumerated with much self-satisfaction on
inscriptions: construction of public buildings, distribution of food,
money, and presents; and games and spectacles of all kinds.

Such munificence was obviously not peculiar to the African
bourgeoisie. It was displayed throughout the Empire. Probably
the Carthaginian nobility practised it already, for in towns where

the Phoenician tradition was particularly strong, like Leptis in Tripolitania or Maktar in Tunisia, special entitlements translated from the Phoenician have been found. The purpose of these seems to have been to honour their authors: the names *amator civium,* and *ornator patriae,* which occur in the dedications, were apparently no empty rhetorical phrases, and appear to have referred to some definite social promotion, won by displays of munificence.[55]

Aristotle refers to certain clubs (*hetairiai*)[56] which existed in Carthage and whose members met for communal meals (*syssitiai*). They were corporations by public law. It is very probable that the cost of their banquets was defrayed by the leaders of their association, who subsequently benefited from the support of their colleagues in their political careers. Movers, Gsell,[57] and other scholars were of the opinion that these *hetairiai* were religious brotherhoods, and their public banquets were, in fact, as we have seen, given under the temple porticos.

It is evident that the people were completely in the hands of the nobles, and, except in the relatively democratic period which followed the War of the Mercenaries, they had a very limited voice in the management of affairs, in spite of the existence of a General Assembly as early as the sixth century. Effective power resided in fact in restricted bodies—the Senate and a Committee of five members, who perhaps formed select committees entrusted with the direction of certain affairs.

The Carthaginian 'constitution', if one may use the word—for the Punic Republic, like most cities of antiquity, never had a written statute, but only a collection of laws and customs, rather like the British Constitution today—was very similar to that of the Greek oligarchies, a comparison emphasized by Aristotle.[58] Its most original feature was the existence of a body of non-political magistrates who, from the revolution of the fifth century onwards, imposed a rigorous civic and moral discipline. It was by founding this Court of the Four Hundred, which Aristotle compares with the *ephors* of Sparta,[59] and recent scholars with the Venetian Council of Ten, that the Carthaginian aristocracy consolidated their power after the fall of the Magonids.

When Hannibal sought to deprive them of their strength, he persuaded the people to revoke the law of irremovability of these magistrates. Their authority, which was all the stronger for being ill-defined, was exercised over the people as well as over the executive. After the fall of the monarchy, the executive power was shared by two *shofetim*. This title, which the Romans translated as *suffetes*, means 'judges'. It was the title borne by the elders of the people of Israel before the institution of the monarchy. This similarity shows that the role of these magistrates was not essentially to administer the law, for they were undoubtedly deprived of this function by the institution of the aristocratic courts. They were in fact political and military leaders resembling the Roman consuls, although their prestige was not so great. One of the serious faults of the Carthaginian aristocracy was their inveterate distrust of all personal initiative. This was one of the chief causes of the weakness of their foreign policy. During the First Punic War, four generals were crucified by order of the Four Hundred.[60] Not having at their disposition the specialized police forces used by modern authoritarian States to subdue their subjects, the Carthaginian oligarchs compelled theirs to obedience by fear of the executioner.

It is clear, therefore, that the most remarkable features of Carthaginian society can be explained by its colonial origins. The position held by the priesthood was certainly justified by the supreme importance of religious affairs in Semitic societies, but even more by the fierce affection for its traditions shown by a people cut off from their roots and surrounded by hostile foreigners.

The preponderance of the aristocracy was the more easily established because they never had occasion to overcome the opposition of a popular class of their own race. The rich Tyrian merchants in Africa had brought with them only completely subservient workers. When they later became a landed nobility, it was at the expense of an uncivilized foreign population, and not of a peasantry, who would certainly have claimed an honourable place in the city, as they did in Greece and Italy. Nevertheless, the conditions by which Carthage developed gave birth to a proletariat of very mixed origins, side by side with the colonizing aristocracy; they too came to consider that they were Punic citizens. This proletariat will form the subject of our next chapter.

REFERENCES

1. Eratosthenes, quoted by Strabo, I, 4, 9.
2. Strabo, XVII, 3, 15.
3. J. Beloch, *Bevölkerung der Gr. Rom. Welt*, p. 467.
4. R. Dussaud, *Religion des Phéniciens*, p. 375. For the poems of Ugarit see above, p. 257, n. 4.
5. MC, pl. 77–8.
6. P. Cintas, CRAI, 1951, pp. 17 sqq.
7. A. Héron de Villefosse, *Mon. Piot*, XII, 1905, p. 79.
8. C. Picard, *Catalogue Mus. Alaoui, Nlle série*, pl. LXXXXVI, Cb 637.
9. MC, pl. 60.
10. G. G. Lapeyre and A. Pellegrin, *Carthage punique*, pl. III, 2.
11. MC, pl. 60, 2.
12. *Ibid.*, pl. 55, 2.
13. On Punic religion in general see our *Les Religions de l'Afrique antique*, Paris, 1954.
14. The identification of the Punic gods still presents some very complex problems; cf. for example, G. Levi Della Vida, *Rendiconti Acc. Naz. Lincei*, VIII, X, 1955, pp. 550 sqq.
15. The problem set by the word MLK in Punic script is still a very obscure one. Without wishing to take part in a controversy on which only experts in Semitic philology and epigraphy are qualified to express an opinion, we will merely point out that this group of letters appears to correspond to two or three homonyms:
    1. a term qualifying a particular form of sacrifice. It was first so deciphered by O. Eissfeldt, *Molk als Opferbegriff im punischen und hebraischen und das Ende des Gottes Moloch*, 1935; cf. R. Dussaud, CRAI, 1946, p. 371; J.-G. Février, 'Molchomor', *Rev. Hist. Rel.*, 1955, pp. 8 sqq. and lastly, *Journal asiatique*, 1955, pp. 52–3. The exact meaning of the word is not yet definitely established.
    2. an epithet entering into the composition of certain names of divinities (cf. in the Leptis inscription quoted in the previous note, MLK'ASHTART), p. 552.
    3. the word meaning 'King', which may or may not be identical with the preceding use. It is certainly no longer possible, after the work of Eissfeldt and Dussaud, to deny the existence of homonym 1, as advocated by C. A. Schaeffer, *C. Rend. Ac.*

inscr., I, 956, p. 67. Schaeffer even casts doubt on whether human sacrifices ever took place in Carthage and considers the *tophet* to be nothing more than a cemetery for children who were still-born. This is in direct contradiction, not only to texts and inscriptions (the latter are even more explicit in Cirta than in Carthage, cf. J.-G. Février, *op. cit.*, p. 11, and 'Un sacrifice d'enfants chez les Numides', in *Mel. Isidore Levi*), but also with the excavators' observations and the laboratory analysis of bones found in the urns. Pending the publication of the results of researches by Dr Muller and Dr Leclercq on the Salammbô discoveries, see L. Poinssot and R. Lantier, *Rev. Hist. Rel.*, 1923, p. 26; Dr Henry has confirmed the presence of teeth, some of which belonged to new-born infants, and others to children two or three years old. In addition, in the largest urns, were found remains of birds and quadrupeds (calves, sheep, lambs, goats), generally in conjunction with human remains, but sometimes by themselves. The same thing has been found at Hadrumetum: P. Cintas, *Sanctuaire punique de Sousse*, has noted that in the lowest level (sixth century to seventh century), the urns contain only children's bones, but in the second layer (fourth century) some contain lambs' bones, either by themselves, or, as in Carthage, mixed with human ashes. The proportion of animal remains then increases, and after the Roman conquest, they are the only sacrificial remains found. This progressive replacement of human by animal victims would be enough to prove beyond any possible doubt, that the *tophets* received the remains of holocausts and not of persons cremated after a natural death; it is hardly likely that anybody will maintain that the animals were still-born! The presence of remains of children some years old, which is perfectly well explained by literary texts (they had been fraudulently preserved from sacrifice for several years, as Diodorus explains), is also quite incompatible with Schaeffer's thesis. Finally the dedicatory inscription is exactly similar to that used for the consecration of a statue (cf. the Leptis inscription, quoted in previous note), and is completely different from the way epitaphs were worded.

16. Silius Italicus, III, 23–7.
17. A. Merlin, CRAI, 1916, p. 262, and G. Ch.-Picard, *op. cit.*, p. 125.
18. Tertullian, *De exhortatione castitatis*, 13.

19. J. Carcopino, *Aspects mystiques de la Rome païenne*, pp. 24–9.
20. *Catalogue Mus. Alaoui, Suppl.*, p. 63, C 1076, and G. Ch.-Picard, *op. cit.*, p. 188.
21. G. Ch.-Picard, *op. cit.*, p. 156.
22. MC, pl. 6.
23. G. Contenau, MAO, III, p. 1476, fig. 897.
24. C. Picard, *op. cit.*, p. 147, Cb 442.
25. *Ibid.*, p. 298, Cb 1075. MC, pl. 34.
26. M. Hours-Miedan, *Cahiers de Byrsa*, I, 1950, p. 62, pl. XXXIV, d.
27. *Catalogue Museum Lavigerie, Supp.*, I, pl. II, 2 and pl. III. MC, pl. 61.
28. J. H. Reynolds and J. B. Ward Perkins, *Inscriptions of Roman Tripolitania*, pp. 318 and 347.
29. A. Héron de Villefosse, *loc. cit.*
30. S. Gsell, HAAN, IV, pp. 410 sqq., and G. Ch.-Picard, *op cit.*, pp. 130–1.
31. R. Dussaud, *Religion des Phéniciens*, Collection Mana, p. 375.
32. G. Ch.-Picard, *op. cit.*, pp. 100 sqq.
33. Justin, XVIII, 6.
34. R. Dussaud, *Rev. Hist. Rel.*, CVIII, 1, p. 40.
35. Polybius, I, 71, 1.
36. Diodorus, XX, 8, 3–4; Polybius, I, 29, 7.
37. Quoted by Columella, I, 1, 18; cf. Pliny, XVIII, 35.
38. Varro, *Rust.*, I, 17, 4 sqq.
39. M. Hours-Miedan, *op. cit.*, p. 66, pl. XXXI.
40. Varro, *op. cit.*, I, 52, 1.
41. Columella, V, 5, 4.
42. M. Hours-Miedan, *op. cit.*, p. 46, pl. XX.
43. *Ibid.*, pp. 45–6, pl. XIX.
44. Pliny, XVIII, 63.
45. M. Hours-Miedan, *op. cit.*, p. 52, pl. XXV.
46. Varro, *op. cit.*, II, 5, 7–8.
47. M. Hours-Miedan, *op. cit.*, p. 51, pl. XXII g.
48. P. Cintas, *Céramique punique*, pl. LXIX, 255.
49. R. Dussaud, *l. l.*
50. C. Picard, *op. cit.*, I, pp. 262 sqq., Cb 963–Cb 974. MC, pl. 77–8.
51. M. Rostovtseff, *Social and Economic Hist. of the Roman Empire*, pl. XLIII.
52. C. Picard, *op. cit.*, pp. 295 sqq., Cb 1067–Cb 1070. MC, pl. 79.
53. G. Ch.-Picard, *op. cit.*, pp. 120–2, fig. 11. MC, pl. 76.
54. Justin, XXI, 4, 3.

55. G. Levi Della Vida, *Africa ital.*, VI, 1935, p. 105. *Rendiconti Acc. Naz. Lincei*, IV, 1949, pp. 405 sqq.
56. *Polit.*, II, 8, 2.
57. S. Gsell, *op. cit.*, II, p. 232.
58. *Polit.*, II, 8, 1–4 and III, 1, 7.
59. *Ibid.*, 8, 2.
60. *Infra*, pp. 205–6.

CHAPTER IV

THE PEOPLE, INDUSTRY, AND THE SOCIAL PROBLEM

OUR information about the Carthaginian proletariat comes from archaeological rather than literary sources, the latter being more concerned with the deeds of the great. According to the law of chance, more graves of the poor should come to light than of the rich. The humble objects found near their mortal remains make it possible to reconstruct the lives of these simple folk, who intervened in political affairs only in moments of crisis, when their wretched lot became too hard to bear.

The Carthaginian proletariat, as we have seen, lived mainly in the city itself. It included sailors, workers in the arsenal, and elsewhere, market-gardeners from Megara, employees in the trading establishments, and slaves. There were also foreign settlers and, forming a separate class altogether, the professional soldiers, whom the State had to maintain to defend the city, in view of the inadequate numbers of the population.

THE METAL-WORKERS

The workers were relatively numerous, although there were obviously no factories employing hundreds of men. The most important industrial enterprises, managed by the State, supplied the needs of the army and navy. In Cartagena, the Carthaginian settlement in Spain, which was founded by the Barcids as the capital of the overseas empire, there existed an arsenal in which 2,000 people were employed.[1] It was certainly organized on the lines of one in Carthage itself. Some idea of the capacity of the Carthage factories can be obtained from the peak output figures at the beginning of hostilities in 148 B.C., after the Romans had demanded the surrender of all war materials in the city. When these conditions were made known, the Carthaginians decided to resist, and in one month manufactured 3,000 shields, 9,000 swords, 15,000 lances, and 30,000 catapult-darts[2] although there had been no general mobilization of industry. The potters, for example, continued to ply their trade, for it would not have been wise to employ unskilled workers on such specialized work. The figures available correspond to the output of 300 or 400 forges, each employing four or five workers. To them must be added the carpenters who made the wooden parts of weapons. The armourers were probably employed in several large workshops, similar to the one which the father of Lysias the orator owned in Athens at the end of the fifth century, and which had 120 workers.[3]

But in peacetime, many metal-workers worked on their own account, or for private patrons. Stelae have been found which were dedicated by smelters of iron and copper, and makers of body-scrapers and tweezers.[4] Some of the tools and products of their trade have been found in graves, while others are represented on stelae:[5] axes and hammers, weapons of various kinds, knives, scissors, fish-hooks, scrapers, and spoons. In the next chapter we shall discuss articles of the toilet and of personal adornment. Bronze vases, with varying degrees of ornamentation, were also made, though the Carthaginians produced no original work in this field; they imitated Greek originals, mass-producing endless copies of models already long out of date in their country of origin.

The metallurgical industry was supplied from overseas. Copper was imported from Spain, tin also from Spain and from the Cassiterides, and iron from Elba. The remarkable thing is that the Carthaginians, who had access to such abundant supplies of raw materials, never attempted to sell their finished products abroad. This would have brought in a handsome margin of profit and their failure to do so can only have been due to the inferiority of their workmanship, compared with that of the Greeks, by whom they were outclassed from the seventh century onwards. In consequence, the Punic workshops produced only enough to satisfy internal consumption; not a single article made in Africa has been found in the countries of the European Barbarians, such as the Celts whose ports were, nevertheless, visited frequently by Carthaginian ships.

The singular inferiority of Carthaginian metal-work can be explained historically: while Carthage remained a port of call for Oriental ships sailing to the West—i.e. until the great landmark of the fifth century—no attempt seems to have been made to work the ores which came in transit through the harbour, except perhaps for the manufacture of a few trinkets. The policy of self-sufficiency imposed by the Carthaginian government after Himera forced them to produce for themselves at least the indispensable necessities, and may have obliged them to bring in fresh teams of craftsmen from Phoenicia. But most of the workshops were apparently not established until the great Sicilian War (409–338 B.C.), during which prisoners of war who had been rounded up in the ravaged towns of Sicily were brought in, notably from Selinus and Agrigentum. These slaves showed no great zeal in working for their new masters and were content to go on copying models they were familiar with, rather than trying out new designs. In time they adopted Punic customs, and probably purchased their freedom, but never rose above their inferior status. The Carthaginian craftsmen never achieved the initiative and inventiveness which were shown by the agriculturists; such qualities develop only in men enjoying some measure of social importance and respect.

THE WOODWORKERS

The workers in wood seem to have enjoyed more prestige. The Phoenicians in Asia, who sold Lebanese pine and cedar to Egypt and Palestine, had already made a reputation for themselves as carpenters, and Solomon called upon one of them when building his temple. Some of these workers joined the first African colonists. In the first century A.D. wooden beams were still to be seen in Apollo's temple in Utica, which had been there for more than a thousand years. The most important work of these woodworkers was obviously the building and repairing of ships, at which they were past-masters, as the Greeks willingly acknowledged. The extension of the Punic empire in Africa soon brought supplies of local timber very similar to what was produced in Asia. Cedar was especially valued; today it grows only in Morocco, but then it probably grew on the Tunisian mountains. The dry African climate has preserved several wooden chests which had been used as coffins, but which had previously been articles of furniture. They are made of very thick planks of cedar or cypress, put together with wooden or lead dowels.[6]

This method of construction shows how even in a privileged

trade, the Carthaginians staunchly resisted any changes in technique. The invention of nails during the third millennium made
possible entirely new types of structure, and yet no nails were
used in Carthage before the third century. Even then, they were
nails with gilded heads, used to attach some external decoration
and not for constructional purposes.

Carthage also possessed very skilled wood-carvers. A head of
Demeter in gilded cedar, dug up at Sainte-Monique in a recess
beneath the temple of the goddess,[7] shows, in spite of some superficial deterioration, a remarkable purity of line, although it was
almost certainly copied from a Greek model.

TEXTILES

The textile industry was one of Carthage's main activities. As in
all ancient societies, everyday attire was made by the women of
the house, who spun and wove wool or flax. Their spindles and
shuttles generally went with them to their graves. But inscriptions
often mention professional spinners[8] and we know that large
workshops were sometimes installed in the women's quarters of
noble houses, in which dozens of slaves worked under the direction of the mistress of the house, or of her overseers.

On the inland pastures belonging to the Carthaginians or to
the natives, an abundance of raw material was produced.
Cushions and embroidered carpets found a market even in
Greece in the fifth century. Tunisian women are still skilled at
this craft and the decorative motifs which they hand down from
generation to generation perhaps go far back into antiquity.
Carpets, like tent-cloth, which was also often decorated, are today
indispensable to the nomads and are often the only furnishings
they possess. Yet the Libyans of early antiquity preferred to live
in crude huts, called *magalia*, and were probably satisfied with a
few skins to cover the ground. Carpets were probably invented in
Syria, and in all probability the Phoenicians, who soon became
acquainted with them, introduced them into North Africa. 'We
may suppose', writes M. Poinssot,[9] 'that the Tyrian and Sidonian
traders taught the neighbouring pastoral populations to copy
Asiatic fabrics. They were obliged to take into account the
barbarous state of their subjects or protégés, and so had to choose
as models plain rectangular designs, which would be the easiest to

copy. Perhaps they were like the carpets and hangings, decorated with diamonds, chequered patterns, scrolls, and saw-tooth designs, which were reproduced in the eighth and ninth centuries B.C. on some Phrygian monuments, some of which were votive or religious, and others burial-stones.'

In addition to the heavier woollen fabrics, the Carthaginians also made fine linen muslins which were largely used for wearing-apparel.

Spinning, weaving, and embroidery rarely went beyond the stage of family production, but dyeing was a veritable industry supporting large numbers of people. The Tyrians are presumed to have invented the purple dye which was obtained from the decayed flesh of the *murex*, a shell-fish found on the shores of Africa. On many sites of antiquity, from Djerba to Morocco, the broken shells have piled up on the beaches together with fragments of pottery and of walls. Some of these sites were never reoccupied after the fall of Carthage as, for example, Dar Essafi, near Kerkouane.[10] This little town, whose prosperity has already been mentioned, gained its livelihood more from the sea than from tilling the soil. Round its small harbour at the mouth of a *wadi*, numerous vats hollowed out of the solid rock were used to hold the flesh of the *murex* while it was decomposing. Because of the smell, these vats were usually sited down-wind. The shells were usually left round them and are still there. Together with fishing, but more important, this industry was the chief source of the wealth of the inhabitants. The purple did indeed fetch a very good price, and was doubtless taken into Carthage for the dyeing processes.

Leatherwork, like the woollen industry, grows up naturally among nomad populations. The Libyans adopted it even in the Neolithic Age, and it is very likely from them that the Carthaginians learnt to make a kind of morocco—sheep- or goat-skin dyed red, which was much esteemed by the Romans for its skilful workmanship.

CERAMICS

But the industry which found the widest markets, and the only one still active today, is that of pottery. The importance of terracotta, for the ancient inhabitants of the Mediterranean shores, can scarcely be exaggerated. Except for the choice metal vases of the well-to-do, receptacles of all kinds were made by the potter, from amphorae which took the place of barrels, and sometimes even of cupboards, to minute phials to hold perfumes and precious liquids. Clay was also used to make a large number of common-place articles and cheap trinkets. Potsherds strewn over a site are often the first indication of some ancient building whose walls have long since vanished. They also give the approximate date of its occupation.

There is therefore no better proof of the economic dependence of Carthage on Tyre, at least during the early centuries of its existence, than the fact that its everyday crockery came from Tyre, although the low value of such wares could hardly have made them a very attractive proposition for the merchants who sold them. There can be only one explanation for this: the round-hulled ships which went to fetch ore and metal from the West needed a heavy cargo to fill their holds on the outward journey, and the Tyrian jars served this purpose admirably. For the same reason, the Greek colonists received vases and domestic articles from the motherland. Later, under the Roman Empire, the ships which carried Carthaginian wheat to Ostia brought back bricks from the Imperial factories in Italy which must have had a monopoly of African markets, for no other bricks have ever been discovered. Tyrian pottery is therefore found in the lower layers of the *tophet*: heavy two-handled jars decorated with a wide bright red band, beneath which groups of three vertical strokes are painted at regular intervals, or vases without handles, and with tall bell-shaped necks like thistle flowers.

Before long, however, workshops were set up to use the local clay, and when eventually trade with Tartessus declined, they were able to produce enough themselves to meet the demands of home consumption, as well as the needs of foreign customers.

The discoveries of P. Gauckler and of Poinssot and Lantier give a vivid impression of the work of these Carthaginian potters. Workshops which are practically intact have been uncovered near the harbours, and especially round the Dermech burial-ground, where the potters waited for the families of the dead to sell them the articles required in the tomb, such as jars for oil, wine, and milk, lamps, perfume phials, and statuettes of protecting deities.

The clay was dug from the Carthaginian peninsula itself, just north of the burial-grounds;[11] near the Hamilcar station red cliffs tower above the beach—they are composed of sand bound together with bright red clay. Although it was heavily worked by the Carthaginians, this seam is still being excavated in open-air quarries today, with little concern for the possible collapse of the hill. Another deposit reaches the surface on the southern slope of St Louis Hill. Although this clay is of excellent quality, it was apparently very little worked, for fear of undermining the foundations of the citadel.

In the country, the Libyan women still made their crude household pottery with their bare hands, as their Neolithic ancestors had done before them, and as their Bedouin descendants still continue to do today.[12] In graves on Cape Bon and the Sahel, and also in the wheat plains of the Medjerda, bowls, cooking-pots, and jugs have been found similar to those on sale today in the villages. The women who modelled them sometimes tried to imitate the shape of Punic vases, and especially of lamps.

In the Smirat graves, a vase which was modelled by hand stands side by side with its counterpart turned on a potter's wheel. In the towns the Carthaginian potter used a wheel,[13] a crude machine consisting of two blocks of stone. One, a plain stone hollowed out in the shape of a bowl, formed the pedestal, another, shaped like a mushroom, had a foot which pivoted in the cavity of the pedestal. It took two men to work the device. One squatted on the ground and spun the wheel as fast as possible; the other stood and shaped the clay, which was stacked ready in slabs beside him.

On the other hand, their kilns were fairly advanced. P. Gauckler[14] excavated one at Dermech which had been left exactly as it was when it was abandoned, in full operation, during the capture of Carthage by Scipio. It is perfectly preserved to a height of 20 feet, 13 feet of it lying beneath the level of the soil in Punic times. It consists of an elliptical hearth surmounted by a tall cylindrical chimney; the latter, which could be closed at the top by a dome-shaped cover, was divided internally into two concentric zones by a tubular column in two sections, one above the other. The hearth communicated with the workroom by large square apertures arranged round the clay floor and by ventilation holes round the central pillar. A draught was thus created by the concentric zone round the inner chimney, where the coarser pots were stacked. The vases were placed, according to the degree of heat they required, in the two superimposed compartments of the central chimney, where the firing was more regular, and where they were protected from scorching and from the smoke and dust which escaped through the square apertures. The kiln opened through a narrow arched doorway, on to the furnace, which was at a lower level, and which, when excavated, still contained heaps of ashes and clinker, and decayed wood, the remains of the fuel prepared for the fire. There were also fragments of pots and rejected pots.

This cellar, which had no window, was situated below the workroom proper; the floor between them was on a level with the potter's room, enabling the potter to pass straight in there; on shelves, were piled the vases of raw clay which were awaiting their turn to be fired, each one carefully separated from its neighbours by bone rings to prevent them sticking to each other. There also were piled the pots that had been tried and tested, before the flawless specimens were put into store.

The store-rooms were joined to the workshop by a narrow corridor some fifteen or sixteen feet long. There we found a collection of moulds and a few pots containing white or brown pigment for painting or decorating the vases. There were also thousands of vessels of all shapes and sizes arranged according to type ready for sale.

The most striking of these vessels were the bowls around the outer rim of which were welded seven smaller cups. We shall see later for what strange purpose these were used.

These Punic kilns are identical with those used nowadays by Tunisian craftsmen. The clay is first washed in vats, then piled in circular heaps which are trodden down by an assistant, a technique known to the ancient Egyptians, and certainly to the Carthaginians. From these heaps were taken slabs of about twelve pounds in weight, which are wedged or kneaded by hand. Apprentices pick out the stones with a reed. The prepared lumps are then placed on the wheel, which is of a much more advanced design than that used by the Carthaginians. The vase comes to life on the wheel under the craftsman's fingers. It is cut away

with a wire, dried for an hour or two in the sun, and then kept
for several weeks in a cool damp room to get rid of the water
used while it was thrown. If it were fired too soon, it would split.
The kiln has not changed since ancient times. The vessels are
walled up in the kiln for three days, the first for firing, and the
other two for cooling.

The fact that these techniques have lasted so long does not
mean that they cannot be improved. The Punic potter was never
an artist like his Greek counterpart. The shapes which grew under
his hands were heavy and clumsy. The clay was generally left
bare, with neither colouring nor glaze, the only decoration on its
surface coming from the firing. The few exceptions are ancient
vases partially or completely coated with red. Painted vases were
extremely rare, and even these were crudely decorated with a
plain band surmounted by triglyphs like the ancient Tyrian vases,
or later with childishly stylized ornamentations. On one amphora
is an amusing scene showing two ostriches drinking from a vase
on a stand.[15]

The sole preoccupation of the Punic potter was uninterrupted
production in vast quantities at a very low price. When we think
of the thousands of jars and pitchers of all sizes and the lamps
which came from the graves and the *tophet*, and of all the pottery
required for daily use, for carrying supplies, including water, and
even for building, it is not difficult to imagine that the Carthaginian potters had very little time to be fussy over their work.
And yet it would have benefited the economy of Carthage if it
could have saved itself the expense of importing from Greece
whole cargoes of vases *de luxe*, right up to the fifth century. Then
the rigorous policy of the aristocracy put a stop to this drain on
the economy, but it either could not or would not create a replacement industry which would have made the State self-sufficient in
this respect.

Only religious requirements persuaded the potters to depart in
any particular from their normal routine. Ritual vases of fairly
complicated design were required, like the *kernoi*,[16] the main
bowl of which had around its lip a number of small cups resembling sconces. They were used for a peculiar ritual in honour of
Demeter, in which the priestess fastened one on her head after
lighting the sacred flame in the central bowl, and placing in the

surrounding cups the grain offered as first fruits. Preparations for celebrating this festival were being made in the spring of 146 when the city was captured, and the potters had already put the necessary *kernoi* in the kiln to fire them.

The potters, or at least the most skilled of them, the *coroplates*, supplied most of the religious imagery used in Carthage. Even large life-size statues used in the temples were often made of clay. Even the Greeks used such idols up to the fifth century, but after that date they were hardly ever made except in the countries on the margins of the Hellenic world, in Etruria, for example. We possess a fairly large number of Punic terracotta statues. Some were discovered in the Salammbô chapel by Dr Carton;[17] others, collected from humble country shrines on Cape Bon, are later than the destruction of Carthage but are certainly copies of Punic models. Some are not without character, like the half-horse, half-lion statue of Tanit from Thinissut, which is full of fierce disdain.[18] But others were simply cast from Greek models, like the *Cereres* of Korba;[19] others again preserve the crudity of ancient idols, like the Soliman Demeter.[20] The Mediterranean religions demanded the constant presence of the divine image. The faithful had to have statues to place in their private chapels, in the graves of their dead, or as ex-votos in their temples placed beside the vases containing the sacrificial ashes.

Our museums therefore possess hundreds of figurines, many bought in Greece, like the decorated vases. The Carthaginians gave to these imported statues the name of their own gods who most resembled them. They preferred those which had the most ornamentation: goddesses wearing heavy crowns, or wrapped in a sheath-like garment draped with enormous pendants,[21] like the *Lindia* of Rhodes. Moreover the Punic potters made casts of these figures and reproduced them by the gross. They also made their own miniature images of their national gods. Numerous terracotta medallions representing Baal Hammon on his throne, in a pose similar to that of the venerable statue in the temple of Hadrumetum, have been found.[22]

Seventh- and sixth-century graves, and the corresponding levels of the *tophet*, often contain masks made of clay. Young women, wearing a veil falling on either side of the head like the Egyptian *klaft*;[23] young men with the grace and smiling serenity of the *korai* and *kouroi* of ancient Greece.[24] But side by side with gracious beauty are some nightmarish horrors: faces with deformed bone structure, or with the skin covered with warts and tattoo-marks, or faces distorted into a horrible leer.[25] Some archaeologists have regarded these as true-to-life portraits and have referred to Punic realism.

They are in reality magic objects intended to secure for the living and the dead the protection of the gods, represented by the smiling masks, and to ward off, by the principle of *similia similibus curantur*, evil spirits, represented by the grimacing masks. These dread spirits were first evoked in ritual dances by masked performers. Such practices, still familiar today to black witch-doctors, were common among most Mediterranean peoples. In Latin, the word *larva* designated both the spirit and the mask. In Sparta, within the sacred precincts of the Temple of Artemis Orthia, similar grimacing figures have been dug up.[26] After the ceremony, the actors hung up their masks as ex-votos. This practice survived after the dances were no longer performed, on account of their value as a means of scaring away evil spirits. As for the busts of smiling goddesses with *Kouroi* heads, these were doubtless full-length statues reduced to their essential parts, in which their magic powers resided. In this, then, as in other branches of ceramic art, the Carthaginians confined themselves to following the example of the Greeks. The only initiative of their own was to embellish the original with a few suitable accessories: the grimacing masks, for example, sometimes wear on their foreheads an inverted crescent on a disc, the astral symbol of Tanit and of Baal. Some *Kouroi* have silver rings in their ears and even in their noses.

After the fifth century, however, almost the only masks that have been found are of Silenus or of Saturn, and in the later days of Carthage only dramatic masks. For the cult of Demeter, which soon became naturalized, in addition to the *kernoi* statuettes, busts were made to serve as incense-burners, in which the *calathos* of the goddess was hollowed out to receive the burning embers.[27] The Hellenic fashion was adopted rather late, but it was the only one which brought some measure of inspiration to the routine-ridden Carthaginian craftsmen.

There are, however, in existence a few original figurines which give expression to popular fantasy, like those produced by the potters of Nabeul when their taste is not spoiled by their being sent to Sèvres, and when they are allowed to make amusing rococo display pieces, full of flowers, trees, and animals. A statuette of a devotee[28] raising his hands in homage to a god is hunched up in his '*djellaba*' of coarse wool; another, on the other hand, is clothed in a rich tunic of pleated and embroidered muslin, with a cape;[29] others represent donkeys carrying water in pointed jars fastened to a pack-saddle, just as they can be seen today trotting through the narrow village streets.[30] These make one regret the snobbishness of the wealthy Carthaginians and their bad taste, which led them to prefer Greek trash to these crude trifles, so full of natural charm!

THE GLASS-BLOWERS

The Phoenicians were reputed to have invented glass; this is not true, but it is explained by the skill they acquired in this industry. In Carthage, small phials have been found, shaped like jars, made of opaque dark blue glass, embellished with bright yellow bands and geometrical decorations. P. Gauckler[31] has made a very precise study of the way these were made. 'The pattern', he says, 'was obtained by designs fixed inside the glass. The phial was first roughly shaped, after being impregnated with the background colour, generally dark, blue-black or indigo, though occasionally it was light (silvery white). Then, while the glass was still hot and viscous, light cuts were made in which threads of a light colour were inserted (yellow ochre, citron, white, or turquoise). These protruded beyond the cuts and were left standing in relief. Sometimes they remained in this state, but more frequently the glass was re-heated. The colours, expanding in the heat, became fused in the glass, which was subsequently buffed on a wheel, so that the surface looked perfectly smooth.'

Other phials[32] represented the Nile god, Hapi, or a squatting monkey holding a vase between its legs.[33] Glass was also used to make striped beads, resembling agate, which were used for necklaces or for covering a corsage or for decorative knobs on a casket. From glass, cheap scarabs and a multitude of charms were also made. The most curious of these represented either men, whose bright yellow skin contrasted strongly with their dark blue or black beards and shiny curly hair,[34] or else young men or women with pale skins. All had large hooked noses and large staring eyes, to scare away demons. This glassware, frequently found in Carthaginian tombs of the fourth and third centuries, is also found all round the shores of the Western Mediterranean as far away as Gaul. It is important to settle where they were made. S. Gsell[35] thought they were made in Egypt and E. von Bissing in Greece.[36] The author agrees with J. Vercoutter, that the Phoenician glass-blowers soon learnt to imitate Egyptian models and were responsible for the production of most of the specimens so widespread in the West.[37]

Ivory and bone, which are sometimes difficult to distinguish from each other, were used to make a host of small objects in everyday use. Reference has already been made to the carved combs found in seventh- and sixth-century graves, which probably came from Asia. P. Cintas discovered in Utica the grave of a bone-worker which he dates as early fourth century.[38] Near the skeleton had been placed 'everything that was likely to be on his work-bench on the day of his death, as though everything had been hurriedly swept off it to be put with him. His humble craftsman's tools: a hammer, a hatchet, an iron knife, a hard stone polisher; crude raw materials: sheep's ankle-bones, pebbles, and shells. Half-finished objects also: bone medallions, rubbed-down pebbles, mother-of-pearl shells, polished on one surface; and finally, completed articles: a delightful small polished capsule intended as an ornamentation for a casket.'

This craftsman was by no means poor; he was wearing a necklace with five pendants, and a solid gold ear-ring decorated with very delicate filigree-work. Curiously enough, there was nothing else besides the jewels and the tools: no lamp or vase to accompany the dead man. This fondness for souvenirs of the earthly life, emphasized by a disdain for the traditional burial ritual, is so violently in contradiction with Carthaginian habits that this bold spirit may not have been a Carthaginian at all. He may conceivably have been a foreigner, who died far from his native land without having adopted the cult of his new country, and who was buried by his neighbours, who did the best they could, but were ignorant of the proper funeral ritual.

Decorative ceramics, glass-blowing and ivory-carving are

artistic crafts. We have mentioned the jewellers, and workers in wood and bronze. Another body of workers had adopted a particularly interesting technique already popular with the Capsians,[39] namely, that of decorating ostrich eggs, on which large eyes were painted to make them look like female faces, or on which were engraved geometric patterns, or even sometimes human figures.[40]

GENERAL CHARACTERISTICS OF CARTHAGINIAN INDUSTRY

In spite of their number, and their indispensable activities, the workers of Carthage, as we have seen, did not play the important part one might have expected them to play in a mercantile organization, which had at its disposal abundant supplies of raw materials and a vast market for its products. They just managed to supply the everyday needs of their compatriots, and were never able to compete with their Egyptian or Greek rivals, even when an authoritarian policy prohibited the entry of finished products from abroad.

One is tempted to attribute to this excessive protectionism the mediocrity of their products, which were immune from competition and, except in Carthage, needed only to satisfy barbarian populations, who cared little about the quality of the trash they received in exchange for the materials they contributed. But it is disconcerting to come across so few articles made in Carthage in the vast territories washed by 'Tyrian Seas'. The reason was certainly the lack of creative power and technical ingenuity of the Carthaginian craftsmen. This inferiority is all the more remarkable because the Greeks, themselves experts, paid tribute to the skill of Carthaginian traders and because the farmers, as we have seen, succeeded in bringing their methods to a high state of perfection. On the other hand it should be noted that all North African societies appear to have shared the Carthaginians' lack of interest in industry.

In Roman Africa, where agriculture was so prosperous, artisans played a very minor part in comparison with their counterparts in Italy, Gaul, and Egypt. In the Africa of the Middle Ages only routine occupations were carried on, far inferior to the crafts of the Moslem States in the Near East. Even today, industrialization has scarcely touched the Mahgreb, although it has been under Western influence for more than a century, and although most of its skilled workers are of European origin.

There may be some justification for thinking that the African is by nature allergic to technical activity, and also to practical intellectual disciplines which seek to discover natural laws and to make use of them to improve the lot of man. The Phoenicians may have been influenced by the physical and racial environment in which they found themselves in Carthage. However, it must be recognized that they did maintain a technical superiority over the native peoples and that it was this which helped them to survive after the destruction of their city. The Numidian princes, like other Berber rulers, were well aware of the inferiority of their own peoples in this respect. Indeed, according to an ancient Dido legend Iarbas, King of the Gaetulians, employed Tyrians as professors of civilization.

At any rate, Masinissa and his successors settled within their kingdoms a large number of 'Punic technicians', by whose help they were able to transform the 'douars' and 'casbahs' in their domains into veritable cities. The inscription on a second-century mausoleum in Dougga[41] describes as a 'Punic technician' an architect named Abarish, son of Abdashtart, who was beyond all doubt a Carthaginian; he had under him two assistants, Zamar, son of Ateban, and Mangi, son of Varsaco, who were Numidians. The team consisted of three masons and two carpenters, all natives, and two iron-workers who were probably Phoenicians.

The role of the Carthaginians, therefore, seems to have been to enrol and train native workmen. The inscriptions of the *tophet* of Cirta[42] mention scribes, a doctor, a smelter, a sculptor, carpenters, and a bow-maker, and they all have Punic names. The influence of these *emigrés* was remarkably rapid and far-reaching, penetrating even to the rustic highland peoples who were generally extremely resistant to outside influences. Thus at the end of the fourth century A.D., in the district round Hippo, a patois was still spoken, which was doubtless very much crossed with Libyan, but contained enough Punic words for St Augustine's flock to recognize it as a near relation of Biblical Hebrew, and to proclaim themselves proudly as Canaanites.

THE FOREIGNERS

Although Carthage was not a very hospitable city, it was, never-theless, obliged by the needs of trade and commerce to admit foreigners. Merchants of all nations had free access to its port, which was the only outlet for the vast territories whose trade was controlled by the Carthaginian navy. They therefore set up permanent agencies around which, from the beginning of the fourth century, fairly large alien colonies developed. Later, when the severe restrictions of the oligarchic régime were relaxed, the growth of these colonies was obviously further encouraged. In view of the good relations which existed between Carthage and Etruria, it is not surprising that the Etruscans formed one of the largest and probably the most respected of these groups. Many inscriptions in their language have been found in Carthage. They soon established with the inhabitants of their adopted land not only business relationships, but also what we call today cultural exchanges. For example, in the Tarquinia burial-ground in Italy, a sarcophagus was found which was adorned with a male statue exactly like those from the Sainte-Monique burial-ground, but which contained the remains of an Etruscan. This remarkable discovery sets a very difficult archaeological problem, which will be discussed in the next chapter.[43]

The perpetual conflicts and the racial hatred which alienated Greeks and Phoenicians did not prevent Hellenes from settling in the new Tyre. The first evidence of a numerous colony dates from 396 B.C., when the Punic authorities called upon its most distin-guished members to organize the cult of Demeter, which had just been officially adopted.[44] These Hellenes were of very mixed origins. Many of them, doubtless, were Sicilians from towns which had been obliged to accept the Carthaginian protectorate; others were merchants from the free cities of Sicily or from Southern Italy; or they were sometimes political refugees (one of the opponents of Agathocles, King of Syracuse, at the very end of the fourth century took refuge in Carthage and married a Carthaginian woman by whom he had two sons, Hippocrates and Epicydes, who were among Hannibal's best officers). We shall recount later the story of Ophelas, a Macedonian adventurer whom Agathocles lured into Africa and assassinated; after his death and Agathocles' hasty return to Sicily, many mercenaries, who had come from Greece or from Cyrenaica to take part in the expedition, agreed to transfer their services to Carthage. A certain Agesandros of Cyrene, whose daughter Pamphila was buried in the Dermech burial-ground,[45] was doubtless one of these. Most of these soldiers of fortune, however, went back home after completing their term of service with Carthage, as did for example Xanthippus of Sparta.

The scope of the intellectual exchanges between Greeks and Carthaginians has been frequently emphasized. But the Carthaginians borrowed infinitely more than they gave. Greek sculptors, for example, certainly established workshops in Carthage. Their handiwork is recognizable on the Sainte-Monique sarcophagi,[46] and their influence was also felt in Carthaginian techniques, like the stone engraving processes used in the decoration of stelae placed in the *tophet*.

Carthage was also the home of a famous worker in bronze, Boethus, son of Apollodorus, whose signature has been deciphered on the pedestal of a statue at Ephesus. Incidentally this artist has presented us with one of the most complicated puzzles ever to face archaeologists, and one which might almost be the invention of some mischievous sprite. It transpires that he bears the same name as another more famous worker in bronze, Boethus of Chalcedonia. In Greek, the countries of origin of these two artists are written identically, except for one letter—Carthaginian was *Carchedonios* and Chalcedonian was *Calchedonios*. To make matters more difficult, the masterpiece of Boethus of Chalcedonia, an *Agon*, or deity of the *Palaestra*, was lost when the Roman ship which was carrying it sank in a storm off the Tunisian coast, near Mahdia; it was finally recovered from the sea in 1907 and is now in the Bardo Museum!

The intellectual activities of the Greek settlers in Carthage are even more interesting than their artistic productions. One of the last Platonists of ancient times, Iamblichus,[47] refers to a famous Pythagorean School which existed in Carthage and at the head of which were successively four scholars whose names he gives as: Miltiades, Anthon, Hodius, and Leocrites. Even assuming that the last of these lived at the time of the destruction of Carthage, the foundation of the school must have gone back to the previous century, that is, to the middle of the third century, a period when Carthage was most receptive to Hellenism. *A priori* it is not unlikely that a sect which had established itself in Tarentum in Southern Italy should have founded a branch in the great African city, as it did in Rome, at that time.

Of all the forms of Greek thought, the Carthaginians were best equipped to understand the doctrines of Pythagoras, though their 'alogical' minds must have been highly resistant to the rigorously intellectual principle of Pythagoras according to which all natural laws appeared as the reflection of mathematical relationships. But the Carthaginian disciples of the sage of Samos were able to' enrich their master's ideas with many strange developments! Instead of following the example of other sects who tended towards a more or less materialistic rationalism, they arrived at a form of mysticism which, by a boldly symbolical interpretation, succeeded in reconciling with ethics and reason all the stories of mythology; and which, while accepting polytheism, developed it into a kind of 'henotheism' in which all the gods of the pantheon were subordinated to one supreme god.

This attempt coincided exactly with that of the Carthaginian priesthood, who as early as the fifth century had striven to subordinate all the gods of Tyre to the Tanit-Baal Hammon couple. It was most appropriate also that Pythagoras identified the supreme god with Apollo, whom his disciples did not hesitate to believe to have been reincarnated in the person of their master. Now, in Carthage, a god who was particularly revered was one whose Phoenician name was probably Reshef, and who was identified by the Greeks with Apollo. This god, like his Greek counterpart, was a musician and played on the lyre. Pythagoras taught that a similarity existed between the harmony of the seven strings of the lyre and the harmony which kept the spheres of the universe in their places; their movement produced a mysterious music which was audible in moments of ecstasy to the soul of the initiate. One of Pythagoras' disciples, the musician Arion, was cast overboard by treacherous sailors, but was saved by a dolphin (a creature sacred to Apollo) which had been charmed by his playing. The School of Pythagoras contributed more than any other to the acceptance of the idea that the souls of the departed rose up through the air, and that the most deserving found peace in a paradise on the planets,[48] and particularly, on the moon. All these doctrines were tolerated later in neo-Punic religious circles.

An illustration of this is provided on the stelae found in La Ghorfa and Althiburos, in a Numidian district which was strongly influenced by Carthaginian civilization, but scarcely touched by Roman influences. On the Dougga mausoleum[49] which was built at the time of the destruction of Carthage, the idea of the soul's flight through the air had been symbolized by the statues of sirens which flank its crowning pyramid. These bird-women, themselves originally winged souls of the departed, were charged with the task of escorting the dead through the perils of the atmosphere, with its winds and harmful demons. The soul's upward flight is shown in a most picturesque fashion on the Althiburos stelae, dating from the first century A.D.[50] Deceased 'astronauts' are borne aloft on the backs of birds, which is very logical—but also on the backs of dolphins, which would seem much less logical if we were unaware of the Babylonian belief in the Upper Ocean, which had been preserved in Carthage, and which, moreover, was part of the Pythagorean cosmology. There is possibly also a connexion between the myth of Arion, saved by the music of his lyre and by the help of Apollo, and the fate of the righteous soul, carried aloft by celestial dolphins through the sidereal seas. Such concordances may be multiplied. There are, for example, the regulations of the Aesculapius-Eshmoun temple at Thuburbo Majus, which included a ban on the eating of beans, one of the chief items in the disciplinary manual of Pythagoras. We may therefore conclude that there was an intimate and fruitful relationship between the mystic sect which the Greeks established in Carthage and the Punic priesthood. At about the same time, the doctrines of the sage of Samos were attracting the attention of pious and scholarly Jews in Alexandria who founded the strange Essenian sect, whose principles have just been revealed by the Dead Sea Scrolls.

Moreover, the Pythagoreans were not the only Greek mystics who settled in Carthage. We have already referred to the success which the cult of Demeter enjoyed in Africa. It had come from Sicily as early as the beginning of the fourth century and had been enriched, in particular, by contact with the mysteries transplanted from Eleusis to Alexandria by order of Ptolemy I. Others were attracted by the identification of Dionysus (or Bacchus) with Shadrapa, the healing child god, also associated with the Egyptian god Horus. Now Shadrapa was directly associated with Tanit and Baal Hammon.[51] It was by these associations that Bacchic symbols reached the decorations on the stelae of the *tophet*; the eschatological hopes put forward by the religious brotherhoods of the god complemented the teachings of the *Kohanim*. However, in these matters the Greeks sometimes did more than bring their ideas to Carthage. Some allowed themselves to be attracted by Carthaginian gods to the extent of taking part in the *mol'k* sacrifice itself. Stelae with Greek inscriptions are rare in the Carthaginian *tophet*, but seventeen have been dug up in the Cirta *tophet* where these human sacrifices took place.

Finally, there were a large number of Asiatics in Carthage. First, there were the Phoenicians, who were welcomed as fellow-citizens; then Cypriots, whose ancestors, according to tradition, had supplied Dido's companions with wives and a High Priest—doubtless from Anatolia. One of the towns founded by Hanno on the Atlantic coast of Morocco was named in Greek: 'Wall of the Carians'. If this name is not the approximate rendering of an imperfectly understood Phoenician term, it provides evidence of the immigration into Carthage in the fifth century of inhabitants of the province of Caria numerous enough for the Admiral to recruit from their midst several hundred colonists. It does indeed seem as if Carthage encouraged foreigners who came seeking asylum, to go and settle in new colonies, where they would be able to preserve their national traditions without harming the unity of Carthaginian civilization. Thus the town of Acholla, on the coast of Byzacium, appears to have been founded by Maltese, and Sicca (today Le Kef) in Western Tunisia, seems to have been founded by Elymaei from Sicily.

THE SOCIAL PROBLEM

The population of Carthage, therefore, contained elements which differed widely in origins and culture as well as in wealth and social standing. Yet there seems to have been little serious class conflict. We know practically nothing about the urban slaves, except that they must have been very numerous: they seem to have harboured no violent hatred against their masters. At the beginning of the fourth century the ambitious, high-born Hanno the Great started a political and social revolution in the hope of making himself supreme ruler.[52] He called upon the slaves to rise, but seems to have had little success with those who worked in the city and lived with their masters. Bomilcar, who also tried to make himself dictator during the war with Agathocles, relied on his mercenaries and appears to have found no support among the urban proletariat. Finally, in 149 B.C., at the time of the supreme crisis, the Punic Senate decreed the liberation of all slaves. There could have been no fear, therefore, that they would side with the Romans, and the trust that was placed in them was certainly justified, for they fought to the end with the greatest courage.

The real social danger lay elsewhere: in the first place, among the Libyan farmers. These rebelled in 396 B.C. and in 379 B.C., and on each occasion threatened the very existence of Carthage.[53] Archaeology has shown that their standard of living was very low. Although they were free men, the obligation imposed on them to pay a tribute which in time of war might rise to a quarter or a half of their harvest was obviously a heavy burden. Nor must it be forgotten that, until these last years, the *Khamessat* remained in force throughout North Africa. This was a contract for payment of rent in kind which gave the landowner four-fifths of the income from his land. These Africans remembered their recently lost liberty; the economic system which was forced upon them must have been most irksome, and they would obviously have preferred to return to their nomadic way of life, and keeping flocks and herds. The final incentive to revolt was the near presence outside the Carthaginian domains of their compatriots who were still free. The rural slaves who worked on the estates of the Carthaginian aristocracy were also dissatisfied with their lot. These two classes provided troops for the fourth-century peasant risings, also the 20,000 men whom Hanno was able to rally to his cause after the failure of his attempt at a rebellion within the city itself.

The mercenaries were another disturbing element. We shall describe later how dangerous for Carthage was the presence of this explosive force, ready at any minute to destroy, rather than protect, the city. But mention must be made here of the great war which broke out in 240 B.C. and which, thanks to Polybius[54] and Flaubert, has become the most famous episode in the history of Carthage. It was, above all, one of the great social crises which occurred in the Ancient World in the period between the death of Alexander and the restoration of order and stability by Augustus. The dynamic element in the army which the Carthaginian government was imprudent enough to assemble at Sicca, was the body of men whom Polybius describes as 'half-Greeks', the former slaves of deserters from Sicily and the Greek mainland.

At that time those countries, with Asia Minor, were centres of great social unrest. They had been the battle-ground of three great civil wars, which the Romans had had to put down in 134, 103, and 73 B.C., and in them all were vast numbers of ill-treated slaves, incited by revolutionary propaganda from the East and urged to rebellion by wise men or philosophers who dreamed of a great social revolution. Spendius, who was the real instigator of the rebellion by causing a last-minute breakdown in the agreement which Gisgo had just negotiated, was one of the half-Greeks from Campania who had been enslaved by the Romans. As soon as the breakdown occurred, the mercenaries regrouped the fugitive slaves, who were the workers from the Carthaginian estates who had risen against their masters. The Libyans also revolted in a body. Polybius gives a detailed account of the pitiful condition to which these wretched folk had been reduced by the harsh tribute exacted by the Carthaginians during the war with Rome. Many of the men had been imprisoned for failing to meet their obligations, but the women had been able to put something aside—usually their personal jewellery.

This they willingly handed over to the mercenaries, who thus got the money they needed for the war and for their arrears of pay. This detail is reflected in the present-day customs of the Mahgreb Bedouins: the meagre savings that they are able to make are invested exclusively in silver jewellery, large clasps, bracelets, and ankle-rings, which are never touched except at moments of dire necessity.

The mercenaries also found support in the Phoenician towns, which complained that Carthage treated them as subordinates and not as equals. The merchants in these ports obviously suffered severely from the Carthaginian monopoly of overseas trade. Opposing interests proved stronger than ties of blood; during the last war against Rome, the seven most important towns, led by Utica, abandoned Carthage for Rome, and thanks to their defection were able to preserve, within a Roman province, their theoretical independence.

This element of civil strife and revolution explains the atrocities of the 'truceless war', as the ancients called it. Gisgo and the other Carthaginian ambassadors taken prisoner by treachery and buried alive after their noses and ears had been cut off and their limbs broken; captured mercenaries crushed by elephants; the long-drawn-out agony of the rebel army in the narrow defile, and the 'shameful torture' of Mathos. These horrors have been made known by Flaubert's novel. The cold impersonal account in Polybius seems more impressive today than this pathetic fresco, which one is inclined to consider as inaccurate or overdrawn. But the facts are the same in both, and their authenticity seems beyond dispute.

The social problem in Carthage, therefore, did not come from a class conflict within the city, but from a clash with men of different nationalities employed on a variety of economic tasks. All the Carthaginians, rich or poor, free men or slaves, stood together because they all benefited, even if unequally, from the city's prosperity, and because even the most wretched knew that they stood to lose everything if the city fell. What happened in Spain when Cartagena was captured by the Romans, shows that this feeling was by no means illusory.[55] That town contained two elements: a middle class, mostly traders, and a working class mainly employed in the arsenal. We do not know the exact status of these latter, but at least they were legally free men. Scipio was careful to leave this hierarchy intact. He sent the citizens home and told the artisans that they would henceforth be slaves of the Roman people, but that they would be freed at the end of the war if their work had been satisfactory; in the meantime, they were organized on military lines into squads of thirty men, each under a Roman overseer. The remaining prisoners were sent to the galleys.

Unlike the Carthaginians, the Libyans had only been kept in subjection by fear. The Spaniards were the same. Here was a weak spot in the Punic empire which the Romans skilfully exploited. Polybius[56] emphasizes Scipio's cleverness in posing as the liberator of the Iberians, at pains to treat with the utmost consideration the hostages which the Carthaginians had collected. These were, for the most part, the families of the native chiefs, held responsible for the loyalty of their tribe. 'Having had all the hostages brought before him, to the number of more than 300, he began by caressing and praising the children in turn, promising them that they would soon be restored to their parents. . . . He gave ear-rings and bracelets to the girls and daggers and swords to the boys. Thereupon the wife of Mandonius, brother of Indibilis, King of the Ilergetes, prostrated herself at Scipio's feet, begging him with tears in her eyes to see that the wives were treated with more consideration and respect than they had been by the Carthaginians. . . . Then Scipio, understanding what she meant, and seeing the youth of the daughters of Indibilis and several other noble ladies, could not refrain from bursting into tears. This young woman's remark was enough to reveal to him all that these young women prisoners had been obliged to suffer.'

This moving passage, whose tender charm is well rendered by Buchon's archaic translation, shows that the propaganda methods used today to undermine a colonial empire, have changed very little since ancient times. The psychological warfare department of the Roman army had very conscientiously compiled its dossier of 'Punic atrocities', and, in the absence of journalists, historians were given the job of bringing these charges before public opinion in civilized countries, namely in Greece, where the international conscience of those times was moulded. It would obviously be absurd to treat as Gospel truth war propaganda of this kind; its insincerity is clear. In fact, Carthage did not lack skilful colonial administrators who succeeded in winning the trust of their subjects. One of the best was Hasdrubal, the son of Gisgo, who secured the allegiance of Syphax by giving him in marriage his daughter Sophonisba, a lady herself endowed with all the talents and charms of a beautiful spy.[57] But at that time a spirit of nationalism was awakening among the Libyans and Carthage was the first obstacle in the way of their aspirations. Syphax, who did his best to hinder its development, was obliged to yield to Masinissa who contrived to harness it to his own advantage. Thus Carthage perished because it failed to solve the very difficult problem which is always created in colonies where two populations live side by side, but whose standards of living and civilization are too blatantly at variance.

REFERENCES

1. Polybius, X, 17, 9.
2. Appian, *Pun.*, 93.
3. Lysias, *Contre Eratosthène*, 19.
4. *C.I.S.*, 3014. *R.E.S.*, I, 6; *C.I.S.*, 330–2, 338, 346.
5. M. Hours-Miedan, *Cahiers de Byrsa*, I, 1950, p. 65.
6. Coffin from Ksour es Saf, A. Merlin, *Mon. Piot.*, XVII, 1910, pp. 128–30, figs. 2–3; from Thapsus, Epinat and Novak, BAC, 1900, p. 157; from Mahdia, Hannezo, *Recueil de la Soc. arch. de Constantine*, XXVI, 1890–1, p. 296.
7. No description so far published but it is preserved in the Bardo Museum.
8. Unpublished inscription from the *tophet*.
9. L. Poinssot and J. Revault, *Tapis tunisiens*, p. 11.
10. *Supra*, p. 47.
11. P. Cintas, *Céramique punique*, pp. 31–2.
12. *Ibid.*, pp. 447 sqq.
13. L. Poinssot and R. Lantier, BAC, 1923, p. LXXIII. P. Cintas, *op. cit.*, p. 23.
14. P. Gauckler, *Nécropoles puniques*, II, pp. 513–14.
15. P. Cintas, *op. cit.*, p. 335, pl. LXIX.
16. *Ibid.*, pp. 535 sqq.
17. L. Carton, *Un sanctuaire punique découvert à Carthage*, Paris, 1929.
18. A. Merlin, 'Le sanctuaire de Ba'al et de Tanit près de Siagu', *Notes et Documents*, IV, 1910, pp. 44 sqq., pl. III; MC, pl. 61.
19. MC, pl. 64.
20. *Ibid.*, pl. 63.
21. P. Gauckler, *op. cit.*, I, pl. CLXXV, 1.
22. A. Merlin, *op. cit.*, pp. 40–1.
23. MC, pl. 24.
24. *Ibid.*, pl. 25.

25. *Ibid.*, pl. 26.
26. Dawkins, *The Sanctuary of Artemis Orthia*, pp. 163 sqq.
27. *Catalogue Mus. Alaoui, Suppl.*, pl. LXXV, 2, p. 149, I, 164.
28. MC, pl. 68.
29. *Ibid.*, pl. 69.
30. *Ibid.*, pl. 30.
31. P. Gauckler, *op. cit.*, II, pp. 308–9, pl. CCXXXIX.
32. MC, pl. 21.
33. P. Gauckler. *op. cit.*, pl. CLXX.
34. MC, pl. 57, 58, 59.
35. S. Gsell, HAAN, IV, p. 99.
36. E. von Bissing, *Studi Etruschi*, VII, 1933.
37. J. Vercoutter, *Les objets égyptiens et égiptisants du mobilier funéraire carthaginois*, p. 342.
38. P. Cintas, *Karthago*, II, 1951, p. 37.
39. Palaeolithic tribe who lived on the steppes of Southern Algeria and Tunisia.
40. M. Astruc, *Libyca*, II, 1954, pp. 9 sqq.
41. J.-B. Chabot. *Corpus Inscr. Lib.*, I, p. 1, no. 1.
42. A. Berthier and R. Charlier, *Le sanctuaire punique d'El Hofra à Constantine*, pp. 77–83.
43. *Infra*, p. 163.
44. Diodorus, XIV, 77, 5.
45. G. Ch.-Picard, BAC, 1950, p. 118.
46. J. Carcopino, *Mem. del Pont. Accad. Rom. Arch.*, 1921, III, *Memoire*, vol. I, part. II, pp. 109–111.
47. Amblichus, *De Pythagorica Vita*, XXVII, 128 and XXXVI, 267.
48. F. Cumont, *Recherches sur le Symbolisme funéraire des Romains*, p. 183.
49. On the subject of the stelae from La Ghorfa and Althiburos cf. above, p. 94, n. 50. On the Dougga mausoleum, cf. MC, pl. 82–3.
50. *Ibid.*, pl. 80.
51. G. Ch.-Picard, *Religions de l'Afrique antique*, pp. 96–7.
52. Aristotle, *Polit.*, V., 6, 2.
53. Diodorus, XIV, 77, 3.
54. Polybius, I, 65–88.
55. Polybius, X, 17, 7, 10.
56. *Ibid.*, 18, 5–15.
57. S. Gsell, *op. cit.*, III, p. 197.

CHAPTER V

EVERYDAY LIFE

PHYSICAL CHARACTERISTICS

Unfortunately—and it is their own fault—we know less about the physical appearance of the Carthaginians than of most ancient peoples. Their meagre art has left nothing to compare with the Egyptian frescoes, the Greek painted vases, or the Roman stelae and mosaics, all of which depict the individual going about his daily task, reproduce his clothes and his tools, and reveal his pleasures and his troubles. Most of the Carthaginian monuments, under the influence of strict religious rules, represent gods rather than men, or else represent men in such a stylized fashion, that no precise information can be obtained from them.

The anthropological examination of skeletons found in tombs proves that there was no racial unity;[1] the so-called Semitic type, characterized by the long, perfectly oval face, the thin aquiline nose, and the lengthened cranium, enlarged over the nape of the neck, has not been found in Carthage, nor for that matter in Sidon. On the other hand, another cranial form, with a fairly short face, prominent parietal bumps, farther forward and lower down than usual, is common in Lebanese burial-grounds and in those of the new Tyre: perhaps it belonged to the real Phoenicians. But most of the Punic population seem to have had African, and even Negro, ancestors.

The skeletons are generally fairly slender; and yet many Carthaginians displayed, on occasion, extraordinary physical endurance. Hannibal astonished his compatriots by his remarkable resistance to fatigue and sickness; we know that although he lost an eye crossing the Tuscany marshes, he was just as active afterwards, and that when he was considerably over fifty, he could still cover the fifty leagues from Carthage to Thapsus in two stages on horseback. Similar physical endurance was a necessary quality in sea-captains braving the Atlantic, and leaders of caravans crossing the Sahara. One of the latter, Mago, boasted of having crossed this desert three times without a drop to drink. We shall see later that Hanno's sailors rowed their way round the entire Sahara coast—a remarkable exploit, even supposing these coasts to be less arid than they are today.

The Barbary nomads have always possessed iron constitutions, coupled with extreme sobriety. These attributes derive from a process of natural selection resulting from a complete lack of hygiene and an enormously high rate of child mortality. It may be supposed that in Carthage the practice of child sacrifices provided an incidental method of getting rid of weakling children. Texts on two stelae from the *tophet* of Cirta, deciphered by J.-G. Février,[2] inform us that a couple who had had a deaf and dumb child—accursed progeny, in the words of the inscription—offered him to the gods in return for the prospect of further normal offspring. After the birth of a second child, the unfortunate first-born, who was by then several years old, was actually 'passed through the fire'.

It seems likely, therefore, that the Punic aristocracy had largely escaped the softening process which often overtakes Oriental peoples in urban and mercantile societies. The inhabitants of Carthage who were not engaged in overseas trade, devoted themselves, as we have seen, to agriculture, and took a personal share in the labours of the farm. Up to the end of the fourth century, the young men served in the army. In the battle of Crimisos, in 339 B.C., 'the sacred battalion' which they formed was annihilated. This led the government of the Republic to be more sparing of their blood on future occasions. Nevertheless, the courage displayed by the whole population during the siege of 149–146 B.C. proves that military virtues were by no means extinct.

The Carthaginians did not share the pious Jews' antipathy to the cleansing properties of water. The Phoenicians, who learnt their architecture from the Cypriots, acquired from them the art of building excellent bathing establishments, complete with drains and heating, like those found in the palaces of Vounos.[3] In Carthage, as we have seen, the houses of the rich had their own perfectly appointed bathrooms, and probably private swimming-pools as well.

There were also public baths, some reserved for the aristocracy and others open to the general public. Excavations have yielded many bronze body-scrapers, which were used to free the body of sweat, oil, and dust, after a hot bath or physical exercises. One was even made of silver. Both men and women used perfume—often to excess. In nearly every grave was placed an *alabaster*, a small phial with a handle,[4] or a minute amphora of iridescent glass,[5] to hold perfume. Aromatic substances were dissolved in oil, which took the place of soap, or were blended into a cream; one stelae was dedicated by a maker of such unguents.[6] In fact, the Carthaginian perfume-makers were famous and sold their products abroad—in particular to the Libyans, who valued them highly, although this did not prevent them from buying other beauty preparations from the Greeks or Egyptians. Naturally enough, the gods shared the tastes of their worshippers: Baal Hammon most probably means 'Lord of the Altars where Incense burns'. The smoke of incense rose ceaselessly in the temples from lofty candelabras or from terracotta burners.

Apart from the priests, who were clean-shaven in the Egyptian manner, most grown men wore beards.[7] The glass masks which doubtless represent a god (perhaps Dionysus) have magnificent blue, curled, corkscrew beards. The statues and terracotta masks, on the other hand, have very short beards which are indicated by a simple spotting of the cheeks.[8]

Nevertheless, the Carthaginians had razors and even considered them as sacred articles. In graves of the sixth to the third centuries, copper blades are found shaped roughly like a very elongated axe-head, with a convex cutting-edge, and with a tine often swan-necked in shape.[9] They resemble the razors used in ancient Egypt and those still used today among certain tribes in Equatorial Africa. However, some archaeologists, including S. Gsell, are inclined to think that these implements are hatchets, and point out that they are found in the graves of women, as well as of men, and, moreover, that the men wore beards. Certainly the 'razors' found in burial-places could not have been articles of everyday use. They have no handle that could be gripped, and, after the fifth century, they were embellished with line-engravings so skilfully executed, that they may be considered as examples of the best and most original artistic productions of Carthage. They represent a varied range of figures: Egyptian gods like Horus and Anubis; a god in Egyptian costume, but with a beard and mitre (perhaps Baal Hammon), and figures carrying lotus leaves, palm trees, or animals.[10] In the third century the Greek gods appear: Hermes; Heracles strangling the Cretan bull; and the monster, Scylla. These razors were therefore either charms to protect the dead from harmful influences, or more probably instruments used in connexion with some rite performed during their lifetime. It will be remembered that in certain initiation ceremonies a 'sacred toilet'[11] was decreed by the Phoenician religion. A stele of the Roman period, which marked the tomb of two persons with Punic names, shows a man being sprinkled with purifying water. Combs carved on other stelae were probably used for dressing the hair of the initiates. It may be concluded that the razors were used by the temple barbers for the sacred toilet and that they thus became a symbol of initiation; the faithful worshipper then had copies made of them which he offered as an ex-voto or preserved all the more preciously because the blade was decorated with figures or inscriptions like a real amulet.

The Carthaginians looked after their hair just as carefully. The Libyans, like their descendants, the Berbers, often had tightly curled hair, and many Carthaginians had inherited from their native ancestors tight curls such as are often found on masks. These required double combs, often made of ivory and richly decorated. Specimens have been found in all the ancient tombs. One has a Syrian king in his chariot on one side, and on the other, two genii with long curved wings on their backs, facing each other on either side of a small palm tree.[12] It comes from a seventh-century tomb and must have been imported direct from Phoenicia.[13] Other combs are decorated with Egyptian subjects, like Isis and Nephthys, accompanied by Mesopotamian genii.

The Phoenicians believed that supernatural power resided in the hair of certain individuals; the story of Samson is based on such an idea. This power was located especially in a lock of the hair which had therefore to be carefully preserved. Thus, statuettes of children, which have been dug up in certain shrines, have a central lock of hair which divides the scalp like the crest of a helmet and on the front of which is fastened an amulet. This custom had been borrowed from the Libyans. The Temehous appear on Egyptian monuments with a short plait which reaches the shoulders. A statue of Hermes found in the Antonine Baths at Carthage and dating from the second century A.D. represents a Berber[14] whose shaven head is surmounted by a plaited crest ending in a crescent-shaped amulet. This prehistoric hair-style is still worn by some tribes in Morocco.

The female *coiffure* was naturally more elaborate than the male. The women of Carthage were very proud of their long hair, which they sacrificed during the siege of 149 B.C. to make catapult-slings. In the sixth century they seem to have adopted the Egyptian fashion. The hair was drawn back behind the ears and fell in· thick curls on either side of the face. At least, that is the *coiffure* found on a sandstone head of that date, which is probably a copy of an ancient Greek original.[15] Later styles kept step with Greek fashions.

The terracotta statuettes, like the heads which decorate the handles of bronze *oenochoai*, all have their hair parted in the middle, with either an irregular fringe over the forehead or a coil over each ear. Feminine figures on stelae have either straight or wavy hair drawn tight on either side of the head.[16] The priestess of the *tophet* who is pouring out a libation has a high chignon and long drooping locks falling to the shoulders.[17] The glass masks, however, show more originality: a head-band keeps the hair close to the forehead, leaving it free to puff out above and on either side. Curled hair-styles with a central crest or ridge are equally common towards the end of the period of Phoenician domination and on neo-Punic stelae of the first century A.D. Bone or ivory pins were used to keep this central erection in place.

Carthaginian mirrors, fairly common in tombs, resemble the Etruscan mirrors; they usually consist of a disc, or sometimes a rectangle, mounted on a handle, and coated on one side with a layer of reflecting silver. But whereas the Etruscans usually engraved the other side, and the Greeks decorated the handle, the Carthaginians, who engraved the blades of their razors, left the back of their mirrors smooth, and contented themselves with decorating the wooden, bone, or ivory handle.

A few *de luxe* specimens were protected by a cover. There is one in the Lavigerie Museum, of fine Greek workmanship,[18] which depicts the left profile of a woman's head. Others are protected by a plain canvas case. Rouge was liberally applied to the cheeks and lips and kohl to the eyes. Make-up boxes of lead or of wood have been found in graves. Shells were also used, the two halves being fastened together by a silver chain. M. Fatter, a chemist living in Carthage, has been able to make rouge with an antimony base, very like that used by the Carthaginians.

It seems that men, and perhaps women as well, indulged in tattooing; it is known that this custom, of barbarian origin, has persisted to the present day among the Bedouins of North Africa, especially in the pre-Sahara steppes. It has even been maintained that the very complicated patterns which are handed down by the specialists of this art (generally aged women) contain motifs which date back to antiquity. Too much importance should not be attached to such uncritical conclusions. Nevertheless, the terracotta busts of the 'smiling goddess' have an indentation on the chin very like the *foula* which adorns the chins of Bedouin women.[19] The ugliness of the 'grotesque' masks[20] is emphasized by a whole series of incised or painted patterns: the forehead is divided by a vertical row of diamond shapes transfixed by an arrow pointing towards the nose. The cheeks have horizontal stripes reminiscent of those with which Negroes and Polynesians decorate their bodies. Others have a single design in relief, often a crescent inverted over a disc, the symbol of Tanit and Baal, which is always placed at the base of the nose; this seems to have been regarded as a vital area in need of special protection. We have already stated that these masks represent, not human, but supernatural beings, perhaps intended to ward off evil spirits. Nevertheless, it is fairly certain that many details, particularly of adornment, were borrowed from real life.

For primitive peoples, tattooing was not just an ornament: it had a ritual significance, protecting the wearer from the evil influences around him. It often indicated, also, that he belonged to some special brotherhood requiring initiation. Carthaginian tattooing seems to have had this double significance of protection and dedication, which explains its genuinely religious symbols, of which the most significant was the crescent.

DRESS

The Carthaginians were clearly differentiated from the Greeks and Romans by their dress, which was enough to give them the name of 'barbarians'. Rigidly conservative in this respect, they remained faithful to the fashions of their country of origin, right up to the end of their civilization. These were no more original than many other aspects of Carthaginian civilization. One of them, which may perhaps be regarded as their real national costume, is Mesopotamian in origin; another came from Cyprus or from Anatolia; a third from Egypt.

The Tyrians, like most Orientals, usually wore a long straight woollen robe with sleeves. It appears in its stark simplicity on a statuette of a worshipper, recently discovered.[21] He wears no other garment, and no belt, as was usual. In Plautus' *Poenulus*, the Greek Milphio shouts to the Punic merchant 'Hey, you there without a belt!' However, it was sometimes necessary, probably, to raise the lower part of the robe for greater ease in walking, thus blousing the upper part. This effect is shown on the famous Baalyaton stele found in Phoenicia and now in the Ny Carlsberg Museum.[22] The long heavy robe was usually a sufficient protection against heat or cold and a cloak was not usually necessary. To quote the *Poenulus* again, the facetious Milphio, catching sight of Hanno, exclaims: 'What is this bird coming along dressed in a tunic? Did he have it made out of his bath-robe?' But the ex-voto of Yehawmilk, King of Byblos in the fifth century,[23] shows the prince wearing a cloak in addition to his robe. It is a kind of shawl fastened over the chest, and completely covering the back. The Christian apologist Tertullian,[24] who wrote in Carthage at the end of the second century A.D., has left us a fairly precise description of Carthaginian dress as worn by certain sartorial conservatives. He speaks of a *pallium* gathered round the neck, fastened at the shoulders by clasps and hanging down on either side. But this dress, a convenient protection against cold and rain, could only have appeared at a fairly recent date as clasps are rarely found in Carthaginian graves and appear to have been used exclusively by women.

The Carthaginians did not like to go out bare-headed. Herodotus[25] mentions that this custom distinguished the Asiatics

from the Egyptians, and states that the latter owed their pro-
verbially hard skulls to their habit of exposing them to the sun
without a covering. The Asiatic headgear, which the Greeks
called a *tiara*, was nearly always a kind of turban, without brim
or peak, and fairly tall. The Asiatic Phoenician had adopted a
fairly low cylindrical turban as worn by Yehawmilk and Baalyaton. We come across it again on the well-known stele of the
priest and child.[26] But the Carthaginians seem to have preferred
a conical hat, probably of felt, which they got from Cyprus.
They also protected their heads with a veil, which was sometimes
fastened across the forehead and hung down at the sides, like
the Egyptian *klaft* or the present-day Arab head-dress, and was
sometimes folded up into a turban.

The feet were protected either by sandals, or by thick-soled
shoes, or by boots.

The Cypriot costume was much more complicated. It consisted of a long under-robe of pleated linen muslin, like that of
the Egyptians, covered by layers of outer garments which got
progressively thicker and shorter. A statuette dating from the
second quarter of the sixth century, found in Cyprus,[27] wears a
pointed *tiara* like a bishop's mitre and four outer garments:
a long straight under-robe, a muslin 'apron' with pleats curving
over the stomach, a kind of jacket rather like a modern tail-coat,
open in front, with the tail reaching to the knees, and over all
this, a short cape finishing just below the chest.

This singularly unpractical costume spread to Africa and lasted
for at least seven centuries. It was worn by women as well as by
men. A statuette found in Carthage[28] wears a very ample robe,
with two belts. The first of these is not visible, but is worn very
high so that the upper part of the robe blouses over it; the second,
at the waist, supports a kind of apron whose flat pleats fan out
over the stomach, and a long embroidered band which hangs
down vertically. The tunic stops short at the knees in front, but
completely covers the legs behind. Gauckler thought this statuette
represented an adolescent boy, doubtless because the robe was
short in front; but the breasts are clearly defined. The short cape,
with horizontal stripes, looks rather like the nineteenth-century
caped coat and recurs on the Leontocephalic statue of Tanit from
Thinissut,[29] and on the figure of the same goddess on the

sarcophagus of the priestess of Sainte-Monique.[30] The pleated muslin apron was also worn by men: on neo-Punic stelae it is seen held up by a belt with shoulder braces and worn over a kind of pleated frock-coat, open in front to reveal a long robe, also pleated.

But in Cyprus and Etruria a sports costume is also found consisting of a tight-fitting singlet and a pair of abbreviated trunks; like a modern swimming-costume. In Gouraya, in Africa, an ostrich egg has been found on which was incised a drawing of a hunter,[31] armed with a bow or small crescent-shaped shield, and wearing a tight-fitting singlet, red, or perhaps bi-coloured, like a medieval doublet, with a stripe in front and a wide gymnast's band round the neck, and breeches fastened tight round the knee. On the head is a round skull-cap, also edged with braid. The shoes have heels and are fastened with laces crossed over the leg.

On the other hand, the Egyptian style of dress was rarely worn. Mention has already been made of the long transparent robe which seems always to have been worn by the attendants of certain temples, and sometimes by those making sacrifices. Razors often show gods and men wearing a loin-cloth.[32] The former are primarily divinities, some direct from the Nile, like Horus and Anubis; others from Carthage, like Baal Hammon, or even from Greece, like Hermes. A man wearing the crown of Lower Egypt and holding a ringed Egyptian cross is doubtless Pharaoh. Not one of these is Carthaginian. This exotic costume therefore distinguishes the Egyptians, and appears never to have passed into common use.

We know even less about female costume, for statues and statuettes are nearly always of goddesses and foreign women. The funeral stelae nearly always carry the image of the dead woman, but details are rarely visible. Moreover none are earlier than the fourth century. One single stele from the *tophet* represents a priestess pouring out a libation.[33] The most interesting evidence, because it is more definite, comes from neo-Punic votive or funeral stelae.

They confirm that the Carthaginian women, unlike the men, soon adopted Greek fashions. From as early as the sixth century perhaps, they wore embroidered robes similar to those worn by Ionian women, as shown on statuettes of that period,[34] which were probably imported. The priestess of the *tophet*, who probably lived in about the third century, wears a very simple pleated robe, gathered to the waist by a high belt. The masons who cut the clumsy funeral-stones showed their clients wrapped in a perfectly straight robe, occasionally with a few pleats, a head-veil, and sometimes a cloak.[35] This is more or less the Greek costume of the goddess Kore from the great sarcophagus of Sainte-Monique. But we have also seen that the pleated robes and capes from Cyprus were worn by women as well as men throughout the history of Carthage, and, after its fall, in the neo-Punic cities. Nearly always a long embroidered band, the Greek *paryphe*, descends vertically the full length of the pleated robes. This decoration, which seems to have been worn only by women, was sometimes separate from the garment and sometimes fastened to the material like a broad stripe.

Attention has often been drawn to the similarity between the Punic costume and that which is worn today by the Moslems of North Africa; but in fact the Tyrian robe resembles the Egyptian *galabieh* more closely than the flowing *djellabah* of the people of the Mahgreb. The hooded cloaks, the *burnous* and the *cachabias*, which had no equivalent in Carthage, probably originated from the Roman *cucullus*. Nevertheless, Oriental attire has remained remarkably unchanged throughout the ages, in marked contrast to the capricious changes of European fashion.

E.-F. Gautier[36] has drawn from this fact a number of conclusions which seem on the whole to be correct. In ancient times this difference in clothes was regarded as the mark of a different civilization. The Greeks and the Romans violently condemned the long seamed robe with sleeves, and the *tiara*. In all probability the Romans borrowed the tunic from the Carthaginians. The Phoenician origin of the word is accepted by philologists and, moreover, it is well known that until the time of the Punic wars only a kind of loin-cloth, the *subligaculum*, was worn under the toga; the aged Cato expressed himself as quite satisfied with it. But in fact, in Rome, the word tunic meant, very early on, if not from the beginning, the Greek *chiton*, a length of material without seams, which was fastened by clasps and which left the arms and legs bare; the *tunica talaris et maniculata* which was a reproduction of the Tyrian robe, was only worn by libertines.

The clasps or safety-pins which became so essential a part of European dress that their shape is used by archaeologists to distinguish different civilizations, were rare in Carthage, and used almost entirely by women.

The Asiatic costume was certainly not very practical for violent exercise. It was based on a conception of the human body which was completely at variance with that of the Greeks. As early as the sixth century, the latter placed high in their scale of values the idea of the body beautiful—an idea held in abomination by the Orientals. Clothes were for the Hellenes a trivial accessory; their gods and heroes are represented as strong young men completely naked. The Oriental, on the other hand, sought to inspire respect, not by his strength, but by his dignity and wealth; he cared little for muscular symmetry; instead he preferred to cultivate a portly figure more suggestive of his opulence, and a luxuriant beard and head of hair; and to wrap himself in ample robes. A man of importance, even if he were young, would try to look old, in order to impress others with his appearance of wisdom. Oriental gods are never naked: all the Carthaginian idols were clothed, with the exception of a few lewd examples not later in date than the fifth century,[37] whose stylized caricature of the body and obscenity suggest that they were fertility charms rather than real figures of divinities.

This disdain for the human body led the Carthaginian artists to anatomical distortions, not because of lack of skill, but to emphasize the parts in which the magic potency of their works resided. This conception is still preserved in Islam today and explains why the Moslems remain faithful to a traditional costume which is not for them, as it is for us, a mere means of adornment; the strictest Moslems insist on the beard and the robe, and even the modernists among them who have been won over to Western ways, cannot bring themselves to abandon the *chechia* or the *tarboosh*, the round hat without brim or peak which resembles so closely the turban of antiquity, and which, as the fez, has become the symbol of their faith.

JEWELLERY

This philosophy of dress also accounts for the exuberance of Carthaginian jewellery, which disdained the strict sobriety of

Greek aesthetics. The most surprising fashion was the wearing of nose-rings; in Genesis we read that the Canaanites wore them and that they were called *nezem*. Several terracotta masks, both male and female, have this singular form of adornment.[38] Ear-rings are so common in graves that every Carthaginian, regardless of sex, must have possessed them. Moreover, in the *Poenulus*, Milphio suggests that Hanno's slaves must have had no fingers, since they wore their rings in their ears! The plainest are small gold rings; others are lengthened by the addition of a pendant in the shape of a ringed cross, the Egyptian hieroglyphic representing life; others again have suspended from them a tiny casket filled with beads, or a pendant in the shape of an egg.[39] The bronze head which decorates the lid of a mirror-case has a silver rosette in the lobe of the ear. Sometimes a ring was worn in only one ear.

Diadems were not necessarily a sign of distinction. Several of the women shown on funeral stelae wear them, and they are found in graves belonging to ordinary individuals. The famous Lady of Elche wears a veritable helmet of jewellery: rows of polished uncut gems framed by two enormous discs on either side of the head which are in turn encircled with other gems round their rims. But this figure must represent a goddess, for it is doubtful whether such a massive head-dress could really have been worn by a mortal. The tall round crowns and gem-studded *tiaras* on some statuettes are also symbols of divinity.

The most beautiful jewels in our collections are necklaces: one had as its centre-piece a turquoise crescent over a jacinth disc;[40] from this hung symmetrically twelve cylindrical pendants, four plain crescents, two crescents inverted over the disc, two round pendants with a central *umbo* and indentation below, and lastly two circular pendants with nine-pointed stars in relief round the edge. Often the necklaces are made of tiny beads connected together by a technique apparently invented by the Phoenicians, who disseminated it throughout the Mediterranean, and which the Etruscans adopted and perfected.

Jewels were not only used for necklaces. Many, like the example just described, were grouped round the inverted crescent and disc, the astral symbol of the supreme Carthaginian deities; a gold medallion represents a squatting bottle-shaped idol in a niche;[41] a Tanit symbol on an altar is framed between two rearing cobras.

Very often the pendant, a golden cylinder decorated with the head of a sacred animal, or a crystal acorn with a golden cup, forms a vertable reliquary,[42] containing, not the bones of a saint, but a scroll, or parchment, or gold-leaf, covered with inscriptions and magic formulae.

The poor contented themselves with stringing together glass beads and shells, with bone or terracotta charms. The latter generally represented Egyptian gods and all kinds of magic protective symbols, also of Egyptian origin, such as the eye of Horus, the cobra or *naja*, a papyrus, an altar, or a divine throne. Vercoutter and Cintas[43] have made a detailed study of the distribution of these charms found in graves. Generally speaking, figures of gods become less frequent in later periods, giving way to simple amulets. This seems to indicate that in the lower classes, at any rate, religious feeling tended to decline and to degenerate into plain superstition. Also, the cultural influence of Egypt, at first very profound, continued to weaken after Carthage was cut off from the East towards the beginning of the fifth century.

Naturally, both men and women wore bracelets, either plain rings or spirals, and the women also wore massive anklets, as Bedouin women do today.

Seals merit special consideration, for they served as jewels, and as charms, besides fulfilling their normal function. In all ancient and medieval societies the impress of a seal was indispensable to the authenticity of a deed. Seals therefore became the symbol of their owner's personality and the designs engraved upon them were not chosen solely for their decorative value, but also for their religious efficacy which guaranteed the deed they sealed, as it were, under oath. Anyone who broke a contract sealed with the imprint of his tutelary gods, committed sacrilege and exposed himself to their vengeance. The two great civilizations from which Phoenicia drew its spiritual sustenance, Mesopotamia and Egypt, had adopted a very special kind of seal, the choice of which had been dictated by the fundamental principles of their religion: in Babylon it was a cylindrical roller of precious stone, whose entire surface was engraved with scenes, often very complicated, from Chaldean mythology; it was rolled across the still moist clay of the writing-tablet. In Egypt, the seal formed an exact reproduction of the scavenger-beetle which was regarded as the representation of the Heliopolis sun god, Kheperi; the ball which the beetle rolled represented in miniature the planet which Kheperi was believed to push in front of him across the sky. The actual seal was the flat under-belly of the insect, on which were engraved hieroglyphics forming New Year good wishes, or prayers to the gods asking them to confer long life on the owner, both in this world and the next.

The Phoenicians adopted both the Mesopotamian cylinders and the Egyptian scarabs in turn, but after the foundation of Carthage the former began to disappear. Only five have been found in Carthage, and some of these had Egyptian designs, though one made in jasper depicts the Babylonian god Mardouk strangling a winged monster.[44] This, with the comb already described, is one of the rare traces of Mesopotamian influence in Africa. Rollers and scarabs were both mounted in a stirrup or ring made of precious metal, in which the seal could turn, and which was worn round the neck on a cord. The scarab rings were often small enough to be worn as finger-rings. The mount varied according to the wealth of the wearer, and the period. In the seventh and sixth centuries B.C. only china scarabs were used; these were made in Egypt in the Greek trading centre of Naucratis, which was to the empire of the Pharaohs what Shanghai used to be to the Chinese. In the fifth and fourth centuries B.C., the Carthaginians began to make seals from jasper and cornelian. They then abandoned Egyptian designs in favour of Greek ones. And towards the end of the fourth century, the seal, which had, as it were, been the symbol of the bond uniting the new Tyre with its Oriental traditions, went out of fashion in its turn, in favour of the Greek intaglio.

The Carthaginians showed themselves to be good craftsmen in the art of engraving on precious stones and indeed in all forms of engraving. The design of an archer, and of a Pegasus found in Utica,[45] bears comparison with the best productions of Greek or Etruscan craftsmen.

GOODS AND CHATTELS

Carthaginian houses, which were very plain and narrow, did not usually contain very much furniture. In those of the poorer classes, as in the *douars* of the present-day Kabiles, whose social traditions go back to antiquity, only a few large jars were found. The Greeks called them *pithoi* and they were used in place of cupboards for storing food, and even clothes. The recent excavations in Ensérune, in the province of Roussillon,[46] have revealed dwellings which were contemporary with the Punic wars. In these, an enormous jar stood in the centre of the only room. The few indispensable household utensils which the poorer folk required were all made of terracotta: the brazier,[47] the *kanoun* of the Arabs, was used for cooking, and also, in spite of the risk of asphyxiation, for providing a little warmth on wet winter days. The simplest of these, like those still sold by Djerbian grocers, consist of a shallow bowl of which the brim is raised to form a crenellated support for the cooking-pot. Others, more elegant, are shaped like a small tower, with holes in the side to provide the necessary draught. They are decorated with triglyphs and lozenges and are very similar to the domestic incense-burners. In fact, there was very little difference between the altars on which incense was burnt and where the humble daily sacrifices were offered to the household god, and the brazier used for cooking.

Terracotta lamps were used for lighting; Phoenician lamps were extremely rudimentary—a bowl, with the rim pinched inwards to hold the wick, was placed on a saucer to catch the oil which seeped through the hot clay. As in the tombs, the lamp normally stood in a niche in the wall. Apart from a few very ancient exceptions, the Carthaginian lamps had two necks.[48]

In about the fourth century, it occurred to some potter to close up the oil receptacle by folding in the lips of the bowl before the clay was fired, and thus prevent the oil from spilling when the lamp was carried. But this shape was less elegant than that of the Greek lamps, which had a round enclosed reservoir for the oil, with a hole for filling and a long tubular neck. These latter were imported in large quantities from Rhodes and Alexandria during the last two centuries before the fall of Carthage. Some of them were real works of art;[49] one specimen is carved in hard stone: on the upper part is a bearded male figure, doubtless a god, whose eyes in black enamel inlaid with a fine gold circle, give it a strikingly life-like effect. Its body merges below into that of a frog.

This strange conjunction, reminiscent of the hybrid monsters of the Gnostics, can be explained by reference to Egyptian symbolism. The tadpole, which emerged without any visible origin from the Nile mud, to change into a frog, seemed to the Egyptians to represent the human soul which survived the bodily vicissitudes of life and death.

This magic lamp must have been carved in Alexandria to accompany a dead man and to illustrate his future resurrection. Another stone lamp, found with this one, is shaped like a human head, and is probably a Carthaginian copy of a Greek original. The Carthaginian potters popularized this type of lamp by making large numbers of inferior copies. Today a modest forger has established himself in an ancient water-reservoir near Malga, and having secured a mould of one of these bearded lamps produces copies by the gross which he does not even bother to fire. Many tourists carefully bring back with them these crude travesties which are sold by urchins at the station exits.

The Carthaginians also had veritable chandeliers with numerous cups, but these were religious objects, which Cintas has compared with the *kernoi* used in the worship of Demeter,[50] already mentioned, as well as with the famous seven-branched candlesticks used by the Hebrews. In fact, the cups are arranged in groups of seven: on the centre of one is the bust of the Egyptian goddess Hathor; on another, figurines in the Greek manner, similar to those which are found on bronze vases.

These oil-lamps gave a fairly bright light, provided that the wick was trimmed so that it did not smoke. The light was improved by dropping a few grains of coarse salt on the wick. When Tunis was liberated on May 8, 1943, the city and its suburbs were without electricity for several months, as the Germans had destroyed the generating station before surrendering. Since candles were unobtainable, and oil was sold everywhere without restriction, we made use of antique lamps. This unintentional experiment allows us to state that the Carthaginians could see just as well as our great-grandparents before the invention of the Carcel lamp.

For the Carthaginian housewife, the terracotta jar served one very essential purpose—that of carrying water. Modern sociologists have commented on the great importance of water-carrying in Barbary. A few years ago some of them undertook an extensive inquiry into the various methods used throughout the Mahgreb. The installation of wayside fountains as a first step towards bringing water into the home, is in process of killing customs which, as the Bible reminds us, were of the utmost importance in daily life. It was at the well that Eliezer found Rebecca, and Christ met the woman of Samaria.

The Carthaginians, who had none of the highly developed conduit systems of the Roman engineers, followed the same procedure as the Hebrews. The water-carrier was an important person. He led a donkey or a horse, laden with two plaited conical baskets, in each of which was a pitcher with a pointed bottom. These are illustrated by a number of amusing statuettes. This kind of pitcher, shaped like an inverted cone, was in widespread use in the Mediterranean. Although it appears very impractical to us, it fitted very well against the flanks of a pack-animal; in a cellar, the point sat in a hole specially made for it, and even on board ship it went into a special support down in the hold, with the neck protruding above deck.[51]

This pottery, cheap and easy to replace, was the chief stand-by of the Carthaginian household. It also provided the dead with a means of facing the restricted but eternal life beyond the grave. A childish belief which the theologians soon abandoned, but which remained more or less unconsciously rooted in the popular mind (and the trouble we take over our graves proves that we have not entirely banished it), conceived of the tomb as an eternal abode within which the dead carried on the normal activities of everyday life. An assortment of articles was therefore placed beside the corpse, as decreed by strict religious and legal rules dating from the sixth century to the fourth century: a pitcher, a pot, two ewers, a lamp, and a saucer. These were the essential provisions for a journey, permitted the dead person to manage alone without having to come back and bother his heirs.

Those who enjoyed a higher standard of living could buy for themselves real articles of furniture such as wicker-work, carpets, and hangings. The chief ambition of every family was to be able to acquire one of those fine cedar chests, made to last for ever, in which jewels and materials could be stored more conveniently than in jars.[52] The father of the family would probably sleep on it, using a carpet as a mattress, thus making sure that his wealth was adequately guarded. One day the chest, the symbol of his thrift, would do duty as his coffin. The baskets sometimes shown on monuments, have also left their imprint on the floors of tombs; they were used mainly for gathering fruit. The Carthaginians wove pannier baskets for the donkeys, and it is permissible to imagine the Carthaginian in the market-place stowing his purchases in a wicker basket, like his Tunisian descendants. The word *cophinus* has been current throughout the Mediterranean area from prehistoric times, for the simple reason that it designates an article that has always been essential to their way of life.

Mago mentions rush mats, which took the place of carpets among the poor, and mentions among plants worth cultivating, those which could be used for wickers or basket-work.[52] The Carthaginians made no use of the African esparto grass, which was too short for their liking; they preferred the Spanish grass. Finally, as we have seen, they taught the Berbers to weave carpets and to work patterns in them.

In the later Carthaginian period, the richest citizens adopted Greek furniture, as they did Greek domestic architecture. We know that they developed a craze for ceremonial couches which were used especially for banquets. These sumptuous pieces of furniture, decorated with bronze, silver, and gold, were made in the East by famous artists, of whom the best known, Boethus of Chalcedonia, flourished in the second half of the third century B.C. Now, by a singular chance, a collection of these *fulcra*, as the Romans called them, resembling one of Boethus' masterpieces, were brought to Tunisia. They may have come from the workshops of his successors.

The Mahdia galley, which left the Piraeus shortly after Sylla had sacked Athens, with a cargo of works of art bound for Italy, sank off the coast of Tunisia. Besides the Agon group signed by the Chalcedonian sculptor in bronze, it carried bronze and marble statues, and couches which Poinssot and Bréchot have patiently pieced together.[54] The couches consisted of a wooden frame, mounted on metal-covered feet, and on which lay a metal mattress made of interlaced bronze lathes. The elbow-rests had applied ornaments, themselves miniature works of art: busts of Athene or of Nike, life-like heads of neighing horses, and heads of ducks. Stelae, or Punic (or neo-Punic) funerary *naskoi*,[55] show guests reclining on such couches in the Greek or Etruscan manner. The food was placed within reach of the guests, on small three-legged tables. There were also richly carved seats: the thrones of the statues of divinities found in the Salammbô and Hamilcar chapels are decorated in the Greek manner with 'winged victories' carrying weapons, as were doubtless, too, the armchairs used by the Carthaginian nobles.

Like all Mediterranean peoples, the Carthaginians lived primarily on cereals and olive-oil. Bread, and also a kind of porridge, were made from wheat and barley. Cato gives the recipe for *puls punica*: 'Put one pound of coarse-ground cereal in water and allow to soak thoroughly; pour into a clean trough; add three pounds of fresh cheese, half a pound of honey and one egg. Stir well and cook in a new saucepan.'[56] This sweet dish probably played the same part in Punic feeding as the *couscous* of the Mahgreb Arabs. Plautus describes the Africans as 'porridge eaters', although the Romans were themselves just as partial to this *pasta* as their descendants are today to spaghetti and polenta.

The Carthaginian pastry-cooks were renowned: their confections were elegantly shaped in terracotta moulds: some of these were in the form of fishes or animals; others of birds, shell-fish, and even of men on horseback—fantastic figures borrowed from Egypt or Greece.[57] In Carthaginian cookery, as in the Tunisian, sweet and highly spiced dishes must have alternated. The peasants grew a very strong kind of garlic, which they used to excess. The most prized vegetables were the cabbage, the chick-pea, and the artichoke which probably originated in North Africa. It grows wild on the *sraouat*, or High Tell plateaux, and on the scarcely less arid slopes of the Sicilian mountains. Like most of the Semites, the Phoenicians abstained from eating pork; nevertheless, they hunted the wild boar which swarmed in the *maquis* and forests of Tunisia. But they ate dogs, a custom which seemed just as abominable to other nations as child-sacrifices.

The great King Darius, it is said, ordered them to cease both practices. He was not obeyed, and even today dog-eaters are found in the neighbourhood of Gabes, some even in the peninsula of Carthage, to the great detriment of stray dogs. Meat was mainly eaten when sacrifices were offered. The priests took great care to lay down what their share of the victim was to be. They claimed 300 pounds of the flesh of an ox offered as an expiatory sacrifice, and were generous enough to allow the faithful to keep the offal, the bones, the hide, the legs, and the feet.[58]

Fortunately for the poor, fish were plentiful. The coasts of Tunisia are well stocked with grey mullet, sea-perch, sea-eels, sole, dolphins, and especially, tunny fish, which come every year to Cape Bon. The port of Missua, today Sidi Daoud, probably owed its growth to its tunny-fishing industry. Salting-stations were set up in the south, at the entrance to the lake in the Biban Mountains, and all along the coast of Byzacium. Tunny were also brought from the Atlantic, and fishermen from Gades even went as far as the Sargasso Sea to catch them. The fish were then salted and packed in jars for sale.

The innumerable long pointed wine-jars which have been found in Carthage prove that wine was a favourite drink. Nevertheless, Plato[59] maintains that it was forbidden by law to soldiers, slaves of both sexes, magistrates in office, judges, sea-pilots, and also to both men and women before indulging in the sexual act. But the philosopher, if he did not invent this stern regulation himself, must have freely interpreted some sacred law, like that of Aesculapius in Thuburbo Majus.[60] The epithet 'sober', applied to certain gods, and the Latin epitaph of a priestess of Hercules-Melkart, seem to indicate that wine was in fact forbidden on certain occasions, or to certain people.

This prohibition, however, was far less wholesale than that of the Koran, for the Carthaginians certainly cultivated the vine and made wine. They even earned a certain reputation for a kind of malaga or sherry which the Romans called *passum*. Mago describes how it should be made:[61] 'Gather well-ripened grapes early in the morning, removing those which are mouldy or damaged. Drive rows of stakes or forked sticks into the ground four feet apart and join the tops with poles; spread reeds on these on which to expose the grapes to the sun; cover at night, to prevent the dew from making them damp. When the grapes are dried, pick them off the stalks and drop them in a pitcher or jug. Add enough best-quality must to cover the grapes. On the sixth day, when they have absorbed the must and have swollen, place them in a basket and crush in a press, collecting the liquid. Next tread the residue and add fresh must made from other grapes which have been left in the sun for three days. Mix well and press. Decant the liquid from this second pressing into jars and seal immediately to prevent it from going bitter. Then, after twenty or thirty days, when fermentation is complete, strain into other jars. Coat the lids immediately with plaster and cover with a skin.' The Tunisian Jews use a similar method today in the district round Bizerta.

However; most African wine was not held in very high esteem. The Greeks as well as the Romans maintained that lime or even plaster was mixed with it to neutralize its acidity. But it may be thought that their own habit of adding pitch or resin to their wine was not much better.

CHILDHOOD AND UPBRINGING

A terracotta statue from the Temple of Thinissut[62] represents a young woman whose head is covered with a curious tight-fitting round hat. She has a snub nose and a broad mouth, which give her a homely rustic appearance. She is preparing to suckle her child, which she is holding on her lap. This was how the humble folk who frequented the sanctuary imagined the great Courotrophic Demeter, but it can be assumed that this rustic Madonna was modelled from a real peasant woman feeding her child. The goddess-nurse also appears elsewhere; for example, in a niche behind the throne of the Tanit with the Sphinxes in the Lavigerie Museum. Thus the Punic religion, which on the one hand exacted the horrible tribute of babies burnt alive, paid honour also to the sanctity of motherhood, and could portray it in the most touching manner.

It is only fair to point out that apart from the atrocities of those ceremonies in which children perished, the Carthaginians were no more cruel in their treatment of new-born babies than other peoples of antiquity. In the Mediterranean world, economic and social conditions, as well as the sexual practices which were tolerated, made it universally inexpedient to rear every child that was born. In fact, the Greeks and Romans reproached the Carthaginians with conferring a religious and ennobling value on a melancholy but necessary practice, which they indulged in themselves in shameful and secret ways. A baby born in Carthage ran very little more risk of being burnt alive on the day of the *mol'k* than did a baby in Athens or Rome of being abandoned at some street-corner, on a heap of filth, where it was left to the tender mercies of wild animals; or if the best happened, slave-dealers might come along and take it.

It must not be thought that the Carthaginians neglected their children. Like the Romans, they had goddesses whose special function it was to watch over child-birth. A curious bas-relief which was found near Béja, portrays seven divinities, probably Numidian, but whose names and appearance prove that their worshippers came under the cultural influence of Carthage.[63] At the feet of a goddess called Vininam, a wailing baby lifts itself up towards her as though appealing for her protection. She is holding an elliptical object which A. Merlin thinks is a pair of forceps. If it is, Vininam was a kind of African Lucina.

Perhaps new-born boys were circumcised. The Phoenicians, like the Jews, borrowed this custom from the Egyptians, who, in their turn, had probably borrowed it from African Negroes. Originally it was an initiation rite signifying integration into the community—a relic of the practice of mutilation (like knocking out teeth) which was practised by primitive peoples, such as the Capsians who lived in Tunisia in the Palaeolithic Age. Apparently the Libyans also practised circumcision. Did the Carthaginians later give up a custom which the Greeks and Romans considered barbarous and shameful? S. Gsell,[64] at least, thought so, since none of the rather crude jests that Plautus directs against the Carthaginians makes any references to this mutilation. But in Italy there can have been few opportunities of confirming this! However, there may have been a religious reason why circumcision was eventually given up by the worshippers of Baal: it was regarded as a means of claiming back from the god the person who underwent the operation; the Carthaginians paid the human tribute demanded by their gods, through the practice of the *mol'k*. Thus the slaughter of some children made unnecessary the mutilation of the rest.

The conferring of a name on a child was certainly a religious act. Unlike the Indo-Europeans, whose method of naming exalted the individual's human qualities, or his social advantages, the Semites emphasized his dependence on the gods. Many Punic names are formed from the name of the god in question preceded by the word *abd*, which means 'servant', e.g. Abdmelkart, servant of Melkart, which gives Amilcar; Abdastart, Abdeshmoun. Other names are really a short phrase expressing a divine action, e.g. Asdrubal, which is really Azrubaal, 'He who is aided by Baal'. Arab names are like this today, e.g. Abdallah, and all those names in which Abd is followed by a word meaning God. Of particular interest are the Carthaginian names Baalalyaton, 'Baal has given him', and Muttumbaal, 'gift of Baal'. Carcopino has demonstrated, in considering their Latin equivalents[65] *Donatus* and *Concessus*, applied to Africans in the Imperial period, that these names designated victims intended for the *mol'k*, but who had been spared through the form of substitution known as *molchomor*. The Carthaginian name system survived for a long time, and the African Christians who later invented such monstrosities as Quodvultdeus and Deogratias, were still observing its essential rules.

We have very little information about the kind of clothes worn by Carthaginian babies. The divine child of the goddess Thinissut is quite naked, and the African climate would allow a child to be so for several months of the year. A number of feeding-bottles have been found; they are simply small egg-shaped vases with a funnel-shaped neck and a very tapering spout, around which was wrapped a cloth to serve as a teat.[66] A complete set of doll's crockery has also survived—a collection of minute jars, jugs, cups, plates, and moulded clay lamps.

Information about the Carthaginian education system is equally meagre. According to the Emperor Julian, Carthaginian children were sent from their home at a fairly early age, with the injunction to live by the fruits of their labours and to avoid all shameful acts.[67] Seen from this angle, Punic education must have been very practical, and nearer to the idea of living by one's wits than the Greek *paideia*.

It may be that this kind of practical training was given especially to children whose families destined them for trade and distant enterprises. Priestly families probably had their own schools within the precincts of the temples, like those of the

Jewish rabbis. There, the children would be taught to read and write Phoenician, and to learn the poems and rules in which mythology and ritual were handed down. To this study of the Phoenician 'Bible', the apter pupil would add the subtleties of theological controversy. It would be impossible to understand how the Punic religion could have attained the heights of abstraction suggested by some monuments, if 'universities' had not existed comparable with the Talmudic circles, and, in some respects, with the Islamic *medersa*.

The lay nobility, at least in the later years of Carthaginian history, sought to give their children a more liberal education. Many Carthaginians had learnt Greek in Sicily, or even in Carthage itself, although under pressure from the conservative elements, the Senate had contemplated a ban on the study of Greek, on the pretext of preventing communication with the enemy.[68]

Some Carthaginians were attracted by the humanistic ideals of the Greek *paideia* and wanted to bring up their children in the Hellenic manner: the great Hannibal had studied military strategy in Greek text-books, and probably acquired a smattering of other disciplines as well. Sophonisba, we are told, was just as accomplished in the humanities as she was in music, so women, apparently, were not denied an education. Perhaps they were even allowed to devote themselves to the non-utilitarian arts, while the boys were directed at an early age into practical activities.

It is tempting to assume some connexion between the meagre knowledge we have of the Carthaginian educational system, and the poverty in intellectual and artistic matters we have already noted. There was certainly no Punic humanism. In so far as they are conscious of their reasons, this deficiency may perhaps explain the enthusiasm of certain modern admirers of Carthage who happen to be hostile to the classical tradition, precisely because they have had little share in its benefits. The exclusively practical training the Carthaginians received was a great handicap to them when they found themselves competing with other nations who had a less utilitarian conception of culture. Their failure in this respect is all the more remarkable because their intellectual ability was unanimously recognized by their contemporaries.

Moreover, all that has survived and endured in Carthage was the work of those sections of the population who received some spiritual training: the priests and the Hellenized nobles.

COURTESY

The Greeks and Romans accused the Carthaginians, and indeed all Asiatics, of a servile attitude towards those in authority. But this was merely an exaggeration of over-refined Oriental politeness.[69] The Carthaginians saw no shame in humiliating themselves before those whom they sought to honour. When the tide of war demanded that they should seek mercy at the hands of Roman generals, the most important men of the city did not hesitate to prostrate themselves and even to kiss the feet of their conquerors. The Romans were irritated by such fawning, but nevertheless borrowed from the Carthaginians some of the courtesies that were lacking in their own tradition: the greeting *Ave* is of Phoenician origin.[70]

THE FAMILY

The tight control exercised by their Government gave little opportunity for the Carthaginians to satisfy their obviously sensual nature. One can readily believe the ancient writers who, like Voltaire later, affirmed that 'vitriol and fire flowed in the veins of the inhabitants of Mount Atlas and the neighbouring lands'. But little indulgence was shown to the weaknesses of the flesh. The religious reform of the fifth century and the decline of Astarte in favour of Tanit, had purified religion of most of its sexual practices, which had their origins in fertility rites. Sacred prostitutes survived only in the single temple of Sicca.

Moreover, the structure of the family and the status of women did little to encourage masculine licence. Monogamy was generally, if not universally, practised, and many tombs contain the skeletons of married couples. There is no evidence of a harem or of eunuchs. The women of the aristocracy, who, as we have seen, received an extensive education, were able to exercise considerable political influence. They could also become priestesses, with complete control over all the temple personnel, both male and female.

There appears to have been little homosexuality in Carthage.

The Roman general L. Quinctius Flamininus, brother of the 'liberator' of Greece, had a Carthaginian boy-friend. One day he cut the throat of a deserter from Gaul purely to amuse this youth who had missed a gladiatorial combat;[71] but a slave's depravation must be blamed on his masters rather than on his native land.

AMUSEMENTS

On the whole, Plutarch[72] was probably right to describe the Carthaginians as a stern people, hostile to pleasures and amusements. Their city must have seemed very dull to the Greeks. Theatres and public games were unknown. The only public festivities were religious ceremonies, and there was nothing amusing about them. The feasts organized by important personages soliciting popularity were usually orgies. In this community of business-men, the arts were regarded as useless accomplishments, and soon languished. Music alone seems to have been held in some respect, although a number of indented bone or ivory tablets which have survived and have been regarded as the bridges of stringed instruments are more likely to be casket hinges.[73] However, the gods were often represented as holding a dulcimer or zither,[74] and this would indicate the use of music for religious ceremonies. It was also used as an accompaniment to ritual dances. The Ugarit poems, the Bible, and classical texts show that the Phoenicians, like the Hebrews, honoured their gods by performing rhythmic evolutions; a shrine near Beirut was in fact dedicated to Baal, the god of dancing. Sometimes the steps of these ritual dances were slow and dignified, like those still performed today by Greek and Sicilian peasants; sometimes they were wild and frenzied, to arouse the divine power inherent in all things. Flaubert based his description of the frenzied leaping of the fanatics of Baal on the Aissaouas. He would have been interested in a small Phoenician monument found in Sardinia and which has been described just recently by P. Cintas.[75] Three completely nude women, and a man dressed in an Egyptian loin-cloth (probably a priest) are executing a frenzied dance round a *betyle* (a kind of ritual stone). They are probably engaged in stimulating the fertilizing energy latent in the stone, so that it may pass into the bodies of the dancers, who appear to be rubbing

their naked bodies against it, just as Breton women did not long
ago against the dolmens, to ward off sterility. Such ceremonies
satisfied neither the seeker after beauty nor the seeker after
pleasure. Moreover, it seems likely that in Carthage itself they
died out completely, or were at any rate made more respectable
after the reforms of the fifth century, and that they survived only
in some of the remoter provinces.

SUPERSTITION

The melancholy and barbaric temperament which made the
Carthaginians so odious in the eyes of other nations was the result
not of avarice alone, but of another feeling which appears to have
dominated their entire being, namely, superstition, or, as the
Greeks called it, 'fear of the Demon', *deisidaimonia*. From the
cradle to the grave, the Carthaginian felt himself surrounded by
hordes of evil powers, against whom he waged ceaseless but un-
equal combat. Nothing has been more lasting than this conviction
which neither the later changes in religion, nor all the progress
of science have been able to eradicate from the Mediterranean
mind. Even today, the Tunisian, be he Moslem or Christian, still
believes in the evil eye, in magic spells, and evil genii, as well as
in beneficent saints chosen indiscriminately from among the
disciples of Jesus or the companions of Mahomet. Most of the
means he employs to protect himself from evil influences go back
to remotest antiquity. For example, the fish which was often
carved on the Punic stelae or which figured in Roman mosaics, is
still painted on the *arabas*, or carts used to carry vegetables to
market; and superimposed upon it, as in heraldry, is the 'Hand
of Fatima'; this has no connexion with orthodox Moslemism at
all but is an exact reproduction of the 'Hand of Baal' which
appears on the pediment of some of the stelae from the *tophet*.

SICKNESS

The demons were imagined as deformed and grimacing beings
and are so represented on the masks, which were supposed to
ward them off by facing them with their own likeness. When in
the dog days the sirocco blew and from the Lake of Tunis came
a stench as of rotten eggs, the consul, Censorinus, was afraid
that he would lose his whole army. He therefore ordered it to

abandon its camp on the isthmus. But the demons came in upon the wind and swooped down upon the young children, smiting them with a form of dysentery which killed them in a few hours. Many parents had sacrificed their first-born to Tanit and Baal, in the hope that they would protect the remaining children. But even these great gods were not always sufficiently powerful to ward off the accursed evil spirits, and all the parents could do was to bury the tiny corpses in jars, in the hope that the earth, receiving the bodies intact, would give them another life.

Sometimes the demons did not kill their victims. Instead they maimed them, and the bone deformations are still visible in many a skeleton. Or else they infected the eyes of their victims with trachoma (granular conjunctivitis), and cut them off from the light of day. Nowadays, in spite of medical progress, the streets of Tunis swarm with such wretches: bandy-legged, lame, hunch-backed, and blind. They have no other resource than to touch the hearts of the passers-by through the spectacle of their misfortunes.

The Carthaginians were not ignorant of the arts of medicine. We have several doctors' stelae. But their knowledge was not far removed from that of the sorcerers: we do not know what they prescribed for their patients, but Mago has preserved for us a number of veterinary treatments. They are not very reassuring. To cure a horse suffering from asthma, he recommends[76] that it should be bled in a dozen different places for three days. Then a mixture should be made of carefully measured quantities of saffron, myrrh, spikenard, white pepper, mead (hydromel), rose-petal oil, and lentils: the mixture to be cooked in a new jar, in the presence of a dog which had been kept indoors for ten days; then there should be added more mead and one egg. The resulting mixture to be administered for at least ten days.

To cure retention of urine, a simpler treatment was used: it was merely necessary to file the animal's hooves, to pound the filings and to mix them with wine; the resulting mixture was administered via the nostrils. In face of such charlatanism, many Carthaginians probably preferred to trust their gods! Eshmoun no doubt cured the sick, like the Greek god of medicine, Aesculapius, with whom he was identified. Another healing god was Shadrapa who was identified with Horus, and particularly with Dionysus.[77] He healed principally the bites of reptiles and other poisonous creatures, which have always been feared in Africa. Snakes abound in the immediate vicinity of Carthage, but most of them are harmless grass-snakes. Then, as now, their presence inside the house was probably regarded as beneficent, for snakes were one of the manifestations of the household god. A species of viper, which is about as long and thick as a man's arm, and whose bite is quickly fatal, is found in the *maquis* on Cape Bon and as far as Bou Kornine. But the cobra and the horned viper are found only in the steppeland south of the Atlas chain. Scorpions swarm throughout Africa; they are still found in Carthage and even at Sidi Bou Said, where according to local legend, they do not attack those who make no effort to kill them. The commonest, the small black scorpion, is relatively harmless, but the very dangerous large yellow scorpion is not unknown on the peninsula. The Arabs greatly fear them, and also certain kinds of lizard, like the gecko, which they regard, quite wrongly, as poisonous.

Against scorpions, the ancients took very similar precautions to those used today: they rubbed the legs of their beds with garlic, or stood them in a cup of water (today camphor or fuel oil are used). But magic was naturally resorted to, as well: scorpion-shapes were cut out of thin sheet-lead and buried under the threshold—an application of the well-known principle: *similia similibus curantur*. Egyptian talismans were also used, for example miniature stelae of black granite showing Horus trampling the crocodiles and covered with hieroglyphics.[78] We found one of these charms near the Antonine Baths. Vercoutter could not have known of it, but he had already shown that the magical signs engraved on gold-leaf and worn round the neck, rolled up in a case, resemble those on the stelae.[79]

Amulets representing Ptah Patecus were also used as a protection against snakes.

FUNERAL RITES

Whatever precautions were taken against demons, a man ultimately succumbed to them. The survivors then had to take great care to safeguard the repose of the dead man. Otherwise he might become an evil spirit seeking revenge against those who had not given him what he needed. However, the Carthaginians were not so obsessed as the Egyptians with anxieties about the next world. Their parsimonious tendencies conflicted with their superstitious beliefs, and, taken together with a natural hardness of heart, obliged the dead to make do with a minimum of strict necessities. Reference has already been made to the lengthy survival of the very primitive idea that life beyond the grave was a pallid extension of earthly existence within the confines of the grave, from which the dead would not seek to emerge providing they were supplied with a certain amount of comfort, and left in peace. It sufficed, therefore, to bury the corpse deep enough to make sure that his grave was not interfered with, and to supply him with a few provisions and useful articles.

The poor contented themselves with burying their dead in a grave, but the rich sheltered theirs within stone vaults whose massive architecture protected them from thieves and gave them a rough approximation to the house in which they had lived.[80] Later, as an additional precaution, the funeral-vault was excavated in the side of a shaft, as deep down as possible.[81] In the necropolis of Sainte-Monique they reach a depth of sixty to a hundred feet.

When a body was buried in a tomb, it was either wrapped in a shroud or immersed in aromatic resin as a simple kind of embalming; the corpse was then enclosed in a wooden coffin— sometimes just a household chest. From the seventh century to the fifth century the coffin (or sometimes a simple litter such as the Arabs use for their funerals today) was given the further protection of a crude limestone sarcophagus.

Later, marble sarcophagi were bought from the Greeks—frequently they were decorated with paintings.[82] In Asia Minor, from the earliest times, the Phoenicians, and particularly the Sidonians, had copied the Egyptian anthropoid sarcophagi, though these were eventually altered through Greek influence. Anthropoid sarcophagi have been found at Caanita in Sicily, and in Andalusia, but the Carthaginians, apparently, never adopted them.

The marble sarcophagi decorated with statues, that were found in the Sainte-Monique necropolis, and which date from the end of the fourth century or beginning of the third century, follow quite a different tradition[83] The effigies are not recumbent, but stand upright with their feet on a plinth. Are they the images of the deceased, as has been the generally accepted view? There has been no certain example found in Carthage of a personal effigy on a tomb; the only funeral-portraits were the statues and stelae erected above the surface of the cemetery to receive offerings and tributes of respect on behalf of the deceased. On the other hand, there are innumerable examples of idols and small images representing divine figures, which were buried beside the corpse to protect him from demons. Masks, terracotta statuettes, and amulets come within this category. Moreover, at least one Phoenician sarcophagus from Cyprus has effigies of protecting gods carved upon it: the figures of Bes and Astarte are repeated four times on the short sides.[84] There is, then, no *a priori* reason for saying that the Sainte-Monique effigies represent men rather than gods. Do their attitudes or their clothes help us to decide? Two sarcophagi have been found with female effigies, and two with male. The well-known statue of the woman arrayed in the plumage of a huge dove is beyond all doubt wearing the attire of a goddess—the same, in fact, as that worn by the Leontocephalic Tanit from Thinissut. The theory that it is a priestess's robe is pure conjecture, without any archaeological or textual basis. The fact is that on all the Punic monuments we possess, the god is distinguished from his worshippers by his stature and by his attire, and this is fully in keeping with the Phoenician conception of the transcendental nature of the gods.

For similar reasons, we cannot accept that this female figure represents a dead woman who has joined the gods; such an apotheosis, familiar enough to Greeks or Romans, would be in direct contradiction to Punic religious ideas. Another statue, in Greek costume, is a conventional figure, and in Greece could have represented Kore, just as well as a deified woman. But a stele found in Hadrumetum[85] would seem to prove that the Carthaginians preferred to represent divine figures. On this stele, bearded men wearing *epi-togas* are holding a closed box in one hand, and raising the other in a gesture either of prayer or of benediction. They may be interpreted as being a Hellenized form of Baal.[86]

The sarcophagus with effigies so attired which was found in the necropolis of Tarquinia,[87] contained the remains of an Etruscan named Laris Partiunus; it confirms rather than contradicts our theory. An Etruscan who had come to live in Carthage might very well have placed himself under the protection of the Punic Baal, as did many Italians or Greeks who had settled in Cirta, and even offered the *mol'k* sacrifice. But it is very unlikely that when he got back to Italy he would go on wearing Punic costume, even supposing that he had worn it in Carthage, which is most improbable.

The origin of these divine effigies, so different from anything produced by Punic artists, and the identity of the sculptors who executed them, remains a matter of conjecture:[88] Carthage itself, Sicily, and Etruria have all been suggested. The latter may be dismissed at once: the costume and the attitudes of the male statues are incontestably Carthaginian. The figure of a woman holding aside her veil, belongs to a commonplace Greek type, and like so many others, was part of the repertoire of the Greco-Punic sculptors.

There remains the goddess clothed in dove's plumage—her costume is almost certainly Egyptian. It therefore seems clear that all these Sainte-Monique statues were executed by Alexandrian artists working in the service of Carthage. The statues represent a clumsy compromise between the Greek funerary statue and the covered sarcophagus which had been in use in Phoenicia for a long time. The adoption of such a compromise might very well have been facilitated either in Alexandria or in Carthage by memories of the Egyptian anthropoid sarcophagi. The Etruscan Laris Partiunus may have been attracted by the purely superficial similarity between these and the sarcophagi with recumbent figures of his own country. But there can be no very close relationship between these three families of funeral-monuments.

A funerary casket from an adjacent necropolis in Sainte-Monique[89] illustrates an even more developed adaptation to Punic traditions of this compromise. On the lid, a Hellenized image of Baal is engraved by a specifically Carthaginian technique. Another casket, however, with the image carved in relief,[90] shows the next transitional stage.

Whether one considers the behaviour of the living or their notions of the after-life, it must be admitted that in Carthage, in the second and third centuries, a process of evolution was taking place which was freeing the individual from the material and moral constraint which had been imposed on him by civic discipline as well as by the national tradition.

This change, which showed itself in all domains, would have given the new Tyre a much more human aspect, if it had not been brutally arrested. But it would also have effaced the last traces of originality; and it is just this originality which is interesting in the customs of the Carthaginians. For technical progress and refinement of manners and customs seem, in all times and places, to lead inevitably to uniformity in individuals and to the disappearance of their traditions.

REFERENCES

1. S. Gsell, HAAN, IV, p. 177.
2. J.-G. Février, *Un sacrifice d'enfants chez les Numides, Annuaire Hist. de Philol. et d'Hist. Orientales et Slaves*, XIII (*Mél. Isidore Lévi*), 1953, pp. 161 sqq.
3. E. Gjerstad, *Cyprus Swedish Expedition*, IV, pp. 25 sqq.
4. MC, pl. 11.
5. P. Gauckler, *Nécropoles puniques*, I, pl. CXLVII, 1.
6. *C.I.S.*, I, 3056.
7. MC, pl. 57–8.
8. *Ibid.*, pl. 36.
9. *Ibid.*, pl. 55.
10. J. Vercoutter, *Les objets égyptiens et égyptisants du mobilier funéraire carthaginois*, pp. 302 sqq., pl. XXVII and XXVIII.
11. G. Ch.-Picard, *Les Religions de l'Afrique antique*, pp. 136 sqq.
12. *Catalogue Mus. Alaoui, Suppl.*, pp. 361–2, pl. CVI 1 and 2.
13. Cf. Ch. Decamps de Mertzenfeld, *Inventaire des Ivoires phéniciens.*
14. MC, pl. 3.
15. C. Picard, *Catalogue Mus. Alaoui, Nlle série*, I, p. 35, Ca 1.
16. *Ibid.*, pl. XI–XVII.
17. MC, pl. 11, 1.
18. G. G. Lapeyre and A. Pellegrin, *Carthage punique*, pl. X, 2.
19. MC, pl. 24. Cf. E. Gobert, 'Centenaire de la Soc. Hist. algérienne' (*Revue africaine*, C, 1956), pp. 501 sqq., part. p. 514.
20. MC, pl. 26.
21. *Ibid.*, pl. 68.
22. G. Contenau, MAO, III, p. 1476, fig. 897.

23. *Ibid.*, p. 1475, fig. 896.
24. Tertullian, *De Pallio*, 1.
25. Herodotus, II.
26. MC, pl. 6.
27. E. Gjerstad, *op. cit.*, p. 102, pl. III.
28. MC, pl. 7.
29. *Ibid.*, pl. 61, left.
30. *Ibid.*, pl. 61, right.
31. M. Astruc, *Libyca*, II, 1, 1954, pp. 99 sqq.
32. Cf. n. 10.
33. MC, pl. 11.
34. *Ibid.*, pl. 13.
35. C. Picard, *op. cit.*, pl. XI–XVII.
36. E.-F. Gautier, *Mœurs et coutumes des Musulmans.*
37. MC, pl. 17.
38. P. Cintas, *Amulettes puniques*, pp. 51 sqq., pl. XII.
39. MC, pl. 18.
40. *Ibid.*, pl. 18, no. 4.
41. *Ibid.*, pl. 18, no. 6.
42. *Ibid.*, pl. 18, nos. 1, 2, 3, 11.
43. J. Vercoutter, *op cit.*, p. 348; P. Cintas, *op. cit.*, pp. 122 sqq.
44. *Catalogue Mus. Alaoui, Suppl.*, p. 348, no. 130, pl. CV.
45. MC, pl. 56.
46. J. Jannoray, *Ensérune*, pp. 188 sqq.
47. P. Cintas, *Céramique punique*, p. 488, pl. XLIV.
48. MC, pl. 28.
49. *Ibid.*, pl. 47.
50. P. Cintas, *op. cit.*, pp. 534 sqq.
51. P. Cintas, *op. cit.*, pp. 482 sqq.
52. MC, pl. 70.
53. Pliny, XXI, 112.
54. G. Ch.-Picard, *Revue archéologique*, 1947, II, pp. 178–239.
55. C. Picard, *op. cit.*, p. 246, Cb 917.
56. Cato, *De Agricultura*, 85.
57. *Catalogue Mus. Alaoui, Suppl.*, 1, pl. XCIX, XCX.
58. G. G. Lapeyre and A. Pellegrin, *op. cit.*, p. 200.
59. Plato, *Laws*, p. 674, a.
60. A Latin inscription discovered in an Aesculapius-Eshmoun sanctuary in Thurburbo Majus (A. Merlin, CRAI, 1916, pp. 212 sqq.); it gives a list of restrictions imposed on those seeking admittance to the sanctuary: abstinence from certain foods, temporary chastity, etc.

61. Columella, XII, 39, 1–2.
62. A. Merlin, 'Un sanctuaire de Ba'al et de Tanit près de Siagu', *Notes et Documents*, IV, pp. 48–9, pl. IV.
63. A. Merlin, CRAI, 1947, pp. 355 sqq. G. Ch.-Picard, *op cit.*, pp. 22 sqq., fig. 1.
64. S. Gsell, HAAN, IV, pp. 188–9.
65. J. Carcopino, *Aspects mystiques de la Rome païenne*, pp. 47 sqq.
66. P. Cintas, *Céramique punique*, p. 488, pl. XXXIII.
67. Discours, I, 15, b–c.
68. Justin, XX, 5, 12–13.
69. S. Gsell, *op. cit.*, p. 189.
70. Ernout and Meillet, *Dict. étymologique de la langue latine* s.v.
71. A. Aymard, *Rome et son Empire*, p. 130.
72. *Praecepta gerendae reipublicae*, III, 6.
73. S. Gsell, *op. cit.*, p. 101.
74. Goddess with the Dulcimer, *Catalogue Museum Lavigerie*, I, pp. 111–12. Woman playing a Harp, G. Ch.-Picard, *op. cit.*, p. 149, fig. 15.
75. P. Cintas, 'Centenaire de la Soc. Hist. algérienne' (*Revue Africaine*, C, 1956), pp. 275 sqq.
76. *Hippiatriques grecs*, ed. Grynaeus, Bâle, 1537, p. 95.
77. A. Caquot, *Syria*, XXIX, 1952, pp. 74 sqq. G. Ch.-Picard, *op. cit.*, p. 94.
78. MC, pl. 22.
79. J. Vercoutter, *op cit.*, pp. 311 sqq.
80. MC, pl. 14.
81. G. G. Lapeyre and A. Pellegrin, *op. cit.*, p. 152.
82. A. Héron de Villefosse, *Mon. Piot.*, XII, 1905, pp. 77–111.
83. *Catalogue Museum Lavigerie, Supp.*, I, pl. II.
84. Picard, *Sculpture antique*, I, p. 217, fig. 60.
85. *C.I.S.*, I, 17, 6, pl. XLIX (preserved in Turin Museum).
86. The statues of Baal-Saturn of the Empire period are shown holding an exactly similar casket, which presumably contained *sacra*. C. Poinssot, *Karthago*, VI, 1957, pp. 75–6.
87. E. Boucher-Colozier, *Mél. École Française, Rome*, LXV, 1953, pp. 78 sqq., pl. 1, 4.
88. See bibliography given in the article quoted in note 87; cf. especially, J. Carcopino, *Mem. Pont. Acc. Archéol.*, I, 1924, pp. 109 sqq. and M. Pallottino, *Mon. Antichi*, XXXVI, 1937, pp. 433 sqq.
89. *Catalogue Museum Lavigerie*, I, pl. IX, 1, 2.
90. *Ibid.*, pl. X, 1, 2.

CHAPTER VI

TRADERS AND COMMERCE

THE 'GUGGAS'

THERE is one section of the population of Carthage which we have not as yet mentioned, but which was in fact the most important and the most widely known: the traders.

In the words of Isaiah:[1] 'Tyre, . . . whose merchants are princes, whose traffickers are the honourable of the earth'. Pliny has no hesitation about describing the *Poeni* as the inventors of commerce. The Hebrews, the Greeks, and the Romans all agree in praising the ingenuity and tireless activity of the Sidonians and Tyrians. They were to be found in all the countries bordering the Mediterranean and even farther afield in the remotest lands of Western Europe. All nations reluctantly accepted their presence, and while cursing their knavish tricks and their relentless pursuit of gain, admitted that they could not dispense with their services.

The Carthaginian traders may aptly be compared with many modern business-men from countries bordering the Mediterranean: Levantines, Armenians, Jews, Greeks, Mozabites, and Djerbians from North Africa—all of whom leave their native lands to make their fortune, are willing to start in some humble trade and to live in uncomfortable and often sordid circumstances, but who eventually amass great wealth through sheer hard work, thrift, and not too scrupulous ingenuity.

However, the Carthaginians had one great advantage over their modern successors: they were backed by a powerful State which was itself keenly interested in trade and neglected no steps to ensure the success of its nationals. This political intervention was mainly directed towards securing a monopoly in certain markets for Carthaginian traders either by force or by diplomacy. But it never occurred to the Carthaginians, or to any of their rivals, to control commercial trends by selective customs duties. The State did indeed exact dues on exports and imports, but never conceived the idea of encouraging some transactions and hindering others, by varying these dues. As will be seen, the Carthaginians had very simple notions about economics—far inferior to those of the Greeks. But it would be a mistake to imagine that their trading activities never varied, or that those who were engaged in them always followed the same procedures. In fact, the picture of the Carthaginian trader, of his aims and his methods, which emerges from the relevant texts, varies according to the period.

In Homer,[2] the Sidonian trader is a familiar figure. He brings embroidered veils and silver goblets from his native land; occasionally he takes passengers on his boat and is not above kidnapping children for the slave-market. Ezekiel[3] and Isaiah both refer to the attraction which Tyre, with its vast overseas wealth, exerted on the poorer children of Israel, mostly peasants or shepherds. To its own undoing, it also tempted the rapacious Assyrians.

Two or three centuries later, Herodotus[4] mentions that Phoenician traders who had been very active in Greece in the past, were rarely seen there in his day. There were not many in Greece even in the sixth century, for they had transferred their sphere of action beyond the Greek and Barbarian lands. A fierce and often bloody rivalry had developed between the Phoenicians and the Hellenes. By the fifth and fourth centuries, the Greek historians refer to the Carthaginians no longer as crafty traders or thieving pirates, but as ferocious warriors and enemies of the State, capable of the worst atrocities; they had become 'Berbers' and 'Saracens'.

During the Hellenistic period, however, the 'Poenulus' was once more a familiar figure in Greek, Macedonian, and Italian ports. Menander, Alexis, and later Plautus,[5] treat him as a comic figure on the stage. In Plautus' comedy Poenulus, one of the characters calls Hanno, the Carthaginian merchant, a gugga. This unflattering term may be roughly translated as 'little rat'. Evidently the Mediterranean peoples were scarcely more polite to each other then than they are today. The gugga had only to appear on the stage wearing ear-rings, but no cloak, and followed by his aged slaves, bent double under bundles of trashy wares, for the audience to rock with laughter.

In the *Poenulus*, Hanno the merchant is an interesting character. He knows Latin quite well, but keeps quiet about it until
the fanciful translations of a scoundrel called Milphio make
him lose his temper. There is nothing morally austere about him
but it seems quite natural for him to stand up for himself against
an enemy. His nephew has a mistress at the procurer's. Hanno
thinks this is a good thing. He himself would like to do the
procurer a bad turn—but not because he objects in principle to
his trade, for in cheating his girls' lovers the procurer was only
doing his job.

In spite of his faults, Hanno is not devoid of sincere and
honourable feelings. In the first place, he is pious: Hanno is
always invoking his gods and regards his good fortune as the
reward of his devotion. He also displays paternal affection: the
memory of his daughters who were carried off in infancy from
Carthage causes him the deepest emotion, which the ruffian
Milphio is quite incapable of comprehending: 'Oh, the cunning
artful rascal! How conveniently he weeps to further the success
of our plan! He is a bigger knave even than I am, and I am
an arch rogue!' Of course it turns out that Adelphasia and
Anterastilla are his own long-lost daughters, and the 'Poenulus',
greatly moved, shows himself to be a good father and a kind
uncle, filled with joy at having found his offspring again, and
even their old nurse, the swarthy Giddenes.

Although this play was very probably performed during the
Second Punic War, it displays no real hatred of the Carthaginians.
Even in matters of commerce, the Greeks and Romans felt no
sense of inferiority—one could always go and do business in
Carthage, provided one had plenty of money and was not afraid
to lose it. Finally, Plautus admits that many Carthaginian children
were kidnapped in the city itself by Greek and Roman slave-
traders. Piracy had not been eliminated, but at least its victims
came from both sides. The destruction of the Carthaginian navy
during the First Punic War, made the great port a profitable
objective for sea-pirates.

In classical literature, the Carthaginian appears in yet another
role: as well as being the Levantine dealer or fighter, he sometimes plays the part of the explorer who crosses the Sahara, sails
his ships over tropical oceans to find Pigmy gold, or braves the

Northern fog and ice to reach the mysterious Thule, the land of the midnight sun.

Yet however different, in character or in methods, the Carthaginians might be, and whether they were traders or pirates, admirals in the navy or explorers, they were all promoters of a common economic policy whose changing requirements dictated the various methods they used.

The economic policy of Carthage must therefore be studied before it is possible to consider these methods or assess their results.

For more than half its existence (815–450 B.C., approximately), Carthage was like a ship at anchor off the coast of Africa. Even when it had made territorial conquests in Tunisia, it remained to Africa what Alexandria was to Egypt—*Alexandria ad Agyptum*, as the Romans said—Carthage, off Africa, rather than in Africa. Doubtless its day-to-day existence no longer depended on the arrival of ships or on the good-will of the Berbers, and it became possible to increase the population and to make better use of the ships available. Doubtless also, a considerable section of the population was no longer directly employed in overseas trade. And yet this trade was never more prosperous than during the last centuries—at least, up to the outbreak of the Second Punic War. It is scarcely an exaggeration to say that only then did 'The House of Carthage' become, from a business point of view, a going concern.

The whole of Carthage's economic policy was dominated by the effort to preserve the mastery of.the Western Seas, or as the Romans called them, the 'Tyrian Seas'. The city was founded for this purpose as an international trading-post on the route to Tartessus. During the first hundred years it had no definite policy of its own; the metropolis of Tyre controlled the activities of its Western outposts which were but the fixed bases, providing rest and supplies for its fleets.

Its great trading organization was designed to secure for the East the mineral ores which it needed so badly. Diodorus of Sicily[6] tells how the Phoenicians had discovered silver-mines in Spain which the natives worked without realizing their real value. The Tyrians were therefore able to secure large quantities of silver in exchange for a relatively small quantity of goods, and thus kept control over the Eastern market in silver for many years. Towards the end of the second millennium there therefore existed a situation very like that which was provoked in the sixteenth century A.D. by the discovery of America. The Phoenicians, like the Spaniards and Portuguese in the sixteenth century A.D., made their fortune by bringing together two economic hemispheres, which up till then had remained completely apart, and in which precious metals had very different values.

But the Tyrians were more fortunate than the *conquistadores* because they found not only silver, whose purely conventional value depended on supply and demand, but also a metal which was absolutely indispensable to the industrial production of that time, but which was rare in the East, namely tin.[7] However, tin was not mined in the Sierra Morena—it came from distant mines, some in the north-west of the Iberian peninsula, and the rest from Brittany or Cornwall.[8] It is a surprising fact that as early as the third millennium, the Atlantic routes from Armorica to Galicia, and north and south to the British Isles and Gibraltar,[9] were in frequent use. There must have been a powerful incentive to make sailors in their frail boats, carrying heavy cargoes of minerals, face the storms of the Bay of Biscay. The centre of attraction was in Andalusia; from the beginning of the Bronze Age, the pre-Tartessians had exploited three of their country's natural advantages: a fertile soil, mineral wealth, and a position at the meeting-point of routes from the Mediterranean to the North and South Atlantic. From then on, their metal industries attained a degree of perfection which gave them for centuries a leading position in the West and allowed them to compete with the great civilizations of the East; their ships sailed across the two oceans, visited the brilliant civilizations of Armorica, and occupied strong-points on the north-west coast of Africa.

Did the people of Tartessus make contact with the Aegeans, who, for their part, certainly sailed beyond the Straits of Sicily? There is no material proof of contact between them, although A. Schulten goes so far as to suggest that the Tartessians may very well have been of Oriental origin.[10] But even if there were no direct contact, the fame of the Western Eldorado must have been passed along the Mediterranean from one people to the next until it finally reached the Lebanese, and attracted the attention of some Tyrian Christopher Columbus. The date of this event, of such capital importance, is unhappily uncertain. The Roman historian Velleius Paterculus[11] placed the foundation of Gades (Cadiz) 'at the time of the return of the Heraclidae', by which he means the Dorian invasion at the end of the twelfth century B.C.[12] This would make it a little earlier than the foundation of Utica.

On the other hand, the first contemporary evidence of trade between Tyre and Spain is in the seven hundredth verse of Isaiah. Some material has been found very recently in excavations in Cadiz.[13] In Andalusian museums, P. Cintas has found very ancient vases contemporary with the foundation of Carthage.[14] But in his opinion these were made much later by routine production of old-fashioned models in distant provinces. For this to be so, their prototypes must have reached Andalusia at the time when they were in fashion in Tyre. Consequently it seems clear that relationships were established between Spain and Phoenicia in the ninth century. In our opinion they existed even earlier. Diodorus,[15] whose evidence fits in with what we know about Phoenician methods, maintains that the Levant traders had frequented the Tartessian ports long before they set up a permanent trading-post near the coast. The choice the Tyrians made from the numerous possibilities of their discovery, is very characteristic of a mentality often found today in many an Oriental trader. It never occurred to them for a single instant to use the raw materials they now had at their disposal to develop a national industry. Having calculated the difference between the current prices of the metals at their source and at their destination, they estimated that even allowing for the enormous cost and hazards of transport, there would still be enough profit for them to be able to buy up the products of all the peoples dwelling on the shores of the Eastern Mediterranean. The lure of quick profits blinded them to the consequences of such a policy: the peoples they hoped to secure as permanent customers were, in the end, the real beneficiaries of a traffic which stimulated their economic activity. Such a choice, and such a mistake, decided the fate for many centuries to come, of both Tyre and Carthage.

On the other hand, it was perfectly clear to the Tyrians that two things were essential before they could maintain this economic policy: on the one hand, complete control of the Tartessian economy, and on the other, complete mastery of shipping routes through the Mediterranean. The first was easy to secure. The natives of Tartessus could offer no more resistance to the newcomers than could those of Peru and Mexico centuries later. A. Schulten is of the opinion that the foundation of Gades was followed by a rapid conquest of the country.[16] This hypothesis, which rests entirely upon an ambiguous passage in Strabo, must certainly be discarded. However unwarlike the Tartessians may have been, it would have needed a military effort far in excess of anything Tyre could have managed, quite apart from the insurmountable difficulties of operating from such distant bases. The only Tartessian king known to us, that wise old man Arganthonius, who reigned in the second half of the sixth century, appears to have been completely free in his foreign policy. Besides, what advantage would it have been to the Phoenicians to make such a conquest? For the first three centuries of the first millennium, they were the only Orientals capable of getting to Spain. They were therefore absolute masters of the market, and the productivity of the country was much better assured by its own rulers than by colonial domination.

It is possible, however, that the Phoenicians took some precautions with regard to their Tartessian allies. The latter had established commercial relations not only with the African coast and the North Atlantic, but also with Morocco. Doubtless they already received from this source tropical produce which came through Mauretania—and in particular, gold from Senegal.[17] It is possible that the Tyrians tried to control this trade by creating a colony at Lixus, near Larache, at the beginning of the first millennium.

Pliny[18] reports, without vouching for its truth, a traditional belief that the Temple of Hercules-Melkart in Lixus was older than the one in Gades. Archaeology has revealed only one trace of that ancient occupation, but it is a very precious one: from Lixus comes the only Egyptian scarab yet found in Morocco.[19] It bears an inscription in the name of Amenophis III who reigned at the beginning of the fourteenth century B.C., though the scarab was certainly made long after that Pharaoh's death. J. Leclant dates it as belonging to the Twenty-second Dynasty which reigned in the tenth century B.C.

COMPETITION FROM GREECE

The Phoenicians ran into no great difficulties in the West until other navigators from the East began to arrive in large numbers. At first, however, a kind of tacit agreement seems to have been reached by which the western basin of the Mediterranean was divided into spheres of influence reserved for each of the invaders. Thus the Phoenicians abandoned any claims on Italy: the northern coasts of that peninsula were occupied before the beginning of the eighth century by the early Etruscans while the Greeks reoccupied the southern perimeter of the 'boot' of Italy, which had formerly been visited by their Mycenaean ancestors.

Today, Bérard's theories have been abandoned and nobody believes any more that the Phoenicians ever controlled the region where Ulysses wandered. The only conflict was over Sicily, which, according to Thucydides,[20] had been completely surrounded by a ring of Phoenician trading-posts; yet the Phoenicians did evacuate without much resistance all the posts in the east of the island, from the second half of the eighth century, only retaining the western outpost of Palermo. This part of the island was inhabited by that curious people the Elymaei, who were perhaps immigrants from Asia. Their capital was at Segesta, and in Eryx they worshipped the great goddess of fertility, in whose temple were sacred prostitutes like those in Corinth and Cyprus. Although the Elymaei had accepted Greek civilization, they remained unshakeably faithful to their Punic allies.

It was vitally important for Tyre to retain control over the most direct route to Spain, namely that along the shores of Africa. This maritime route which was made safe by the foundation of Utica in the eleventh century was even more firmly secured in the ninth century by the foundation of Carthage. It was also covered on the north and east by Eastern Sicily and Malta and by Sardinia, where Nora was founded at approximately the same time as Carthage.[21] *Mutatis mutandis*, this disposition could be compared with that of the British Empire in the nineteenth century, with India taking the place of Tartessus and Gibraltar that of Carthage.

But there were other routes to Spain through Gaul. The
Etruscans seem to have been the first to use this approach.
According to Diodorus, they came into conflict with the Carthaginians over the possession of an island in the Atlantic—
probably Madeira.[22] This was at a time when the Tyrian navy
was at the height of its strength, probably in the seventh century,
before the Phocaeans settled in large numbers along the coast of
Provence. In order to secure the freedom of the seas, the Tyrians
needed unrestricted access to the Tartessian ports. It is highly
probable that they did not look very favourably on this Etruscan
competition but were in no position to oppose it. It was not until
the end of the sixth century, when they had gained complete
control of Andalusia that they took advantage of the Greek
menace to conclude a treaty of alliance with the powerful Italian
Confederation—with a clause guaranteeing their monopoly over
all trade with Southern Spain.[23]

But they failed to secure any such agreement with the Greeks.
As early as the eighth century, sailors from Rhodes and Ionia had
been sailing freely across the Gulf of Lyons.[24] In 630, the Samian
Colaeus, driven by storms all the way from the Egyptian Sea,
discovered Tartessus on his own account.[25] There he was given a
warm welcome by Arganthonius, who was evidently looking for
every possible occasion to escape from Phoenician influence. The
Spaniards had by now realized that they were being devoured
by the Tyrians and hoped to open fresh markets with their competitors. Colaeus brought back to Samos a magnificent bronze
chalice and a sufficiently vast profit on his goods to make him a
rich man for life. This episode confirms the fact that the Tyrians
had been paying the lowest possible price for silver.

The success of this expedition doubtless encouraged the
Phocaeans to head for Provence. They had no sooner founded
Marseilles in 600 B.C., than they extended their colonies all along
the coasts of Gaul and Spain. Arganthonius, faithful to his phil-
hellenic principles, conceded to them a site known as Mainake,
later to become Malaga. Greeks and Phoenicians were now on an
equal footing. Towards the middle of the sixth century, when
the Ionians were threatened by the Persian invaders, they
organized a large-scale emigration towards Sardinia, while the
Phocaeans attempted to install themselves in Corsica. This

disconcerting rivalry, even more than the capture of Tyre by Nebuchadnezzar in 574, made it necessary for the Phoenicians to transfer the supreme control of their Western trading-posts to Africa. Even at the beginning of the seventh century, it had been realized that the continued influx of Greek settlers into the West could only be countered by sending equally numerous colonists from Phoenicia. Then Carthage received a fresh contingent of colonists fleeing from the Assyrian tyranny. Excavations have revealed that in the sixth century fair-sized towns sprang up all along the coast of Africa, including Hadrumetum, Tipasa, and Mogador. In 654, Ibiza, in the Balearic Isles, was permanently occupied. The Carthaginians had once more secured control of their high seas route to Spain.

Thus strengthened, the Carthaginians were able to consolidate the Tyrian heritage in the West by a series of military and diplomatic triumphs. The battle of Alalia in 535 and the conclusion of a treaty with the Etruscans, put a stop to the expansion of Ionian influence and removed a commercial competitor in the West. Marseilles was left isolated, and put up a heroic resistance, determined to preserve its hold over the Catalan and Provençal coasts.[26] But it had to give up Tartessus, which then came completely under Punic rule.

A. Schulten believes that the Carthaginians subsequently reconquered Andalusia. The Arganthonius dynasty did indeed vanish about the middle of the century, but in our opinion it succumbed to the Barbarians rather than to the Carthaginians. It was in fact just at this time that the Celts occupied Castile,[27] and it is unlikely that such incorrigible pillagers would spare the rich and undefended plains in the south. This invasion, in which the Iberians were doubtless also involved, ended when Theron, 'King of Remoter Spain', attacked Gades. This event is recorded by Macrobius[28] who states that Melkart saved the town by a miracle; but the inhabitants felt obliged to appeal to Carthage and to place themselves henceforth under Punic protection. The Carthaginian troops probably never ventured far into the interior, but they kept a tight hold on the coast from a chain of trading-posts. Malaga rose from the ruins of Mainake; the Greeks were driven back whenever they ventured farther south than Cape de la Nao, which was watched over by the Temple of Tanit.

At about this time also, energetic Carthaginian generals like Malchus, and later Mago and his descendants, organized a permanent army in Sicily; it was mainly composed of mercenaries and carried on an almost continuous war against the Greek colonists. However, it succeeded only in preserving the territory of the Elymaei. But it did gain control of Sardinia, thus covering the routes from Carthage to the Etruscan empire, which included most of Italy, from the Alps to Campania. Finally its vigorous intervention prevented Dorieus, the son of the King of Sparta, from founding a Greek colony in Tripolitania, where the frontier was fixed at the far end of the Bay of Syrtes.

All this time, the conquering Persians under Cyrus were imposing peace in the Orient. Carthage, which for a while was threatened by Cambyses, accepted Persian suzerainty willingly enough, since it brought more advantages than burdens. The Asian Phoenicians, under the King of Sidon, who was in command of the entire Phoenician navy, exercised great influence in the Persian Councils, where the Western policies of the 'Great King' Cyrus were decided. They were very largely responsible for his decision to attack Greece. The Hellenic people now found themselves encircled by a vast coalition led by the Etruscans, the Carthaginians, and the Persians.[29] These political agreements were cemented by economic ties. Now that she was mistress of the Western Mediterranean, Carthage continued to convoy to Asia raw materials from the Far West, and to sell them at a very high price. Nevertheless, she had reluctantly to allow some share of this trade to other maritime nations who were also subjects of the Great King. Both history and archaeology prove that direct contacts existed in the sixth century and the beginning of the fifth century between Egypt and Cyprus, on the one hand, and Spain on the other.[30] The inhabitants of Gades, Malaga, Almeria, and Lixus preserved a certain autonomy and developed a relatively new civilization on the European and African shores of the Gulf of Malaga.[31] The Etruscan peace treaty added the richest part of Italy to this common market. Only the Greeks remained outside and both their political and their economic independence seemed to lie at the mercy of enemies who were preparing a combined assault upon them.

But the Hellenes remained superior to their enemies in one

essential respect—that of creative intelligence. We know that in the eighth century and in the beginning of the seventh century, Greece existed on a very simple agricultural economy, and depended mainly on the Phoenician merchants for manufactured products, and particularly luxury articles. But after 650 B.C., enormous advances were made in Greek industries; great towns like Corinth, which was the most prosperous, flooded the whole of the Mediterranean basin, and even the Phoenician cities themselves, with the products of their workshops.

This 'industrial revolution' was due to a number of causes, not the least important being the short-sighted policy of the Tyrians, who supplied their rivals with raw materials in exchange for manufactured articles. Once more, *mutatis mutandis*, there is an obvious comparison between this and the economic revolution which took place in Western Europe in the sixteenth century A.D.; then, as is well known, Spain's vast imports of precious metals, after giving an artificial prosperity to the Spanish kingdoms, completely upset the exchange market, and ended by favouring the Netherlands and England. The economic decline of Phoenicia began by the loss of the internal Greek market, where the Sidonian dealers, so familiar in Homer, were rarely seen after 600 B.C. It is very likely that the arrival of supplies of gold from Tartessus brought about an increase of prices in Greece, and the difficulties facing the Attic farmers at the beginning of the seventh century were in all probability partly the result of inflation. But Solon's example proves that the Greeks were able to weather the crisis by the invention of money, thus stabilizing the prices of precious metals. The Phoenicians in general, however, and the Carthaginians in particular, showed themselves quite incapable of using this vital invention.

This astonishing failure on their part was certainly largely responsible for their loss of Aegean trade. Barter may have been the only possible method of exchange with the Barbarians in the West, but by refusing to convert their precious metals into coinage, the Carthaginians deprived themselves of many facilities, such as loans at interest and banks, which became available to the Greeks. The Carthaginian gold, like that of the Persians, was condemned to lie useless in vaults, although the Persian 'Great King' Darius was wise enough to circulate some of his as gold coins.

It is probable that the absence of money was as much responsible for the continued inferiority of Punic industries as the shortage of artisans. So great was the superiority of the Greeks in this respect that the rigorous blockade by Carthaginian ships did not prevent the Western Barbarians from trying to establish direct trade relationships with Greece. The recent discovery at Vix of the largest bronze bowl that has yet come down to us from antiquity gives some indication of the valuable orders which the Carthaginians lost. At the end of the sixth century, therefore, the prosperity of Carthage was in a precarious state, in spite of her great political strength. The collapse of the great alliance between Persia and Etruria was to reveal this weakness in the most brutal fashion and to bring Dido's city, within a very short time, to the brink of ruin.

This collapse occurred very suddenly and in three different places. First, in Greece and Asia Minor where the Great King's onslaughts on the Greek Confederation were defeated; secondly, in Sicily where in the battle of Himera, fought, it is said, on the same day as the battle of Salamis (480 B.C.), Gelon of Syracuse defeated the mighty army of Hamilcar the Magonid; and thirdly, in Italy, where the Etruscans lost control of Campania and Latium through the combined actions of the Greeks of Cumae and the insurgent Italians. Carthage was less directly hit than her two partners; none of her immediate possessions fell into the hands of her enemies, and her navy was less sorely tried than that of Sidon. But henceforth Athenian maritime supremacy from the Straits of Messina to Egypt, barred to Carthage the routes to the East. Thus her most valuable commercial outlets were closed. The Greeks, no doubt, were still willing to allow business to continue, but Athens, which imposed her economic supremacy on her compatriots, insisted on fixing her own terms in the future.

One thing is certain. These defeats brought about a serious economic recession in Carthage. Precise archaeological evidence of this has been found. Graphs drawn by Vercoutter and Cintas show that at this time, amulets of Egyptian origin disappeared almost completely. It was the same with Greek vases. Black-figured vases made in Corinth or Attica figure extensively in our collections, but red-figured vases, whose production started about 520, are completely absent. Etruscan articles also vanished.

Carthage had thus suddenly ceased all purchases of finished products from allies and enemies alike.

From Sicily,[32] only a few essential commodities like wine and oil were still imported. The consumption of these was probably strictly rationed. If the 'anti-alcohol' bill which Plato mentions was ever enforced, it was probably intended to cut down the consumption of foreign wine, though adequate supplies were not yet available from home production.

We have already shown that this policy of austerity was the result of a veritable political and religious revolution: the Magonid princes were replaced by an aristocratic régime, while Tanit gained pre-eminence over all the other gods.[33] The new régime devoted itself with great energy to the task of finding the necessary resources to make Carthage self-sufficient. The conquest of territories on the mainland removed the gravest of all their anxieties— that of famine. The expeditions led by Hanno and Himilco strengthened the Carthaginian domination in the Far West, and restored the supplies of metals which had been severely cut by the disasters in Sicily. If Thucydides is correct, the Carthaginian war treasury was replenished by 415.[34] However, Carthage continued a policy of Spartan austerity and her traders almost vanished from the ports of Italy and the Eastern Mediterranean. The gold which came from Senegal and the silver from Spain was henceforth used to pay mercenaries and build navies, ready for the hour of revenge.

CARTHAGE RISES AGAIN

The first opportunity to hit back came in 409 B.C. The Greeks in Sicily were several times threatened with total extinction, and finally lost their southern province for ever. Only the great ruins of fallen temples were left to bear witness to the former prosperity of Selinus and Agrigentum.

During this terrible century, war became the most prosperous Carthaginian industry. The value of the spoils far exceeded the cost of the operations, while the prisoners of war, reduced to slavery, provided badly needed skilled labour. The bronze-work shops, which began to operate at the beginning of the fourth century, copied models plundered from cities which had been destroyed. The Carthaginian products remained inferior to the

Greek, but the citizens of the Phoenician towns in the West, the African princes who were beginning to taste the benefits of civilization, the Spaniards, and the Barbarians in Africa and Gaul, had to be satisfied with what they could get.

Having thus strengthened its economic position, the government of Carthage was now able to relax to some extent its severe trade restrictions. Essential contacts had been maintained in the towns in Southern Sicily, like Selinus, which for a time Carthage had hoped to draw within its orbit. When the decision was finally taken to destroy them, relations with Syracuse were extended. But in 398 B.C., Dionysius of Syracuse seized the numerous Carthaginian ships anchored in the harbour, and allowed the population to loot the warehouses which the Carthaginian merchants had established in the city.[35]

In the middle of the fourth century, relations were renewed with the whole of Italy. In 348 B.C., a second treaty was concluded with Rome, which almost immediately afterwards annexed Campania and thus became one of the greatest industrial and commercial powers in the Italian peninsula.[36] The terms of this treaty are given by Polybius: they defined exactly the area which Carthage considered to be its sphere of influence; on the whole they are much less favourable to Rome than the first agreement reached a century and a half earlier. This is explained by the fact that at the time of the first treaty (beginning of the sixth century) Rome was still considered an Etruscan city and thus benefited from the favourable terms which Carthage granted to her allies; while now, the Punic government had greatly intensified its restrictive policy.

At all events, the Romans gave an undertaking to abstain completely from trading or raiding and from founding cities, firstly along the whole of the African coast west of the promontory (Ras el Mekki) which encloses the Gulf of Carthage to the north; and secondly along the Spanish coast west of Mastia (which later became Cartagena). In Sardinia and along the shores of Byzacium in Eastern Tunisia, and in Tripolitania, they were allowed only the right to take on provisions and to get their ships repaired, in case of damage. In no circumstances might they put in for more than five days.

Foreign traders were barred from all ports except Carthage,

and even there were only admitted on a reciprocal basis. These terms were obviously very detrimental to the prosperity of the other Phoenician towns in Africa which henceforth only remained in the Carthaginian alliance through sheer necessity or through fear.

The agreement concluded between Rome and Carthage did not prevent either party from preserving its earlier alliances. Carthage was therefore able to draw closer once more to Etruria; in fact an Etruscan colony probably came and settled in Carthage.[37] Rome, for its part, cultivated its long friendship with Marseilles. This ancient Ionian colony was actually the chief rival of the Carthaginians, who had the whole of Southern Spain under their control, but who, as soon as they rounded Cape de la Nao, found themselves running up against the Ionian customers of King Emporion, who had brotherly connexions with the people of Marseilles.[38]

The descendants of the Phocaeans thus exercised economic domination over all the Iberian, Celtic, or Ligurian tribes in Catalonia, Languedoc, and Provence. Marseilles very probably made efforts to reach the tin and amber countries by going up the Rhône valley and then making use of routes along the valleys of the Loire and the Danube.[39] Experts are not entirely in agreement about the outcome of this policy, which aroused the hostility of many tribes in Gaul.

The Carthaginians were just as resolutely excluded from the sphere of influence of Marseilles as the Greeks were from that of the Carthaginians. Excavations at Ensérune, a small town inhabited by an Iberian tribe, where the road to the Atlantic comes over the Naurouze saddle on to the slopes of Roussillon, prove that the inhabitants of that region depended entirely on the Greeks for their contacts with the Mediterranean world. In such circumstances, it is difficult to see how two men from Marseilles, Pytheas and Euthymenes, managed to pass through the Straits of Gibraltar in about the year 300 B.C., and to explore, the one the coasts of Europe, and the other the coasts of Africa. Perhaps C. Jullian's is the correct explanation[40]—that the anxiety felt by the Carthaginians over Macedonian imperialism led them to grant an exceptional favour to these two Greeks from Marseilles.

RAPPROCHEMENT WITH THE EAST

As soon as Athens declined and relations improved between the Great King and the Greeks, the Phoenicians in the West were able to revive their trade routes with the East. In the process they won back some of the trade in Greece which had been abandoned by their ancestors three centuries earlier. In 315 B.C. there was a Carthaginian in Thebes in Boeotia, who acted as a kind of consul and whose duty it was to receive travellers and to protect their interests.

This revival of trade with Greece is perhaps explained by the crisis which hit the Greek economy, in its turn, at the beginning of the fourth century. At that time, the economic domination which Athens exercised over the Middle East and the Black Sea countries began to weaken. Lacking food and raw materials, the Greeks had to call upon the resources of the Carthaginians and to agree to pay a good price for them. In Punic tombs of this period a number of specimens of Greek pottery have been found, though more of these came from Greek towns in Italy than from Greece itself.

In the second half of the fourth century the barriers dividing Carthage and its empire from the rest of the Mediterranean world finally disappeared. Although it was still in conflict with Syracuse, the Carthaginian State intensified its trade relations with Greater Greece and renewed them with the East, which Alexander's conquests had unified and tied economically to Greece. An event of decisive importance for Carthage was the foundation by Ptolemy I of a maritime empire which with Egypt included Cyrenaica, Cyprus, the Cyclades, and soon Coelesyria of which Phoenicia was a part.[41] Ptolemy broke the unified monetary system which Alexander had established on the basis of the Attic system, and adopted the Phoenician standard for his coinage.

This decision was the main reason why Carthage decided to issue a coinage of its own.[42] In the fifth century its government had doubtless guaranteed coins struck in Sicily (probably at Lilybaeum), which were copied from a currency already in circulation in the island, based on the Attic standard.[43] But the inscriptions on these tetradrachmae prove that they were kept solely for the pay of mercenaries. No more were struck after the end of the fourth century or the beginning of the third century. It seems, therefore, that it was not until this time that a mint was founded in Byrsa to strike coins based on the Phoenician standard.

These handsome coins, bearing the head of Demeter, a palm tree and a horse, symbols of prosperity and prowess in war, were minted in gold or bronze. Silver was not used until later. The absence of silver pointed to a serious state of affairs: at that time Carthage must have lost control of the silver-mines in Andalusia. It was not until the second century that they were recovered by the Barcids. This temporary eclipse of Carthaginian power in Spain has been correctly noted by A. Schulten.[44] But, contrary to the opinion of this German scholar, it seems to have happened much earlier than the First Punic War.

J. Jannoray's discoveries at Ensérune prove, moreover, that this temporary eclipse can scarcely have been the result of a victorious offensive from Marseilles, although it must be considered a possible reason for relaxing the control over the Pillars of Hercules, and allowing Pytheas and Euthymenes to pass them, and to conduct their expeditions along the European and African Atlantic coasts. This historical evidence may perhaps be compared with Cintas's archaeological discoveries. On sites in Southern Spain, Oran, and Morocco, he has found red pottery with a brilliant glaze which could have come neither from Carthage nor from workshops in Marseilles or Campania.[45] It was probably made in Andalusia and disseminated by purely local trade. Perhaps the Phoenicians in the Far West, tired of being exploited by the Carthaginians, had made common cause with the native population, in order to win their independence. They were probably helped in this task by the appearance of a fairly strong monarchy in Mauretania, before the time of the Numidian kings.

The secession of her Western possessions, in which she was allowed to keep only a few strongholds, struck the Carthaginian economy a severe blow. The history of the third-century wars shows that military operations were often hampered by financial difficulties. To remedy to some extent this state of affairs, a kind of token money was put into circulation—much to the astonishment of the Greeks. This took the form of small leather bags, sealed with the public seal, and which it was forbidden to open. They contained an object 'equivalent to a Stater'.[46] It is very unlikely that these counters had any backing in the State reserves of precious metal.

In these circumstances, it is rather surprising that trade with the East was so prosperous. Although the Carthaginian potteries and metal-work shops were able to meet some of the demands of the home market, the city remained largely dependent on imports from Greater Greece, Egypt, and Rhodes. The Campanian potteries, which went into production in the last quarter of the fourth century, flooded Africa with their products. Evidently the severely controlled economy of the fifth century had given way to a greater liberalism. But how were the Carthaginians able to pay for their imports?

The methodical organization of agriculture on African territory had secured Carthage against famine. It must also have contributed appreciably to the goods available for export. The Cape Bon wine was probably not esteemed very highly abroad; in fact the Carthaginians themselves purchased fairly large quantities of better wine from Rhodes: on all Punic sites of the third and second centuries[47] large numbers of amphorae have been found bearing the names of magistrates of Rhodes. On the other hand, equally large numbers of Carthaginian amphorae have been found at various points along the Mediterranean shores.[48] Apparently the Carthaginians sold their wine to the Barbarians in order to pay for good wine bought from the Greeks.[49]

We believe that at this period Africa was in a position to supply much-needed wheat to Greece. There is no definite evidence of this until after the fall of Carthage. Then, Masinissa and his successors exported appreciable quantities of grain to the Balkans.[50] But before the Second Punic War, Carthage controlled the most fertile regions in Tunisia, namely, the valley of the Medjerda and Byzacium. The *chora* produced enough to feed the urban population, and the levies in kind imposed on the Libyans, which sometimes amounted to a quarter, or even a half, of their harvests, were therefore available for export.[51]

Statistics are available on the amount thus contributed.[52] In 201 B.C., Scipio requisitioned nearly 1,250,000 bushels of wheat and over 1,500,000 bushels of barley. The following year, to help Rome in her war against Macedonia, Carthage supplied about 1,000,000 bushels of wheat. In 170 B.C., during the Third Macedonian War, this figure rose to nearly 1,500,000 bushels. The net production of wheat from the Carthaginian domains in Africa can probably be estimated at about 1,500,000 bushels. This is a modest figure. It represents about half the wheat production of the Numidian kingdom in the middle of the first century B.C., and one-thirtieth of what Rome obtained from Africa under the Empire. But the Punic State never exceeded 25,000 to 32,000 square miles in area, which is barely a tenth of Roman Africa. Moreover, the best cultivated regions produced vines and olives. Above all, enough had to be subtracted from the net production to feed the urban population. Even if the population did not exceed 250,000, its total consumption must have amounted to about 1,750,000 bushels.

Production in Sicily and Sardinia was much higher: seven to nine million bushels approximately. In all, therefore, Carthage could place on the market some nine million bushels of wheat. This amount, sold in Greece, would have brought in the equivalent of over two million pounds in our currency. Although the cost of transport would absorb half of this, the remaining revenue would nevertheless be considerable.

Over the long sea routes used by the Carthaginians, it would obviously have been more profitable to carry expensive goods which did not weigh too much. Unfortunately there was only one kind of manufactured goods they could produce which could tempt the Greeks: valuable textiles of various kinds, and in particular their purple cloth. A character in one of Plautus' plays boasts that he has bought his wife a cloak for 400 *denarii* (£70); it is true that at this time the complete wardrobe of the richest Roman ladies was rarely worth more than 1,000 *denarii* (about £175).

In the *Poenulus*, Hanno brings to Rome spoons, drain-pipes (probably made of terracotta) and walnuts. His cargo also included panthers for the public games.[53] The Carthaginians sold all kinds of odds and ends. Their best customers remained the Western Barbarians, who were not fussy about quality, and who paid in precious metals. The Spaniards may have prevented the

Carthaginians from robbing them, but they could not, or did not want to stop them from passing through the Straits.

The wide dissemination of typical Carthaginian glass masks, which have been found even in Switzerland,[54] shows that the rather trumpery Carthaginian products which found few buyers in the civilized countries, were nevertheless in great demand in Gaul. The gold currency was still fed by the gold-mines of Senegal. The Sudan was also reached by way of Fezzan; according to Livy, the customs dues in Tripolitania, the outlet for this trade, amounted to a talent a day.

In the third phase of its history, Carthage recovered the position it had held until the sixth century—that of general purveyor to the East. It was beginning to supply the Mediterranean market with the agricultural produce which was to play such an important part in the economy of the Roman Empire. Having overcome their racial hatred for the Greeks, the Carthaginians joined the economic union which had been founded by the Ptolemies, the richest monarchs in the world at that time. In this way, Carthage was able to enjoy ease and comfort, in spite of the loss of Spain and the burden of the wars in Sicily.

THE STRUGGLE WITH ROME

This prosperity reached its height in the first quarter of the third century. Carthage had just repulsed Agathocles, who had been the first to dare to come and attack Carthage in Africa. After the defeat of this adventurer, who was bold to the point of folly, and whose career suggests that of the Renaissance Italian *Condottieri*, the Greeks in Sicily were unable to find another leader strong enough to unite them. Neither Pyrrhus in Epirus, nor Hiero in Syracuse were able to stem the advance of the Carthaginians, who eventually gained control of most of Sicily. By adding this fresh conquest to their other domains, the Carthaginians now had at their disposal the greatest wheat-producing areas in the Mediterranean, except for Egypt. Then came the clash with Rome.

The collapse of the Punic empire was devastating. The Carthaginians were defeated on land and sea and driven out of Sicily; their home territories were laid waste by Regulus and their ports pillaged by privateers. Carthage was on the brink of bankruptcy. The royal bank of Egypt was approached for a loan of 2,000 talents, but refused to advance anything, on grounds of neutrality. The Libyan farmers found themselves once more in servitude and were compelled to surrender half their crops. The price of peace was fixed by the Romans at 3,200 talents, or more than fifty tons of silver. The Carthaginian treasury was drained. It could no longer pay its mercenaries, who revolted and precipitated a fresh uprising in the surrounding provinces. The Romans took advantage of this development to seize Sardinia and to demand another 1,200 talents.

Carthage was saved by the Barcids. Hamilcar, Hasdrubal, and Hannibal had been trained in the tradition of Alexander. Their strategy was aimed at producing economic as well as military results. Their armies, relatively small and therefore less expensive, moved with lightning rapidity over vast distances to strike at the enemy's vital centres and seize his wealth. Hamilcar's first aim, which he achieved in less than ten years (237–228 B.C.), was to conquer Andalusia. Carthage thus regained control of the famous silver-mines of the Sierra Morena, after having lost them for a hundred years. Fresh veins of ore were probably discovered and improved techniques increased their yield. Polybius states that 2,300 drachmae of silver a day (more than £500) were mined round Cartagena alone.[55] Another mine, at Baebelo, produced more than thirty-six tons a year. The arrears of debt to Rome were rapidly paid off. The mint at Byrsa, and another which was founded at Cartagena, were now able to issue silver drachmae, large numbers of which have been found by archaeologists. They bear witness to the wealth of the Carthaginian treasury.

Nevertheless, further deposits of silver were known to exist farther north in the Spanish peninsula, particularly in Cantabria. Hitherto, their production had been absorbed by Ampurias. The security of the new Carthaginian province could be assured only by subjugating the Celtiberi in Castile. This task was accomplished by Hasdrubal, who thus won a capital for the new empire which he did not hesitate to call Carthage. Master of the main wealth of the Punic empire, and of its only military forces, he became in fact its political leader also.

Carthage had now secured control of Spain as far as the Ebro, and had reached the borders of her old enemies, the Western Ionians. If Marseilles and Ampurias could now be conquered,

the vast Celtic markets would be dominated and the way opened
by river routes to the tin-mines of Brittany, thus avoiding the sea
detour by Galicia and the Bay of Biscay. But just at this moment,
the Gauls tightened their hold on Lower Languedoc and
Provence, where they had hitherto allowed the age-old inhabitants, the Iberians and Ligurians, to remain. They destroyed
Ensérune some time after 250 B.C.[56] However, Carthaginian
diplomacy was successful in pacifying these Barbarian peoples.
Meanwhile, the settlers in Marseilles, realizing the gravity of the
danger which threatened them, appealed to Rome, which immediately intervened. In 226 B.C., agreement was reached that the
Ebro should be the boundary of the Punic sphere of influence.[57]

In our opinion, these economic developments explain Hannibal's astonishing decision to invade Italy overland, via Gaul. His
great march was completely in the tradition of Alexander, whose
exploits were at that very moment being emulated in Asia Minor
by Antiochus the Great. But it entailed vast risks, since the weary
and reduced Carthaginian army would have to face Roman
troops who were completely fresh. It would have been easy to
build a fleet in the arsenal in Carthage which would have been
adequate to neutralize the Roman fleet. Recent discoveries in
Ensérune and Ruscino throw some light on the mystery:[58] several
Punic articles discovered in the first *oppidum* seem to us to prove
that Carthaginian officers lived there for a long time between the
passage of Hannibal and the collapse of the Carthaginian empire
in Spain.

As is well known, the Gauls remained faithful to their alliance
with Carthage, unlike the Iberians in Catalonia, where Hasdrubal
met stiff resistance in 208 B.C. On the other hand, beyond the
Pyrenees he was able to go peacefully into winter quarters without molestation.[59] Again, Claustre has dug up thirty-five Punic
wine-jars in Ruscino.[60] This shows that Hannibal had not lost
sight of the commercial possibilities of his campaigns. Ruscino,
whose name, accidentally or otherwise, has a Phoenician ring,[61]
and particularly Ensérune, whose acropolis dominated the
southern channel, are the Mediterranean outlets of the Aude
valley, which in turn communicated with the valley of the
Rhône by the pass of Naurouze. This route had been used for
a long time to bring tin from the Cassiterides direct to the

Mediterranean.[62] Claustre's discoveries prove, in our opinion, that while Hannibal was pursuing the destruction of Rome, he was also taking steps to secure and safeguard for Carthage the Western resources which would enable her to dominate the whole Mediterranean world.

These great projects were ruined by the indomitable tenacity of the Romans. Nearly all the Carthaginian resources had gone on the prosecution of the war, and after the defeat at Zama she had to buy peace at a cost of 10,000 talents, payable in fifty annual instalments.[63] Her revenues were reduced to those of her African domains, which had also been severely cut down in size by the encroachments of the Numidians. Nevertheless, without imposing direct taxation, Hannibal was able to restore the situation by stopping tax leakages. The subjection of Carthage had at least the merit of saving military expenditure. By 191 B.C., she had paid off her debt to the Romans. But the loss of the Spanish silver-mines devalued her currency. Silver coins minted in the first half of the second century contain more than fifty per cent copper, while gold was alloyed with silver by means of an ingenious process, which left no trace of the operation on the surface of the coins.[64] In Carthage, the standard of living fell sharply. The tombs in the Odeon burial-ground which are of this period, contain only worthless articles, and the ugliness of the more recent ex-votos from the *tophet*, bears witness to the poverty of the faithful.

REFERENCES

1. Isaiah xxiii, 8.
2. Homer, *Odyssey*, XIV, 288 sqq. and XV, 415, 455–6. Cf. Bérard, *Les Phéniciens et l'Odyssée*, I, pp. 219–20.
3. Ezekiel, xxvii.
4. Herodotus, I, 166–7; V, 4246; VII, 158, 165–7, etc.
5. Plautus, *Poenulus, Belles Lettres* edition, line 977.
6. V, 20 sqq. On the proto-history of Andalusia, see R. Thouvenot, *Essai sur la province romaine de Bétique*, 1940, pp. 34–66.
7. The phrase 'Ships of Tharshish' used in the Bible (I Kings, xxii, 48 and x, 22), for the ships of Hiram which sailed the high seas,

would prove that regular trade relations existed between Tyre and Spain at least from the beginning of the tenth century—if only it were certain that the expression is not an anachronism introduced by a later editor.

8. R. J. Forbes, *Metallurgy in Antiquity*, pp. 237 sqq. R. Dion, *Latomus*, XI, 1952, pp. 306 sqq.

9. It is generally admitted that these relations had already greatly favoured the spread of Megalithic civilization. Archaeological evidence placing them in the Bronze Age has been noted by P. Thouvenot, *op. cit.*, p. 41, n. 2.

10. *Cambr. Anc. History*, VII, p. 172. *Tartessos*, Hamburg, 1922.

11. I, II, 4. Cf. R. Thouvenot, *op. cit.*, pp. 55–7.

12. At least, according to the generally accepted chronology, although this is now the subject of considerable controversy.

13. Pelayo Quintero excavations, *Mem. Junta Sup. Excav.*, 76, pp. 8 and 117, p. 7. On the subject of dates, see P. Cintas, *Expansion*, p. 47.

14. *Op. cit.*, pp. 71 sqq.

15. V, 35.

16. *Cambr. Anc. History*, VII, p. 774.

17. J. Carcopino, *Le Maroc antique*, p. 50.

18. XIX, 63.

19. P. Cintas, *op. cit.*, p. 63 and fig. 82. M. J. Leclant has kindly confirmed that in his opinion it is quite impossible to date this object as late as the sixth century, as was tentatively suggested by P. Cintas, *ibid.*

20. Questioned by E. Frezouls, *B.C.H.*, 1955, pp. 170 sqq. We cannot accept the conclusions there stated. The name Thapsus, which is indisputably Phoenician (cf. H. G. Phlaum, *Inscr. lat. de l'Algérie*, II, p. 1), was given to two African sites, one in Byzacium and the other on the Algerian coast. It was also the name of a site in Sicily, north of Syracuse. This latter site possesses all the features which usually attracted the Carthaginians and which are described in detail by Thucydides. F. Villard and G. Vallet (*Mél. École Française, Rome*, LXVIII, 1956), confirm by a study of pottery that relations between Greece and Sicily were interrupted between the thirteenth and eighth centuries.

21. A. Dupont-Sommer, CRAI, January 9, 1948. At this time the interesting *nuraghe* civilization was developing in Sardinia. It was characterized by an indigenous bronze industry probably influenced by the Phoenicians. Cf. M. Pallotina, *La Sardegna Nuragica, Rome*, 1930. G. Pesce, *Ancient Bronzes from Sardinia*.

22. V, 19–20, cf. above, pp. 246–7.
23. E. Boucher-Colozier, *Mél. École Française, Rome*, LXV, 1953, pp. 89 sqq. (the identification of the 'mysterious isle' as Cerne seems to us unacceptable).
24. J. Jannoray, *Ensérune*, pp. 179–82.
25. Herodotus, IV, 152. On these facts, R. Thouvenot, *op. cit.*, p. 63.
26. On these struggles known to Thucydides, I, 13, cf. Jannoray, *op. cit.*, pp., 469–71, who sees in this text an allusion to the battle of Alalia, the outcome of which was disputed.
27. R. Thouvenot, *op. cit.*, pp. 44–5.
28. *Saturn.*, I, XX, 12.
29. C. Jullian, *Hist. de la Gaule*, I, pp. 383 sqq.; cf. our MC, p. 31.
30. P. Cintas, *op. cit.*, pp. 96 sqq.
31. For maritime relations at this time between Spain and what is today called Orania, cf. the interesting excavations of M. G. Vuillemot at Rachgoun, *Libyca*, III, 1, 1955, pp. 7–62. We were not able to consult the numerous papers devoted to this question at the First Archaeological Congress of Spanish Morocco (brief references by M. Leglay, *Libyca*, III, 2, 1955, p. 289).
32. Diodorus, XIII, 81, 4–5.
33. MC, pp. 39 sqq.
34. VI, 34, 2.
35. Diodorus, XIV, 46, 1.
36. Polybius, III, 24; S. Gsell, HAAN, IV, pp. 123 sqq. Bibliography in A. Piganiol, *Histoire de Rome*, fourth edition, 1954, pp. 68 and 533.
37. See the article by E. Boucher-Colozier quoted above no. 23, whose conclusions appear to us to go too far.
38. J. Jannoray, *op. cit.*, pp. 284 sqq.
39. J. Carcopino, *Promenades historiques au pays de la Dame de Vix*, Paris, 1957.
40. C. Jullian, *Hist. de la Gaule*, I, pp. 415 sqq.
41. M. Rostovtzeff, *Social and Economic History of the Hellenic World*.
42. It should be pointed out that until the third century, the greater part of the Western World except for the Greek colonies did not make use of money. (Cf. A. Piganiol, *op. cit.*, pp. 78 and 87.) Carthage had therefore no need of coinage until she had relations with the East.
43. S. Gsell, HAAN, II, pp. 324–7; IV, pp. 130, 459, note 1 (we do not share the opinion expressed in this last note).
44. *Op. cit.* (above n. 10 and 15).

45. *Op. cit.*, pp. 71 sqq.
46. Pseudo-Plato, *Eryxias*, XVII, 399 e–400 a; cf. S. Gsell, *op. cit.*, pp. 321–2.
47. S. Gsell, *op. cit.*, p. 154. Twenty-two handles of Rhodian vases were found in the houses of Byrsa excavated by Father Féron (*Cahiers de Byrsa*, V, 1955, pp. 61 sqq.).
48. See references to these discoveries in P. Cintas, *Céramique punique*, pp. 149–59.
49. We know that the Carthaginians sold wine, chiefly to the natives of the Balearic Isles.
50. M. Rostovtzeff, *op. cit.*, II, p. 275.
51. Polybius, I, 81, cf. *supra*, p. 123.
52. The figures which follow are taken from Tenney Frank, 'Econ. Survey of the Ancient World', I: *Rome and the Italy of the Republic*, pp. 158 sqq.
53. Lines 1010–15.
54. J. Déchelette, *Manuel d'Archéologie préhistorique*, IV, pp. 823–4.
55. XXXIV, 9, 9. Cf. S. Gsell, *op. cit.*, III, p. 318.
56. J. Jannoray, *op cit.*, pp. 403–6.
57. For J. Carcopino, CRAI, *Rev. des Et. Anc.*, LV, 1953, page 258, the boundary was apparently not the Ebro, but another river with the same name farther south, today called the Jucar.
58. Mentioned in the archaeological journals of Avignon, October 1956.
59. S. Gsell, *op. cit.*, III, pp. 147–8.
60. Shape 132 of the P. Cintas catalogue (*Céramique punique*).
61. S. Gsell, *op. cit.*, I, p. 403.
62. J. Jannoray, *op. cit.*, pp. 292 sqq. J. Carcopino, *Promenade historiques au pays de la Dame de Vix*, pp. 62 sqq.
63. S. Gsell, *op. cit.*, p. 322.
64. *Ibid.*, pp. 323–4. On this point only, to give an idea of his methods, we will quote M. P. Hubac, *Carthage*, p. 194. According to him, this is an allegation made by Cato because he was humiliated to discover that the precious metal content of Roman money was inferior to that of the Carthaginians. It would be difficult, however, to maintain that the analyses made by experts in numismatics are invalid on account of anti-Carthaginian bias!

CHAPTER VII

DIPLOMACY, ARMY AND NAVY

DIPLOMACY

THE supreme aim of Carthaginian policy was to acquire wealth. Most of the treaties made by Carthage with other powers were to regulate maritime and commercial relations. The only imperialistic enterprises which were undertaken were the conquest of Spain and of Africa. As we have seen, these were both dictated by the need to restore the economic situation after an unsuccessful war, by seeking fresh sources of revenue. War was a costly business and the Carthaginians resorted to it only after all the possibilities of subtle diplomacy had been tried. The tradition of such diplomacy goes right back to the origins of the city. For thousands of years, wars, alliances, commerce, and trade had obliged the Oriental potentates to exchange ambassadors, to lay down a protocol, and to draw up a kind of international law. The State letters of Amenophis IV, which have been found in Tell El Amarna, reveal all the secrets of a fourteenth-century B.C. chancellory. Many of these documents deal with Phoenicia. Texts which are even more ancient have been found in Ras Shamra. They show the kings of Ugarit manœuvring, not without danger, between the Hittites and the Egyptians, but, as usual, they contain very little information about Carthage. However, in the treaty signed between Hannibal and Philip V of Macedonia after the battle of Cannae, E. J. Bickerman[1] has discovered the characteristic features of an Oriental pact such as the kings of Tyre and Assyria concluded at the time of the foundation of Carthage. Phrases a thousand years older are mingled in a most surprising manner with Hellenistic expressions: 'It is as though Abraham has become a contemporary of Polybius.'

Like the Romans, the Carthaginians kept in stock a whole gamut of treaties for other countries, graded according to their strength relative to Carthage. Thus they had treaties as between equals for allies like the Etruscans, the Romans, and certain Greek cities; others for rather more subordinate allies like the Elymaei; others again for their Barbarian protégés in Spain, Africa, and Sardinia. Finally there were the Phoenician cities which were considered as sister or daughter States, though they were still expected to subordinate their own interests to those of the head of the family.

The Punic diplomats preserved for a long time the Tyrian monopoly in Tartessus, built up the great Triple Alliance with Persia and Etruria, won the support of the Gauls and the sympathy of Macedonia for Hannibal, and brought Syracuse into the Punic camp in 215 B.C.; they deserve to rank in history with the Venetian ambassadors whose achievements have recently been described by J. Allazard.

THE NAVY

The Carthaginian navy enjoyed a very high reputation among all the peoples round the shores of the Mediterranean. Even the rivals of Carthage were unanimous in praising the stoutness and manœuvrability of her ships, and the skill and experience of her pilots.[2] Her navy was very similar to that of the Greeks, about which we are much better informed.

From very early times, the Mediterranean peoples used two kinds of boats, the long narrow boat, propelled by oars, and intended for war, and the 'round' boat, propelled only by sails, which carried heavier cargoes. These all used the rectangular sail stretched on a yard at right-angles to the mast.

The type of rudder used is worthy of special attention. The Carthaginians, in common with all the ancients, knew nothing of the stern-post rudder, which was not invented until the fourteenth century A.D. They used the rudder-oar, belayed to the side of the boat by two ropes. A bar fastened to the head of the rudder at right-angles to its axis, allowed the steersman to work the device. Pictures on stelae[3] show very clearly the three parts: the bar, the shaft and handle, and the blade.

Boats usually carried a port and a starboard rudder. But Captain Carlini[4] has shown that only one rudder at a time was used; the other was kept in reserve in case of loss or damage. However, according to Eliaenus,[4a] the Carthaginians did have

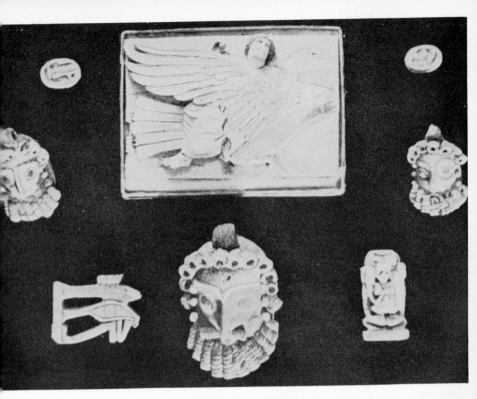

Amulets and ivory lid of a perfume-box (of Greek workmanship): *Musée de Carthage*

Traditional Carthaginian costume depicted on an African stele of the Roman epoch

6. Cedarwood clothes-chest which has been used as a coffin. In front of the chest, and in the glass case above it, the Carthaginian pottery which had formed the funerary furnishings: *Mission archéologique française en Tunisie*

Carthaginian tomb of the sixth century B.C.

two helmsmen on duty at once. He adds that this was not a wise practice and Captain Carlini considers that this system could in fact have serious disadvantages if the movements of both helmsmen were not perfectly synchronized. The same writer admits, however, that in battle the galleys used both rudders simultaneously in order to go about more rapidly, an essential manœuvre in naval warfare. The Carthaginians were in fact past-masters in the use of such tactics. 'Their ships were built to move in all directions with great agility; their oarsmen were experts . . . if some of their vessels were hard pressed by the enemy, their light weight enabled them to withdraw without risk and to make for open water without difficulty. Should the enemy attempt pursuit, they came rapidly about, darted round them or attacked on the beam, continually harassing the Roman ship which could scarcely alter course on account of its great weight and the inexperience of its oarsmen. Many Roman ships were thus sent to the bottom, whereas if a Carthaginian ship was in danger, the others could safely come to its rescue by getting under the stern of the enemy. The Romans could do nothing of this kind. As they were fighting close inshore, they had no room to retreat when they were in difficulties. A ship which was attacked from ahead was wrecked on the sandbanks or on the shore. The enormous weight of their ships and the ignorance of the oarsmen deprived them of the greatest advantage one can have at sea, namely to slip between the enemy ships and to attack from astern those already engaged.'[4b]

The same author also relates the adventures of a Carthaginian captain, who was probably half-Greek, named Hannibal the Rhodian. His mission was to get in touch with the garrison of Lilybaeum (Marsala), which was being blockaded by the Romans by land and sea. He managed to slip into the harbour in a galley. The next day, to prevent his leaving, the Roman consul stationed ten of his best ships on either side of the harbour entrance, and as near as they could get to the sandbanks. Nevertheless, Hannibal was able not only to leave the harbour safely, but to circle round the enemy, raise his oars, stop and defy the Roman fleet, which made no attempt to pursue him. The entrance to the harbour was in fact impeded by sandbanks, between which were only narrow channels. Hannibal had carefully studied their positions. He made for the open sea, then, approaching as though he were coming from Italy, turned his helm so hard in the direction of the tower standing by the water's edge that he could no longer see those towers which face in the direction of Africa. This manœuvre was the only one which would permit him to catch the wind and get back into the harbour. The Romans, incapable of competing with such virtuosity, tried to bar his passage, but the task was beyond them.

The consul Duilius invented a simple counter-measure to the skill of the Carthaginian pilots. It was an inelegant device, unworthy of a real sailor, but effective. His 'crows', gangways armed with grappling-hooks, immobilized the enemy ships and converted a naval engagement into an infantry battle.

The double rudder demanded such a high degree of training that it could only be used in exceptional circumstances. Pictures on stelae clearly show only one rudder in action. One such picture[5] at first led us to believe that a vertical rudder existed, whose axis went down through the hull of the ship, very much in the manner of a modern stern-post rudder. But it was an optical illusion. The vessel is a fairly heavy one and has in reality only one rudder fixed on the port side, so that only the pole and the blade are visible. The non-technical artist drew this blade turned towards the prow, which is obviously absurd. This drawing is unique in that it is probably the only picture from antiquity showing a rudder fixed on the side away from the viewer.

Captain Carlini has explained that the rudder-oar, far from being inferior to the stern-post rudder, made for manœuvrability and was not by any means impracticable for a heavy ship. We have still a great deal to learn about the art of ship-building in ancient times. Progress in underwater archaeology, which makes possible the study of submerged wrecks and their cargoes, will no doubt supply more exact technical information to supplement the meagre documentary and graphic evidence available. Thus the Club for Underwater Research in Tunisia has been able to retrieve the keel of the Mahdia galley, which was 100 feet long and had a beam of over 30 feet; it carried 250 tons of useful cargo.[6]

Although the Carthaginians were remarkable pilots and expert shipwrights, they seem to have made no new discoveries in the art of naval building. It was the Greeks who increased the tonnage and the power of their warships by multiplying the rows of oars. However, the placing of the galley-slaves remains one of the mysteries of naval history. If the shipwrights and engineers of the Carthaginian navy had possessed a marked technical superiority, they would not have been disconcerted by so simple an invention as Duilius' 'crows'. It is also extraordinary that mariners who were bold enough to face the Bay of Biscay and the Moroccan Atlantic, made no attempt to adapt their vessels to the difficulties of the Western oceans by studying the methods of native sailors.

<h3 style="text-align:center">THE ARMY</h3>

The Carthaginian armies had not such a good reputation as the navy. It was generally recognized that the citizens of Carthage possessed exemplary courage and indomitable energy, as was proved by their magnificent behaviour in their hour of greatest trial. But they preferred to entrust the defence of their interests to professional soldiers. This custom, dating from before the sixth century, can be explained by their anxiety to preserve the city's man-power, which could not be easily replaced, and also by their conception of war as an extension of business. It would seem to them quite normal to entrust it to an agent. Moreover, even if they did make greater use of mercenaries than the Greeks, their example was followed by most of their rivals after the fourth century.

From that time onwards, the Carthaginian armies closely resembled those employed by the great Greek cities, and later by the Oriental monarchs.[7] They were all composed of bands of men recruited from a wide variety of nations, who all preserved their national arms and tactics. The main part of the battle units was a phalanx of hoplites equipped in the Greek style with helmet, bronze cuirass, and round shield. They were used for hand-to-hand fighting with lance and short sword. Some Punic stelae[8] show weapons or trophies—figures of men carrying all kinds of weapons, and which were thought of as incarnations of the god of battle. On them can be seen, very sketchily drawn, a large cuirass moulded to the torso, with a kind of tunic below, and greaves to protect the legs; the helmet is represented simply by a triangle.

Other stelae show round shields as well. The Carton chapel in Salammbô[9] contained a ceramic statue of a god wearing a Greek cuirass. He is probably Hadad, the most warlike of the gods in the Phoenician pantheon. Stelae from the Cirta (Constantine) shrine dating from the second and first centuries B.C. also show weapons carved with greater precision than those from Carthage.[10] Several show the round shield, the *aspis* of the Greeks or the *clipeus* of the Romans, together with a sword of a very characteristic shape: the pommel terminates in two superimposed balls at the top, and a V-shaped guard below.[11] This weapon was common among the Italians and the Celts, and was almost certainly introduced into Africa by European mercenaries.

Other stelae illustrate the long oval shield with thickened ridge running down the centre: this is the Greek *thyreos* or the Roman *scutum*, and was made of very light materials. This was also of Western origin and is mentioned in the Roman inventories of weapons captured in Carthage in 149. On one of the Cirta stelae it is shown in a panoply together with a long sword, two javelins, and a conical helmet.[12] These weapons belonged not to a hoplite, but to a light infantryman. The Kbor Klib, a monumental altar dating from the middle of the first century B.C., had a frieze composed of weapons—round shields supported by crossed cavalry sabres, alternating with panoplies which consist of a shaped cuirass hanging on a stake. One of these shields is very similar to the round Macedonian shield, and is ornamented with a fine bust of Artemis in profile.[13] In a similar frieze in Chemtou, a round shield of this kind was decorated with the griffin of Apollo.

The supremacy of the armoured hoplites, which coincided with the most flourishing period of the city republics, was threatened at the beginning of the fourth century by the *peltasts*, or light infantrymen who were less powerful but more mobile. Under Alexander the cavalry played a much more important role. The Carthaginian armies were particularly strong in both cavalry and infantry. Their Balearic slingers were the best in the Ancient World, and fought side by side with Iberians armed with javelins, and Ligurians and Libyans. The javelins mentioned above on the Cirta stele were in all probability Spanish weapons.

Numidian horsemen are represented on the Numidian stelae

from Constantine.[14] Like the infantry, they had no defensive armour other than a small shield, and their only weapon was a javelin which they hurled with a force and accuracy which have become proverbial. But the chief thing which made them such redoubtable fighters was their remarkable skill in riding their diminutive horses bareback and with only a simple bridle. The heavy cavalry, the *corps d'élite*, was chiefly composed of Carthaginian citizens. The Punic equivalent of Mars was, in our opinion, Hadad, who was generally represented mounted; often the horse alone was his emblem. One of the legends concerning the foundation of Carthage relates how an ox-head was found when the foundations of the 'Capitol' were dug. This omen made the site unacceptable as it would have condemned the new city to perpetual servitude. Some distance away, a horse's head was found, and as this was a symbol of might in war, the Capitol was built upon this more propitious site.

If there is anything genuinely Phoenician in this artless story, it would be a reference to Hadad, who in fact was worshipped in Carthage from the earliest times. The horse or head of a horse which appeared with a palm tree on the Carthaginian coinage also represented Hadad. The god himself appears on one stele.[15] He is shown wearing a helmet very like the spiked helmets of the former German army, surmounted by a plumed crest. This is similar to the Italo-Celtic helmet used in the Roman armies, and also to the Assyrian helmet. A long shaft with a small disc on the end to which ribbons are tied, rests across the god's shoulder and probably represents a standard. The Phoenicians probably adopted the use of standards from the Babylonian and Assyrian armies. Among the weapons depicted on the Kbor Klib frieze is a long straight cavalry sword with a hilt in the form of a bird's head. Such swords were used by the Iranian cavalry.

One proof of the 'Westernization' of the Carthaginian armies is their neglect of archers, who constituted an essential part of Assyrian and Persian armies. Arrow-heads have been found in Punic tombs of the seventh and sixth centuries. A magnificent intaglio from Utica shows a nude warrior, with a large helmet on his head, kneeling to draw a bow.[16] But it is only rarely that archers are mentioned in accounts of battles against the Greeks and Romans.

The Carthaginian nobles, who insisted on serving in the army even when the majority of their compatriots were not called upon to do so, were very fond of parading their magnificent armour. Some pieces were too valuable to be used in battle. Hasdrubal, the brother of Hannibal, kept in his camp a silver shield adorned with his own portrait. The Romans captured it and hung it over the gate of the Capitol. Such works of art, with no practical use, were a Greek fashion, as can be seen from the Kbor Klib and Chemtou friezes.[17] A show cuirass has been found in a Punic tomb at Ksour es Saf in Byzacium.[18] It consists of two heart-shaped pieces of bronze, one covering the chest and the other the back. Both pieces are very richly decorated with the same design: at the point of the heart is the head of Athene wearing a helmet; above are two discs. This useless but luxurious piece of armour came not from a Carthaginian workshop, but from one in Campania which specialized in such work, in the third century B.C. It was probably bought or looted by one of Hannibal's soldiers and brought back to Africa. At any rate, its owner regarded it as a specially valuable personal souvenir, since, contrary to custom, he had it buried in his grave with him.

The Carthaginian artillery proved its worth against the Greek towns in Sicily. The Carthaginians were said to have been the inventors of the battering-ram,[19] though the Assyrians already had it earlier. The Carthaginians, to their own disadvantage, probably introduced it to the Europeans. By its aid, Hannibal the Magonid captured Selinus and Himera. He used a version with mobile towers. But the Greeks lost no time in surpassing their rivals. The vital invention was that of the catapult, invented by an engineer from Syracuse at the time of Dionysius the Elder, who used it for the first time against Motya in 398 B.C. The force provided by twisting elastic ropes made it possible to hurl arrows by means of a gigantic bow, or stones by means of a lever. The *onager*, which employed the centrifugal force of a lever worked by a counterpoise, and the *balista* worked by a metal spring, were not invented until the Roman Empire.

The Carthaginians constructed a variety of war-machines called, according to their size, catapults, balistas, or scorpions. In 149 B.C. the Romans commandeered 20,000 such machines which were stored in the arsenals. To replace them, after war had broken out, the Carthaginian women sacrificed their hair. Thousands of limestone bullets, munitions accumulated for the siege, have been found in Carthage. A German general, B. Rathgen, has made a technical study of these missiles, which vary in weight from twelve to over thirty pounds.[20] Some were to be thrown by hand from the top of the ramparts.

The ancients had no field artillery, for their catapults were too heavy and complicated to be readily moved. But the Carthaginians used chariots sometimes and war-elephants always. Chariots were frequently used by the Libyans, especially in the Sahara. The Punic chariots were armoured and were used for making a charge, rather than for transporting troops, as in Homer's time.

Such tactics probably came from Persia. But although chariots were used for centuries, they were never very effective because they were difficult to manœuvre and the horses were too vulnerable. The elephants were much more to be feared. These animals still lived in Barbary in Punic times. They were part of the tropical fauna stranded by the drying up of the Sahara, and as there was not enough vegetation for them to feed on, they were smaller and not so strong as their relatives in Central Africa. They were even less powerful than the Indian elephants. But, like the latter, they could be trained. Fantastic legends[21] praised their sagacity and even their moral and religious sense. They were said to put out forest fires with branches, and to assemble in a Moroccan forest for a solemn purification ceremony by the light of the new moon. They were therefore regarded as 'celestial animals'. In spite of their legendary virtues, the Carthaginians never thought of using elephants for any but warlike purposes, and even this idea was suggested by the example of the Greek kings. In the plains of the Indus Alexander had had to contend with Porus' elephants, and his romantic imagination had doubtless been fascinated as much by their magnificent presence and psychological effect in war as by their effectiveness.

After this, the Greek generals who disputed his kingdom also used war-elephants, while Pyrrhus of Epirus brought some with him on his expedition to the West, thus giving the Romans their first sight of this strange animal. Their peasant sense of humour dubbed them 'Lucanian oxen'[22] from the name of the district where they first met them.

The Carthaginians, too, thought they could put them to good use. Thus the presence of these tropical animals in Carthaginian armies, far from being a survival of Oriental tradition, was yet another example of Greek influence. As the Carthaginians were then at the height of their power, it was an easy matter to capture a very large number of elephants very quickly. We shall see later how and where they caught them. When the great wall was built across the Carthaginian isthmus, enough stables were incorporated in the foundations for 300 elephants. Several hundreds were used against the Romans in Sicily, against Regulus and his mercenaries, and in the conquest of Spain.

Finally, we know that Hannibal accomplished the *tour de force* of dragging forty unfortunate elephants over the Pyrenees and the Alps, to die amid the rigours of winter in Piedmont. One only survived, who became henceforth the bearer of the 'one-eyed leader'. The treaty concluded after Zama deprived the Carthaginians of their remaining elephants and forbade them to train any more of these animals. They had been using them for barely sixty years and it is doubtful whether they had been of any great value. Their psychological effect, however, was certainly tremendous. The Roman legionaries and the rebellious mercenaries were terrified of them, as were the mountain tribes in the Alps. After the defeat of Regulus, the Romans were unwilling to give battle in open country, for fear of these monsters. Their vast size, their sword-like tusks, the astounding skill of their 'snake-like hand', and their ferocious trumpeting, filled the soldiers with terror.

To increase their almost supernatural reputation, the Carthaginians dressed them up and decked them out like actors. Their *mahouts* were doubtless dressed in Oriental garb and had Indian names, even when they were natives of Africa. To make them fiercer and more terrifying the elephants were given prisoners to trample to death, as in India. The horses detested their smell as much as that of camels, and stampeded at their approach.

From the point of view of tactics, the elephants were intended to play the part of tanks in modern armies, to attack heavy infantry and entrenched positions. Their naturally thick hide was reinformed with armour, and turrets full of archers or slingers were perched on their backs. The best defence against their shock tactics was flexibility. The Greek phalanx, too compact to give way easily, could not adapt itself without great difficulty, but the Roman legions, by virtue of their articulated *manipuli*, possessed the mobility which could bring them victory. Nevertheless Regulus committed the fatal error of massing his men into a human rampart, which could not withstand the elephants' assault. Scipio, on the other hand, employed the kind of tactics recommended today against armoured units. He formed lanes or corridors within his battle-legions into which the elephants plunged, only to be encircled and cut off.

But these Carthaginian 'tanks' were not machines. Their intelligence, which enabled them easily to answer to their names, was counteracted by their extremely nervous temperament. The shouts, the sound of trumpets, the pain of their wounds plunged them into a murderous rage which was just as dangerous to their masters as to their enemies. Their riders then had no option but to slay them by driving an iron wedge into an eye-ball with a mallet, a procedure said to have been invented by Hasdrubal, the brother of Hannibal.

THE MERCENARIES

The most difficult problem Carthage had to solve in connexion with the army was the system of command. Professional fighting-men who felt no particular loyalty to the Republic were not very amenable to discipline. There were two possible solutions: the first was the one adopted by the Greeks from the fourth century— they dealt only with *condottieri*. Such leaders, however, might have political ambitions which would be all the more dangerous to the Carthaginians, because they were of Hellenic nationality. One of these Wallensteins of ancient times might very well have conceived the idea of transforming the Carthaginian State into a monarchy, to his own advantage.

This ambition did occur to at least one of them, the Macedonian Ophelas.[23] The story of his career gives some idea of the manners and customs of mercenaries, as well as of the 'truceless war', which since Flaubert's *Salammbô* has become too well known to be related in detail. During the last few years of the fourth century B.C., Agathocles, the tyrant of Syracuse, conceived the plan of freeing Sicily from the Carthaginian menace by carrying the war into Africa. But although he managed to conquer most of the Carthaginian hinterland, his exhausted troops soon became rebellious when they found themselves isolated in enemy territory while the Carthaginian army, which still remained in Sicily, threatened their homeland. There was at this time in Cirene a Macedonian named Ophelas who had once fought for Alexander, and was now an officer in the army of King Ptolemy of Egypt. Like many of his companions, he felt the urge to make himself a king. He had already cast covetous glances towards the West, and had employed geographers to make charts of the African coasts as far as the Atlantic. Agathocles skilfully made use of his ambitions. In return for his help, he promised to go back to Sicily and leave Carthage to Ophelas. The latter allowed himself to be taken in, and sent to Greece to recruit an army of mercenaries, in particular from Attica which he knew well, as he had married an Athenian woman of noble birth, descended from the great Miltiades, victor of the battle of Marathon. The Carthaginians got to know of these activities and sent to Athens two ambassadors, Synalos and Bodmelkart, to thwart them. In their honour, the Demos published a fine-sounding decree, but did nothing to prevent the enrolment of troops.

Ophelas was therefore able to gather together more than 10,000 infantrymen and 600 horsemen. In no way daunted by the climate, he set off at the height of summer along the African coast towards Carthage. After suffering terribly from thirst and snake-bites, the Greeks rejoined their compatriots, whose headquarters were in Tunis. Agathocles spared no effort to alleviate their sufferings. It is even said that knowing the very Greek tendencies of Ophelas, he sent his own son Heraclides to keep him company. Then, taking advantage of the general feeling of well-being, and of the fact that Ophelas' soldiers had dispersed to look for food, he gathered his own troops round him and made a most eloquent address—for he was as eloquent in speech as he was cunning in strategy. He told them that Ophelas was a traitor, whose base designs he had only just discovered. It was time to be rid of him. At once the Sicilians sprang to arms and Ophelas, taken by surprise and unarmed, fell under their blows. His mercenaries wasted no time weeping over his dead body. Agathocles, having surrounded and disarmed them, made another fine speech. It was not difficult to persuade them to accept service under him. They were not particular who their leader was, as long as there was some prospect of plundering Carthage. As for the Carthaginians, they could have seized this opportunity to attack the Greeks, but the magistrate Bomilcar, having recently lost his colleague in battle, chose just this moment to attempt to make himself dictator in his turn, with the help of the mercenaries in his service. According to some authors he was in league with Agathocles. But the people of Carthage put up a stout resistance against these hard-bitten warriors who were hardly less to be feared than their enemies. Decimated in street fighting and cut off in the suburbs, the mercenaries were obliged to surrender. Bomilcar was captured and crucified in the market-place. Through the long hours of his suffering he is said to have had the courage and endurance to remind his compatriots of the injustices committed by the aristocracy against the best defenders of their native land.

It may be noted in passing that it was atrocities like these which dictated the tone of Flaubert's novel. But it is equally evident that the Greeks were just as immoral, treacherous, and cruel as the Carthaginians. This unleashing of unscrupulous personal ambition, this violent contrast between the boundless exaltation of a few individuals and the subjection of the multitude, were very characteristic of the whole Hellenistic period, and particularly of that period of unutterable confusion which for a whole generation followed the death of Alexander. The break-up of the old social framework, in the cities first of all, and then in the newly created Macedonian empire, led to the collapse of all moral values and the triumph of force and opportunism. It let loose upon the world wild beasts in human form whose ambition had been over-estimated by the conqueror's example, but who had none of his nobility of soul.

Never, perhaps, in the whole history of the world, did adventurers, conquering tyrants, and those who make war for the sheer pleasure of it, have such a wonderful opportunity. And never were the peace-lovers, rich or poor, so constantly threatened. The system of raising mercenary armies put them at the mercy of the brutal and licentious soldiery, for the very men they hired to defend them were only waiting to seize the first opportunity to turn on the hated 'townsfolk'. Carthage, with its vast wealth so unequally distributed, was in greater danger than any other city, for the mercenaries could act as champions of the proletariat. As we have seen, the 'truceless war' was, more than anything else, a social crisis.

THE SYSTEM OF COMMAND

The Carthaginian government had taken precautions against such dangers, and by keeping command in the hands of its aristocracy, it sought to keep them at bay. The N.C.O.'s were recruited from the ranks of the mercenaries themselves. This system, which was very similar to that employed for many years in the Roman Empire, could have given good results if the officers had had sufficient authority and prestige. Yet the suspicious security agents of the Hundred Magistrates seemed to make it their special task to deprive their officers systematically of both. If one reads the accounts of the First Punic War, one is reminded more than once of Venice, and of the treacherous snares laid by the Council of Ten to catch their soldiers of fortune.

At the very beginning of hostilities, Hanno, the commander of the garrison of Messina, was crucified for allowing himself to be surprised by the Romans and surrendering. Another Hanno considered himself very fortunate to get off with a fine of 6,000 pieces of gold after being twice defeated. A colleague of his, Hannibal, even managed to keep his command after being beaten by Duilius, but his soldiers took it upon themselves to crucify him. In 253 B.C., after Regulus had been defeated, the Hundred Magistrates had Hasdrubal crucified because he failed to recapture Palermo, and in 241 B.C., the admiral, Hanno, because he had been defeated in the Aegates Islands.

The harshness of the Carthaginian government towards its generals was proverbial. Roman statesmen considered it to be one of the causes of the downfall of their enemies. Be that as it may, their Senatorial class sinned in the opposite direction by protecting its own most dishonest and incompetent generals, in the interests of class solidarity. The implacable attitude of the Hundred was aggravated by the fact that their commanders could not always be trusted. During the same Sicilian War, an admiral named Hannibal, having lost his fleet, avoided punishment by keeping his defeat secret and asking for permission to attack the Romans who outnumbered him. Permission was granted, whereupon Hannibal's envoy revealed the bad news, adding that the admiral deserved no censure, as he had already acted in advance on the Council's decision. In actual fact, the fate of an unsuccessful commander depended less on what he had done than on his political allies. Although we are very inadequately informed about internal politics in Carthage, it seems that military leaders were sometimes chosen outside the ranks of the ruling faction and probably by design. Thus more than a hundred years after the fall of the Magonids, members of the fallen dynasty were entrusted with important commands. This might seem at first paradoxical, if we had not witnessed a rather similar case in France under the Third Republic. Or, if a more ancient comparison is preferred, the kings of Sparta, who derived their power ultimately from the Lacedaemonian aristocracy, remained at the head of the army, although at the slightest misdeed, they were the object of sanctions imposed by the Five Magistrates, whom Aristotle expressly compares with the Hundred Magistrates of Carthage.[24] We therefore find ourselves faced with a particular case of a general historical problem, namely, the natural conflict between military power and the institutions of a republican State.

THE RULE OF THE BARCIDS

Carthage, however, seems to have overcome this difficulty which proved fatal to so many other cities of antiquity. In spite of much idle speculation, which S. Gsell[25] has dealt with as it deserves, there never were in fact any serious conflicts between the Barcids and the government of their country, from the beginning of the conquests in Spain right up to the battle of Zama. But this happy state of affairs was, in our opinion, more apparent than real; the military power was in fact no longer subordinated to the civil power. The maintenance of legal forms was only a façade to hide the setting up of a *de facto* monarchy on the model of that of the Macedonian kings who succeeded Alexander, rather than a product of the Carthaginian tradition.

The Macedonian kings were in effect little more than *condottieri* who ruled over territory they had conquered.[26] Their authority was not based on any national tradition, nor on the consent of their subjects. It rested on a kind of divine right, but the divinity to whom they owed their monarchy was none other than Tyche, the spirit of chance. The real source of their power was the confidence of their troops, and that was based on a more or less superstitious faith in the star of their leader. The test of battle made him legitimate. The conquering leader assumed the royal diadem with his trophy. Should he lose a battle later, he also lost his crown. However, it did happen that a family managed to create the impression that it was in some way predestined to victory. In this way dynasties came into being, but their members were in no way exempt from proving their worth in battle.

The Barcids governed Spain from 237 to 210 B.C., at first with the support of their army and then by virtue of the prestige which Hamilcar's victories conferred on his family. Legally, no doubt, they continued to represent the State of Carthage. But the role of the Carthaginian Assembly and the Senate as far as Hasdrubal and Hannibal were concerned, was limited to ratifying the commanders elected by the soldiers. Now citizens of Carthaginian nationality were in a very small minority among the soldiers; they certainly occupied the highest ranks, but we know that the Hellenistic armies ran their affairs on very democratic lines, and off the battlefield, the votes of officers counted very little more than those of privates.[27]

Moreover, Hannibal seems to have encouraged the international character of his armies; Greeks held important positions, as for example, Hippocrates and Epicydes who decided the renewal of the campaigns in Sicily. An elected general exercised sovereign powers not only in the conduct of operations and the organization of conquered territories, but also in the political and economic administration of a province, and in the conduct of diplomacy both local and on the highest level. When Rome became alarmed at the advance of Carthaginian domination in Spain it approached first Hamilcar, in 231, and then Hasdrubal in 226 B.C. It was with the latter in person that the treaty of that year was concluded which made the Ebro the dividing-line between the Carthaginian and Roman spheres of influence.

Again, on the occasion of the siege of Saguntum, the Roman envoys applied to Hannibal. It was he who, doubtless in order to have some sort of moral support, referred the matter to the Carthaginian Senate, which hastily passed back to Hannibal the responsibility for dealing with the situation. During the Italian campaign Hannibal personally concluded the alliance with Philip of Macedonia;[28] its clauses were binding, not only on the entire Punic empire, but on its allies, such as Utica, as well. The treaty of Syracuse, however, was drawn up by plenipotentiaries of Hannibal, and ratified in Carthage.

On such occasions Hannibal was assisted by a kind of committee of several Carthaginian Senators. Three of these signed the treaty with Macedonia. But these delegates seem to have acted as auxiliary members of Hannibal's staff rather than as supervisors sent from Carthage to keep an eye on the general.

This state of affairs is very like that which existed in Rome at the end of the Republic, when the Senate allowed its proconsuls in the provinces a high degree of autonomy. In Rome, as in Carthage, republican magistrates found themselves invested with powers which in fact went far beyond those of their legal status. The result of this unbalanced division of authority in Rome is well known. It seems likely that the outcome, so far as Carthage was concerned, might have been very much the same, had Hannibal been victorious.

According to Polybius[29] there was a rumour current in Carthage that Hasdrubal was planning to make himself king. Doubtless such rumours were propagated by the political enemies of the Barcids, which does not necessarily mean that they were not without foundation. Hasdrubal's decision to found a new capital in Spain and to give it the name of Carthage (today called Cartagena) had a symbolic significance: in Hellenistic times the founding of a city was the supreme act of kingship;[30] it often followed a victory in which the leader's suitability for kingship had been demonstrated. Moreover, the *Ktistes* became a hero in the town he had created and henceforth became the object of a cult; it has been proved that the divine honours which were conferred on the kings who succeeded Alexander derived essentially from this cult in the cities.[31]

Mention has been made of E. Forrer's view[32] that the word

kart meant not only 'town', but 'capital'. Hasdrubal was thus in effect transferring to Spain the seat of the Tyrian empire, in precisely the same way that Dido had transferred it to Africa. Just as the Roman emperor was considered as another founder of that city, and identified with Romulus, so Hasdrubal became a 'Father of the State' and placed himself on the same footing as Dido. Moreover, it is very possible that he turned to his own advantage an ancient body of religious and mystical lore which forecast a further emigration of the Tyrian people. The importance in Rome of the legends of Troy at the time of the foundation of the Empire is well known. Now, a semi-legendary story, reported by Diodorus,[33] recounts that the Carthaginians had sought to gain possession of an ocean island—probably Madeira —with a view to migrating there if they were driven out of Africa. From the sixth century, therefore, they envisaged the possibility of fresh peregrinations towards the mysterious West, the source of so much of their wealth. Hasdrubal managed to use these prophecies to justify his audacious enterprises, and to clear himself of any suspicion of impiety.

He built a magnificent palace in Cartagena and married an Iberian princess. There can be little doubt that the Iberian tribes, who knew no other authority than that of kings, conferred the royal title upon him. When later Scipio, in his turn, made himself master of Spain, the natives, quite naturally, wanted to proclaim him king, and he had great difficulty in persuading them not to do so. Such an idea would probably not have occurred to them if the Carthaginian leaders had shown the same scruples.

All the peoples of antiquity regarded the monarchy not only as a political and military office, but also as a religious title. The king was the natural intermediary between gods and men. The Phoenician *meleks*, who were priests like those of Israel, surrounded themselves with a ceremonial which was copied from the great royal courts of Egypt and Babylon and which emphasized the holy nature of their office. In the fourth century, Gisgo, the son of Hanno the Great who had been crucified in the marketplace after the failure of his *coup d'état*, was recalled to power to repair the results of a serious defeat inflicted on the Carthaginians by the Greeks. The people handed his enemies over to him so that he could take his revenge; Gisgo had them brought before the

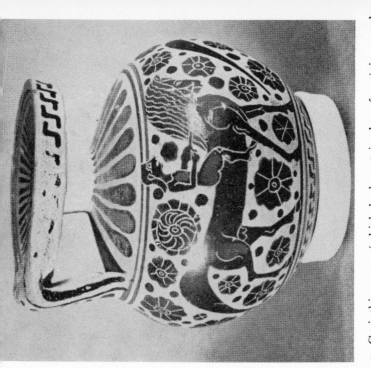

7. Corinthian vase (which had contained perfume) imported into Carthage (sixth century B.C.)

Male mask with ear-ring and nose-ring (sixth century B.C.):
Musée de Carthage

8. Vase of Alexandrine make imported into Carthage (third century B.C.)
Carthaginian war god in the form of a horseman of Hannibal's armies

people in chains and having made them prostrate themselves face to the ground, he placed his foot on their necks three times;[34] after that, he set them free. In this piece of ritual can be recognized a custom of the Pharaohs which was adopted by the kings of Israel, and which later, through the influence of the Bible, became part of the Byzantine triumphal ceremony.[35] In principle, it was applied to captives from foreign countries. The Barcids must have preserved these traditional practices. Moreover, they appear to have placed themselves under the special protection of the Melkart of Gades who enjoyed an immense prestige, not only among the Phoenicians, but throughout the West.[36]

This god, whose name means 'God of the city', and who was the patron of Tyre, was probably regarded as the source of political power, as Jupiter Optimus Maximus was by the Romans.[37] The three Numidian kings of the Masinissa family claimed him as their ancestor. Pompey, Caesar, and Hadrian all attributed their victories to his intervention. In this respect also, therefore, Hannibal was behaving much less like a republican general than like a veritable Greek *basileus*, called upon to reign, not over a nation, but over a world-wide empire.

Against this background it is easier to see the strategy of Hannibal, and of the Barcids in general, in its true perspective. We have already seen that it was dictated by economic considerations just as much as by strictly military intentions. But it differed fundamentally from the former policy of the Punic oligarchy, for whom war was really only business conducted by different means, and for whom it was always strictly subordinated to considerations of financial prudence. In the sweeping range of his ideas and in his temerity, which sometimes exceeded all reasonable bounds, Hannibal was a military leader whose war policies came straight from Alexander.

The son of Hasdrubal had in fact derived all his military education from books and from Greek masters. From Alexander he borrowed the idea of shock troops, few in number but powerful and mobile, who brushed aside all obstacles to reach the enemy's vital spots. The importance of cavalry and the device of annihilating the enemy by encirclement from the wings, which were the most remarkable features of his tactics, all follow from this idea.

Like Alexander also, Hannibal sought to use war to set up an entirely new political order. Polybius bears witness to the fact that he wanted to make Carthage mistress of the whole of the Mediterranean world, an aspiration as far removed as possible from the narrow mercantile ambitions of traditional Carthaginian policy. Unfortunately we know nothing of the plans he had in mind for bringing this about, once Rome was defeated. Almost certainly he intended to use the immense resources and man-power of the Celtic world; he probably envisaged an Italian con-federation freed from the domination of Rome;[38] Campania would probably have been a leading member by virtue of her superior industrial potential.[39] The very keen democratic ideals which were widespread in Southern Italy, the meeting-place of Mediterranean peoples, might have served to bond together such a vast confederation. Then Carthage, enriched by the spoils of all who had fought for her, would become the centre of a great new empire whose might would easily have dominated the already exhausted Greek kingdoms. But it would have been a new Carthage, rescued from her traditional conservatism and from the suspicion and greed which had made her odious in the eyes of so many nations, but which, at the same time, had been the means of preserving her true genius. In this great cosmopolitan city, where the Phoenicians would have been henceforth a minority, would the Carthaginians have succeeded in defending against the pressure of Greek civilization the language, the view of life and of the world, and the religion, which up till then they had so jealously preserved?

REFERENCES

1. E. J. Bickerman, 'An Oath of Hannibal', *Transac. American Philolog. Assoc.*, LXXV, 1944; 'Hannibal's Covenant', *Amer. Journ. of Philology*, LXXIII, 1, 1952, pp. 1–23. The treaty is a pact (*berit*), that is to say it does not include the cursing of whichever side should break it. It is the sole example of this kind of document. The Greek translation made by Polybius is sufficiently clumsy in several places to allow the original Phoeni-cian text to show through it.

2. J. G. Février, 'Les origines de la marine phénicienne', *Rev. hist. et d'hist. gén. de la civilisation*, 1935, pp. 97–125, pl. I–III.

3. M. Hours-Miedan, *Cahiers de Byrsa*, I, 1950, pp. 67 sqq., pl. XXXVIII.

4. M. Carlini, 'Le gouvernail dans l'Antiquité', *Association technique maritime et aéronautique*, June 1935, rebutting the theories of Lefebvre des Noettes, *De la marine antique à la marine moderne*, Paris, 1935.

4a. X. Eliaenus, IX, 40.

4b. Polybius, I, 51.

5. M. Hours-Miedan, *op. cit.*, pl. XXXVIII c. Cf. MC, p. 47.

6. G. de Frondeville, *Les visiteurs de la mer*, Chap. VII.

7. M. Launey, *Recherches sur les armées hellénistiques*, Paris, 1949–50.

8. *C.I.S.*, 269, 1353; C. Picard, *Catalogue Mus. Alaoui, Nlle série*, I, Cb 816 and stelae from the *tophet* (details not yet published).

9. L. Carton, *Un sanctuaire punique découvert à Carthage*, Paris, 1929.

10. A. Berthier and R. Charlier, *Le sanctuaire d'El Hofra à Constantine*, pl. XVIII.

11. *Ibid.*, pl. XV 3 and XVII a.

12. *Ibid.*, pl. XVII a.

13. MC, pl. 72.

14. Cf. le Cavalier d'Abizar, L. Leschi, *Algérie Antique*, p. 196.

15. G. Ch.-Picard, *op. cit.*, pl. 70.

16. P. Cintas, *Karthago*, p. 35, fig. 10.

17. G. Ch.-Picard, *op. cit.*, pl. 71.

18. MC, pl. 71.

19. Tertullian, *De Pallio*, 1.

20. *Zeitschr. für historische Waffenkunde*, 1910, pp. 236 sqq. Trad. *Rev. tun.*, XVIII, 1911, pp. 291 sqq.

21. Recorded by King Juba, they have been handed down to us chiefly through X. Eliaenus, *Nat. animalium*, VI, 56; VII, 2, etc.

22. Pliny, VIII, 16.

23. Diodorus, XX, 40.

24. Aristotle, II, 82.

25. S. Gsell, HAAN, II, p. 256.

26. Cf. eg. E. J. Bickerman, *Institutions des Séleucides*, pp. 11 sqq. A. Aymard, *L'Orient et la Grèce antique*.

27. On the 'democracy' of the armies of the Barcids, cf. E. J. Bickerman, 'Hannibal's Covenant' (*supra*, n. 1), p. 7.

28. *Ibid.*, p. 18. Mr Bickerman supposes that Hannibal had only the

right to conclude a *berit* (cf. *supra*, n. 1), but not a treaty, which would require ratification by the Carthaginian Senate. He must have deliberately chosen this incomplete form of agreement so as not to involve Carthage in diplomatic difficulties with Egypt, who was on bad terms with Macedonia. If this interpretation can be accepted, it would confirm the subtlety of Carthaginian diplomacy, which gave birth to the legend of 'Punic honour' among her adversaries.

29. III, 8. 2, 4.
30. Cf. A. Alföldi, *Museum Helveticum*, XI, 3, 1954, pp. 139 sqq.
31. E. J. Bickerman, *Institutions des Séleucides*, pp. 242 sqq.
32. *Supra*, Ch. II, n. 3.
33. *Supra*, Ch. VI, n. 22 and *infra*, Ch. VIII, n. 83.
34. Polyaenus, *Strategemata*, V, 11.
35. For Egypt, cf., for example, the Karnak stele, R. Breasted, *Ancient Records*, II, 655–62, the Silsilis relief, G. Maspero, *Hist. Anc. de l'Orient*, II, p. 217. For Mesopotamia, the Naramsin stele (MAO, II, p. 674, fig. 469). In Rome, the statues of Hadrian in the style of Hierapytna. For Byzantium, see A. Grabar, *L'Empereur dans l'Art Byzantin*, pp. 127–9.
36. R. Dussaud, *Syria*, XXV, 1949, p. 205.
37. Cf. J. Morgenstern, 'The King God among the Western Semites', *Atti dell' VIII Congresso Internaz. di Storia delle Religioni*, Rome, 1955, p. 257. The views put forward by this author on the evolution of Phoenician theology seem to us questionable; but he has certainly emphasized the link between the cult of Melkart and the development of Tyrian royalty.
38. E. J. Bickerman, 'Hannibal's Covenant', *Amer. Journ. of Philology*, LXXIII, 1, 1952, p. 19.
39. Hannibal had promised Capua that she should be the capital of the Italian Confederation: Livy, XXIII, 102.

CHAPTER VIII

GREAT EXPEDITIONS

CARTHAGE was never in political control of more than one-thousandth part of Africa, at the most, or one-third of Barbary. But for more than ten centuries she was practically the only link between the Mediterranean world and the peoples, black or white, who lived in the western half of the continent, from the Gulfs of Sydra and Gabes in the Mediterranean to the Moroccan Atlantic, and from there to the Gulf of Guinea. At first, the Tyrian colonists had certainly no intention of penetrating into this immense and inhospitable land; but they soon realized that it contained very tempting riches. The dangers and fatigues which had to be faced and overcome to reach them were not sufficient to deter brave and enterprising men, even though they had only elementary equipment at their disposal.

THE SAHARA

This tempting land fell into three parts: Barbary, the Sahara, and the Negro territories. It must be remembered, however, that the very pronounced differences which separate these regions today were much less marked at the beginning of the first millennium B.C. The flora and the fauna of Barbary, for example, were much more tropical.[1] We have already spoken of elephants, but at that time there were also panthers and ostriches, which have now been extinct for more than a century; crocodiles, which are now encountered only rarely in some of the Sahara *wadis*, were then common in the rivers of Southern Morocco. Regulus, for example, claimed that he had met an enormous serpent (probably a boa) in the River Medjerda (Bagradas), and that it had to be destroyed by siege-artillery. Although the Sahara was gradually drying up, it had not reached its present-day desert state;[2] nor was it as vast, because of the greater extent of the North Sudan lakes. It was therefore not too difficult to cross, providing that the great areas of shifting sands (the Ergs) were avoided. The least difficult overland route was by way of the corridor of oases in the Fezzan; it was also possible to follow the coast of Mauretania. These routes led to the great rivers and virgin forests of the tropical zone. The Mediterranean people were aware of the existence of the Niger and generally imagined it to be a continuation of the Nile.[3]

In these vast spaces lived both black and white peoples and, again, their territories were no more rigorously separated than they are today. Gsell,[4] Gautier[5] and others appear to have thought that during the greater part of antiquity the Libyans did not live south of the Atlas and that the desert was inhabited solely by Negroes; and furthermore that the conquest of the Sahara by the Berbers at the time of the Roman Empire was the result of the Mahgreb nomads being driven back by the advance of agriculture. Apparently the Romans, while making life impossible for them in their former territories, were supposed to have given them the means of gaining new ones by introducing the camel, which had hitherto been very rare in Africa.

This tempting explanation, which was for a long time unchallenged, has now been rejected by historians of Roman Africa,[6] as well as by experts on the civilizations of the Sahara[7] and Negro territories.[8] In the first place, it is contradicted by the writers of antiquity. Pliny, for example, states that the frontier between Getulia and Ethiopia, that is to say between blacks and whites, was on a river called Nigris, which, from its description, must be our Niger. Above all, excavations made during the last thirty years or so in the Sahara,[9] and the study of painted or carved figures on its rocks, make it more obvious every day that this desert was not so dried up as it is now and was the centre of a white civilization. The customs of the Sahara Libyans to whom it belonged differed in several respects from those of their fellow-Libyans, whom the Romans called Gutules, on the pre-Sahara steppes. For example, they wore short hide tunics instead of loose cloth garments. But they came under the cultural influence of Barbary, and, probably during the last centuries before the Christian era, they adopted the Libyan alphabet, which they still use to this day. The name Getulia was therefore broadly used to cover the whole of the Sahara.

The centre of this empire of the desert sands was the present-day Fezzan, situated on the most direct route from the Mediterranean to the Sudan. There, throughout antiquity, lived the Garamantes, who were well known to both the Greeks and the Romans. Excavations conducted by Italian archaeologists on the site of the Garamantes' capital, not far from Djerma (the present-day town whose name is derived from Garamantes), prove beyond doubt that the inhabitants were not Negroes; ethnically they were closely related to the Touaregs and their civilization was purely Libyan. Moreover Herodotus speaks of their continual wars with the Troglodytes, who apparently lived in the Tibesti Mountains.[10] They pursued them with light chariots drawn by four horses, and they also used these vehicles to cross the Hamadas whose stony, but fairly level, ground was suitable for this means of transport.

We possess archaeological evidence of the greatest interest which confirms and illustrates the information which Herodotus collected in Cyrenaica. A number of cave-paintings show warriors with plumes, armed with javelins, driving chariots drawn by three or four horses; most of these were found in the Tassili-n-Ajjer, and others in the Ahaggar and Adrar-n-Iforas.[11]

Experts are generally agreed that the oldest pictures of this kind date from the second half of the second millennium B.C. Earlier paintings belonged to a civilization which still used oxen as beasts of burden. These early paintings extended over a long period, and the most recent, very roughly drawn, are sometimes accompanied by pictures of men on horseback. Later, in the first centuries of the Christian era, horses are replaced by camels. The horses and chariots must have been those of the Garamantes and bear witness to their supremacy over most of the Central Sahara.

Again, the style of these cave-paintings is very different from that of the Egyptian frescoes. The representation of horses in the 'flying gallop' position, and the use of the spiral motif, are reminiscent of Aegean influences. One theory has been put forward that the Garamantic civilization was started by Aegeans taking part in the invasion by the 'People of the Sea', and who landed on the coast of Cyrenaica. But this theory must be treated with some scepticism in view of the complete absence of any material evidence of a Creto-Mycenaean colony in Africa.[12] In the present state of our knowledge, it would be wiser to attribute the introduction of the chariot to the Phoenicians, who had been very strongly influenced by the Aegean civilization and who began to frequent the shores of Libya in the last centuries of the second millennium. In any case, we should bear in mind the coincidence between the arrival of the Tyrians on the Tunisian coasts and the formation at the same time of a vast Libyan empire in the Sahara. This unification of the desert was to make it much easier for the Carthaginians to penetrate deep into the hinterland.

Beyond the great shifting sands (Ergs) in the west, other Libyan tribes, of whom the most important were the Pharusians and the Negrites, controlled another route which led across Mauretania to Senegal. Their civilization was very similar to that of the Garamantes, for numerous pictures of chariots have been found all over this region.[13] Later, the Pharusians adopted another mode of transport which is described by Strabo:[14] they rode on horses which had a leather water-bottle slung beneath them. This custom still survives among the Touaregs of the Sudan.[15]

The Sahara has always had two types of inhabitants: the nomads of Libyan descent and the farmers who have settled in the oases. The latter, who today are called Haratim, are able to resist the fevers which prevent white men from settling round the watering-places. On the other hand, they cannot withstand the great variations of temperature which occur in open country. The war-like nomads exploit the settlers whom they hold in subjection. This complementary state of affairs, the result of natural circumstances, was already known in antiquity. Groups of Negroes lived then, as now, in the most northerly oases of the desert, and even in Barbary, where they must have been imported, mostly as slaves. It was once thought that these 'nordic Ethiopians' might belong to the same red-brown race as the Peuhls in Senegal.[16] However, a portrait of a Negro discovered in the Antonine Baths in Carthage, which dates from the middle of the second century A.D. and which very probably represents a prisoner captured by the Romans in the Sahara, near Oran or in Morocco, has the same snub nose as the present-day Sudanese, and not the much thinner nose of the Hamite race.[17] Moreover, there is nothing to prove that the inhabitants of the Tibesti, who have very individual ethnic peculiarities, are the remnants of a population which was once more widespread. When Mediterranean travellers reached the Sudan, they encountered Pigmies like those found today in Equatorial Africa. It seems likely that their habitat was much more extensive, for they were found from Senegal to Nubia.

The Asian Phoenicians, who in all probability came originally from the shores of the Red Sea, had long been in the habit of trading with tropical Africa. On their own account, or on behalf of the Egyptians, they made their way to the Punt territory on the Somali coast, bringing back ivory, precious woods, wild animals, skins and, above all, incense. In this way, Hiram and his ally Solomon got gold, ivory, apes, and peacocks.[18] It was probably not very long before it occurred to the Carthaginians that similar products could be got in Western Africa: there were no aromatic gums, but on the other hand the gold-mines of Senegal were already famous, and remained so until the end of the Middle Ages.

It was not necessary for the Carthaginian merchants to go to the Sudan themselves. In Africa, as in Europe, they were able to use native intermediaries for a long time. The caravans, in return for the payment of heavy tolls, were protected by the Garamantes and went as far as Tripolitania. The Pharusians from Mauretania went as far as Cirta, nearly two thousand miles from their native land.[19] Lastly, Barbary itself produced valuable commodities, especially wild animals and ivory.

The great hunting expeditions were one of the most remarkable ways of exploiting Africa ever used by the ancients. Of the African animals, monkeys were the first to be appreciated in Mediterranean countries, and remained the longest in demand. Paintings found in Crete prove that Minos, like Solomon, kept some in his palace. Even today very ugly, but amusing, monkeys still live in the Kabyle Mountains, but they were far more numerous there in ancient times.[20] The solemn philosopher Posidonius, who saw them during a halt in Morocco, was very amused at their antics.

One of Agathocles' lieutenants, Eumachus, describes how he had seen a district in Krumeria where man and baboons lived together on friendly terms; the Carthaginians bred them as pets. Hanno, Plautus' *Poenulus*, recognized his nephew by a bite which he had got from playing with a monkey when he was a child. One day King Masinissa sent for some Greeks who had come to his kingdom to buy monkeys; he asked them whether the women of their country had no children, since they were reduced to playing with monkeys.

From early times wild beasts, especially lions and panthers, were trapped for the menageries of the aristocracy. A certain Hanno, who may have been the explorer, was said to have kept tame lions as pets, and to have used parrots for his political propaganda, after teaching them to say 'Hanno is God'.[21] The traffic in wild animals became a particularly lucrative trade when spectacles and games in the arena became fashionable and more widespread; in the course of these, wild animals were killed by huntsmen. The Romans indulged in such spectacles as early as the second century B.C. Thus they became acquainted with panthers, which they called 'African rats', ostriches, which were called 'sea sparrows', just as elephants had been nicknamed 'Lucanian oxen'. In the *Poenulus*, Milphio claims to have brought, as part of his cargo, some 'African rats' which he wants to give to the magistrates in charge of the public games. The methods used to capture these animals without too much risk are shown in some fairly late Africo-Roman mosaics:[22] the wild beasts were enticed by goats and sheep shut up in compounds formed by bucklers. When they gathered round the bait, the hunters formed a wall with their bucklers and, with blazing torches, drove the animals towards nets spread to receive them, in which they became entangled. It only remained to put them into cages.

For the herbivorous animals and ostriches no such elaborate precautions were necessary; they were merely rounded up into corrals with the help of large Molossian dogs.[23] On a decorated Punic jar there is a painting of two tame ostriches drinking from a water-basin.[24] As for elephants, they were rounded up in drives organized by the State. For example, a whole army was sent to Numidia to capture them, or perhaps to Morocco, where they were so numerous that elephants' tusks were used to make fences. King Juba recorded the methods used:[25] the elephants were driven into pits; or the trees against which they were in the habit of leaning were sawn through; it was believed that once the animals had fallen over they could not get up again. This ridiculous piece of information, like all the other nonsense which the worthy king recorded on his tablets, does at least prove that the hunters had a fertile imagination and did not hesitate to take advantage of the credulity of their audience, even if it happened to be a king.

The time eventually came, however, when the Carthaginians decided to go themselves over the trans-Sahara routes. Athenaeus has preserved the memory of one of their explorers named Mago, who boasted that he had crossed the desert three times without drinking.[26]

However unlikely this exploit may seem, it was by no means the only one. Aristotle advised confirmed drinkers to follow the example of Andronicus of Argus: by accustoming himself to an exclusive diet of dried salted food, he was able to forget thirst, and twice made the journey to the Ammon oasis without drinking any liquid. J. Leclant compares such stories with the practices which can still be observed today among trained Saharans, who think that salt cheese is the best remedy against thirst: in this way they are able to do without water for three or four days at a stretch.

To the very real dangers of the desert were added psychological hazards: under the burning heat of the midday sun, or in the whirling desert sand, the harassed traveller saw monstrous apparitions, like the creature half-serpent, half-woman, which haunted the sand-dunes and devoured all those who were lured by her beauty. This monster is obviously a near relative of the Scylla of the Straits of Messina, whose legend was well known to the Phoenicians. They doubtless warned their caravaneers against this siren of the sands, the product no doubt of some easily understandable sexual hallucination. After all, Pierre Benoît's heroine Antinéa is a similar creation in modern times.

It was probably in the fifth century that the Carthaginians began their great Saharan expeditions, in an effort to cut out all intermediaries and to get into direct contact with the source of the riches in which they traded. In 1951, English researchers in Sabratha made an important discovery,[27] namely, that although, according to a legend reported by Silius Italicus,[27a] Sabratha was a Tyrian colony, it was in fact not inhabited before the second half of the third century. What is more, it was at first only a seasonal settlement like the one the Pseudo-Scylax describes at

Cerne. Later a modest permanent trading-post was established consisting of houses made of unbaked bricks on stone foundations; archaeologists have noted that there were three distinct phases in its development, which went on right up to the time of the fall of Carthage. Then it was temporarily abandoned until it was entirely rebuilt under Augustus. Sabratha was one of the terminal-points of the Sudan caravan routes. The merchants who came to camp there in the fifth century did so to await the arrival of desert caravans. Very probably they came from Carthage. Leptis was probably a permanent settlement as early as the beginning of the fifth century, but it remained a modest outpost of Carthage. It was only under the Empire that the Phoenicians from Tripolitania revived for their own advantage a trade of which they, better than anyone else, knew the value.

A number of indications point to the existence of a fairly active desert traffic at about this time. Not all the routes ran from north to south. Herodotus mentions a very important one which went from east to west, linking Thebes in Egypt to the oasis of Ammon (Siwa) and continuing into Barbary.[28]

'Above the Libya which is frequented by wild beasts is a sandy ridge which extends from Thebes in Egypt to the Pillars of Hercules. At intervals of about ten days' march along this ridge great lumps of salt are found on the top of sandy mounds. At the top of each mound, amid the salt, springs fresh cool water, and around this are human habitations; here are found the last men to be met in the direction of the desert, above the region of wild beasts. Starting from Thebes, the first people the traveller meets after ten days' march are the Ammonians; after them, and ten days' farther away along the ridge, is another mound of sand like that of the Ammonians, with water and men dwelling round it; and the place is called Augila.'

This information has proved to be remarkably exact: the oasis of Augila has kept its name for 2,500 years. It is situated about two hundred miles west of Siwa and in ancient times belonged to the powerful tribe of the Nasamones. A long ridge still exists, forming the southern boundary of Marmarica, which runs from Siwa to the Nile delta; this is continued westwards by another escarpment running south of Cyrenaica. Behind it is a narrow passage free of sand which is the only means of communication

between the Egyptian oases and Fezzan, north of the eastern
Great Erg. Camel caravans cover this journey in eighty to ninety
hours, which is roughly the equivalent of the ten days' march
mentioned by Herodotus. Beyond Augila, a third stage of ten
days' march led to the land of the Garamantes; and a fourth, of
the same length, reached the land of the Atarants. These people,
like the Nambikwara in Brazil today,[29] placed a taboo on personal
names; this was a magic precaution to prevent their enemies
from taking possession of their personalities by pronouncing their
names. In some cave-paintings a similar taboo prohibited the
artists from representing the human face, which was indicated
by a kind of bar or stick. This taboo survives in the habit of
present-day Touaregs, who are descendants of the Sahara
Libyans, of veiling their faces. Herodotus also noted that the
Atarants abhorred the sun.

They probably lived in the Tassili-n-Ajjer. Rhys Carpenter
supposes that the route from Fezzan turned south towards the
Tibesti Mountains, which were what Herodotus called the Atlas.
But such an interpretation does violence to the text and is all the
less likely to be correct, since rock-paintings show that a route
ran from east to west from Garama to Ahaggar.[30] The mountain
which Herodotus called 'Atlas' and which the natives called 'The
Pillar of Heaven', is described as a very high and slender peak,
perfectly round, a description which fits the extinct volcanoes of
Ahaggar or of Ilamane. The fifth stage of the journey led to the
foot of this mountain; the sixth to some salt-mines, where even
houses were built of salt. It is impossible to situate this with
any accuracy as such deposits of salt are very common in the
Sahara.

Most of the caravan traffic must have left the oasis route,
either in the territory of the Garamantes, in order to go to Tripolitania (a thirty days' journey, also mentioned by Herodotus), or,
a little farther on, to reach Syrtis Minor by way of Cydamus
(Ghadames), an important meeting-place for Mediterranean and
Saharan peoples. These two routes were very extensively used in
the Roman period: in 19 B.C. Cornelius Balbus, an African proconsul, occupied Garama after passing through the defiles of the
'Black Mountain' ('Mons Ater' to the Romans, and 'Djebel Soda'
to the Arabs).[31] Under Vespasian, Septimus Flaccus used a

shorter but more difficult route across the Hamada el Homra. Four or five centuries earlier, the Punic traders must have followed the route described by Herodotus—it enabled them to reach Egypt without going through Greek Cyrenaica, and it must therefore have assumed considerable importance in the fifth century when the Athenian fleet blockaded the Mediterranean. Carthaginian traders must also have visited the oasis of Siwa; Silius Italicus[33] maintains that Hannibal consulted the oracle there on the outcome of his expedition; Pausanias quotes another oracle concerning the hero's burial,[34] but these may be poetic inventions. Nevertheless, it seems certain that Ammon and Baal Hammon were identified with each other at an early date.[35] Gsell's explanation of this is that the oasis cult spread to the Western Libyans, but this seems very unlikely today: it is much more likely that the two gods became one in Carthage. Moreover, it appears that the oracle of Siwa declined in popularity after 146 B.C., which is indirect evidence of the importance of Punic influence.[36]

Carthaginian civilization, however, made less impression on the Garamantes and their neighbours than did the Roman Empire which followed it.[37] The only material evidence of Carthaginian influence is found in the glass beads which were used as currency in dealing with the natives.[38] From their Sahara trade, the Carthaginians obtained precious stones such as carbuncles, emeralds, and chalcedony. In Tiror, in the Tassili-n-Ajjer, H. Lhote[39] discovered a curious ochre drawing with a Libyan inscription: within a rectangular frame decorated with bows at the corners it shows three human silhouettes shaped like hour-glasses and whose outstretched arms are very reminiscent of the bell-shaped idols from which the emblem of Tanit was derived.[40]

From Fezzan, which was a veritable junction for trans-Sahara traffic, it was easily possible to reach the Sudan. In the reign of Domitian (A.D. 79–96), the Roman general, Julius Maternus, was guided by the Garamantes as far as the region of Agysimba 'where the rhinoceros gather'.[41] The attempt to identify this mysterious region has given rise to much speculation. It was probably a region in the Sudan which had already been visited as early as the fifth century B.C. Herodotus describes a journey made by some young men of the Nasamones, who lived in the hinterland of Cyrenaica.

These audacious young men, who came from Augila, decided one day to try to cross the desert. With ample supplies of food and water, they first reached Fezzan. They continued their journey and after crossing the vast expanse of desert, they came upon some trees laden with fruit. While they were refreshing themselves they were suddenly surrounded by diminutive black men who took them prisoner and led them across great swamps to their town, which was on the bank of a river infested with crocodiles. All the inhabitants practised sorcery. In the end, the Pigmies released them and they managed to get back to their own country. According to Rhys Carpenter, this episode must have taken place in the Borkou region between the Tibesti and Lake Chad, where the inland lakes must have been much more extensive than they are today. A picture of a chariot found in Djebel Bou Ghnema, south-west of Garama, seems to confirm the existence of this route, which was that taken by the Troglodyte-hunters. The routes from Fezzan to the Niger are much easier to trace. Pictures of chariots have been found scattered for the most part along the cart-tracks, many of which are still in use today. From Garama a route went to Tassili and round the Ahagger; then came four days' journey without water across the Tanezrouft; then it reached the Adrer and finally the Niger, somewhere near Gao.

The importance to Carthage of all this traffic must not be under-estimated. Its natural outlet to the Mediterranean was in Tripolitania through places like Emporia, Leptis, Oea, and Sabratha. At the beginning of the second century B.C., customs dues in Leptis brought in to the Carthaginian treasury a talent a day (4,800 gold francs).[42] Such a sum could only have been paid, not on local agricultural produce, which was almost entirely oil and dates, but on valuable goods brought from the Sahara, such as gold, ivory, ostrich-skins, furs, and precious stones from the desert. Thus the Sahara trade was one of the main sources of the riches of Carthage and all the more profitable because there were no serious competitors; the Garamantes, who lived on desert tolls, were obliged to keep on good terms with the State that controlled their maritime outlets—otherwise their desert cargoes would have had no purchasers. These incorrigible robbers could do little to prevent the leaders of Carthaginian caravans, like Mago, the record thirst-beater, from making direct contact with the Negroes. After 146, this kind of enterprise was undertaken by other Phoenicians from Tripolitania, and they encountered bitter resistance from the Garamantes.

At the end of the first century A.D., the Sahara tribes tried to take advantage of the rivalry between Oea and Leptis, to seize the latter town. They were cruelly punished by the Romans: mosaics found in Zliten in Eastern Tripolitania, depict Barbarians thrown to the wild beasts in the arena.[43] When a man from Leptis, Septimius Severus, became emperor, he sent a legion to occupy one important sector of the route and Ghadames became a Roman garrison town.[44]

With the decline of the Empire in the fourth century, the Barbarians tried a fresh assault which was nearly successful and which struck a fatal blow at the prosperity of the great Punic city.[45] Meanwhile the Phoenicians in Tripolitania had developed a highly efficient organization for their desert caravans. Indeed it was they who, noticing the increasing difficulties caused to the traffic by the drying up of the desert, introduced camels.[46] These animals may have been used by Alexander to reach the oasis of Ammon,[47] but they were very little used in Africa before the Christian era.

The idea of using camels was probably suggested by the example of the great caravan cities in Syria, such as Palmyra, which, through racial ties, were well known to the Phoenicians. Most of the ancient monuments depicting African camels come from Tripolitania; Leptis possessed at least 3,000 dromedaries in the middle of the fourth century A.D. Mosaics and terracotta statuettes found in Roman Tunisia prove that in the second and third centuries A.D. the Libyans, and even the Negroes, had adopted this new form of transport. The rebel tribes in Tripolitania used them in large numbers in the fourth and fifth centuries A.D. to raid the farmers in Proconsularium and Byzacium.

VOYAGES ALONG THE AFRICAN COAST

It has been categorically stated that the overland routes were the only ones which allowed the Carthaginians access to tropical Africa.[48] This is a paradoxical conclusion, apparently contradicted by a considerable volume of evidence.

Phoenician sailors from the Red Sea had successfully doubled the Somali peninsula in very early times.[49] Herodotus provides evidence, which is all the more valuable because he does not attach much credence to it himself: he relates how in the reign of the young Pharaoh Nechao, at the beginning of the sixth century, Phoenicians, carrying out his commands, made a complete circumnavigation of Africa, starting from the Red Sea and returning by way of the Mediterranean.[50] The voyage took them three years. Each year, at the beginning of the bad season, they pulled their boats ashore, camped out, sowed wheat, and remained until the harvest. Herodotus explains that what seemed incredible to him was, that they said that at first the sun set on their *right* and later on their *left*, a detail which shows that the expedition must have doubled the Cape of Good Hope. Other evidence confirms that the Phoenicians frequented the Equatorial regions as early as the seventh century; for example, a silver libation-bowl discovered at Praeneste in Italy, but made in Phoenicia, depicts a hunter at grips with a man-sized ape without a tail, which must be either a chimpanzee or a gorilla.[51] The recent discoveries in South Africa of cave-paintings in which white men appear, may perhaps throw further light on these mysterious stories.[52]

Carthaginian sailors took no part in Nechao's circumnavigation, nor in the voyage of Sataspes in about 470 B.C. Sataspes was a young Persian nobleman, a cousin of King Xerxes, who was rash enough to take advantage of a young noblewoman.[53] A rigorous law made such an offence punishable by death, and the King, in spite of his relationship to the young nobleman, ordered the execution of the guilty couple. However, he yielded to the entreaties of Sataspes' mother, who was his own aunt, and agreed to spare him on condition that he repeated the circumnavigation of Africa.

Sataspes made his way to Egypt, fitted out a ship, passed the Pillars of Hercules and Cape Cantin (Soloeis), and sailed the oceans for a very long time. At length he landed in a country inhabited by Pigmies dressed in palm leaves, who abandoned their village on the approach of the Persians and fled to the mountains. He was unable to go beyond this point as his ship 'refused to advance'. He therefore came back to Persia, but the

King, suspecting him of lying, had him impaled. The failure of this expedition was probably due to the Equatorial calms. Sataspes had but one ship, which was probably a *kebenit*, a heavy craft not at all easy to handle. The crew were probably weakened by the climate and unable to use their oars when their sails were useless.

HANNO'S VOYAGE OF DISCOVERY

The great Carthaginian expedition along the coasts of Africa probably took place shortly after this event. Mention has already been made of the political and economic circumstances which made Hanno, 'the King of the Carthaginians'—probably a Magonid—equip a large fleet in order to maintain a tighter control over the African 'Far West'. This voyage of discovery is one of the best known of all those of antiquity because an account of it survives: Hanno had it engraved on a stele in Baal Hammon's temple. It was translated into Greek, probably in the fourth century, but with certain alterations which were probably intended to make it less valuable to possible competitors. Unfortunately the master-text contains some obscure and sometimes incoherent passages which make it very difficult to interpret. It has therefore been the subject of endless discussions,[54] and we shall examine the various interpretations and endeavour to arrive at a conclusion.

The aims of the expedition and the means to be employed are very clearly set out in the opening paragraph. 'The Carthaginians decreed that Hanno should sail beyond the Pillars of Hercules and found Libyo-Phoenician towns. He therefore set out with sixty vessels, each with fifty oars, and with many men and women, to the number of about thirty thousand, and with food and other necessities.'

The beginning of the narrative tells how colonies were founded (para. 2–5); the first was Thymiaterion; then, after going round Cape Cantin, where a temple was built to the god of the sea (Poseidon in Greek), Hanno settled the remaining immigrants in five towns; the Wall of the Carians, Gypte, Acra, Melitta, and Arambys.

The Carthaginians next came to a Libyan people called Lixites, from the River Lixus on whose banks they lived. They rested with these people for some time, for they were their allies, and then set off again with Lixite interpreters (para. 7). The Lixites, incidentally, had as their neighbours a wild Negro tribe who lived in a mountainous land swarming with wild beasts. There also dwelt Troglodytes, 'men of strange appearance' who could run faster than a horse.

Leaving the Lixites, the fleet headed south along the desert shore, and then sailed east for one day. Soon a gulf was found with a small island in the middle. Hanno named it Cerne, and established a base there; it was the same distance from the Pillars of Hercules as Carthage.

Next, the estuary of a great river was discovered, the River Chretes (River Senegal). Sailing up it, the Carthaginians found a great lake containing three islands. Above towered great mountains inhabited by savages dressed in skins, who prevented a landing by hurling stones. Hanno left the lake by another stream, full of crocodiles and hippopotamuses and came back to Cerne (para. 9–10).

Hanno then set sail again towards the south, skirting a coast whose Ethiopian inhabitants fled at the sight of his ships. These Negroes spoke a language which was incomprehensible to the Lixites. After twelve days a halt was made at the foot of some high mountains covered with aromatic trees with coloured wood. For two more days the fleet sailed along these mountains which then opened out into an immense gulf whose shores sloped down to the sea. At night fires burned everywhere on the surrounding shores (para. 10–13).

Skirting the coast for another five days, Hanno reached another great gulf, which the Lixites called the 'Horn of the West', containing an island, on which was a lagoon containing yet another island. During the day, nothing but forest was visible, but at night fires burned on all sides, and the music of flutes, cymbals, and tambourines was heard, to the great terror of the navigators; on the advice of their soothsayers, they hurriedly departed from the island.

Next they came to an active volcano, the 'Chariot of the Gods', whose lava flowed down into the sea. For seven days they followed a coast laid waste by fire, and finally entered a gulf known as the 'Horn of the South'. In this bay was an island which, like the 'Horn of the West', had a lagoon with an island in the middle. The island was inhabited by hairy savages whom the Lixites called Gorillas. There were only a few males, who escaped by climbing trees. But the Carthaginians managed to capture a few 'women'. However, they were obliged to kill them because they clawed and bit; their skins were brought back to Carthage.

Lack of food prevented the expedition from going any farther.

The very numerous commentators of this text fall into two groups (apart from those who think it is pure fiction!). One group thinks that Hanno got as far as tropical and Equatorial Africa; the other group thinks that he never got beyond the coast of Morocco. This latter view is so manifestly at variance with the text, that it would be scarcely worth discussing, were it not for the fact that it has again been put forward quite recently by Mauny,[55] whose knowledge of the history of the African Negro makes him a very great authority.

Mauny's main argument is that the means of navigation available to the ancients would not have permitted them to sail round Cape Juby, and that, even supposing this to be possible, they could not have sailed back against the Canary current and the trade-winds. He points out that throughout the entire Middle Ages, Arab sailors were unable to get farther south than Cape Juby, and that it was not until the sixteenth century that the Portuguese succeeded in doing this with the aid of new technical discoveries—and then only after many failures. Mauny must, however, admit that galleys propelled by oars would not have been held up by trade-winds; he would retort that the crews would have been unable to get supplies of water and would have died of thirst on the inhospitable shores of Mauretania. This argument would be valid if the Sahara had been as dry as it is today. But we have seen that the drying-up process has been getting very much more rapid in the last 2,000 years. In the west in particular, *wadis*, which are dry today, were water-courses a few centuries ago. Coastwise trade by means of galleys along the Sahara coasts therefore depended on conditions very similar to those governing expeditions overland; it did not become impossible until the drying-up process necessitated the replacement of the horse by the camel. This turning-point in history occurred at the beginning of the Christian era, which explains why the Romans were unable to continue the trade connexions built up by the Carthaginians.

Furthermore, if one insists that Hanno could not have got farther than the Rio de Oro, one would have to admit either that his account is pure fiction and wonder by what miracle he was able to describe with such astonishing accuracy the flora and fauna of tropical Africa; or else it would become necessary to believe that the climate and inhabitants of Morocco were at that time entirely different, not only from what they are today, but from what they were in Roman times; and also to explain by what miracle this region could have preserved tropical natural conditions which disappeared several thousand years earlier in other regions in the same latitude.

All this would demand climatic conditions vastly different from those of today. Even admitting that such a hypothesis could be entertained, which we cannot accept, it would still rule out any argument based on the present prevailing winds. It seems, therefore, that the Carthaginian admiral could very well have accomplished this exploit, thanks to the precautions he took to adapt his methods to the conditions he knew he would meet. This explains why he succeeded where Sataspes failed. Knowing that the voyage would have to be made with oars and that it would be difficult to get food and water for his crews, he took a fleet of light ships with only fifty oars, whereas the normal war-ship of that time was the trireme.

This use of galleys cannot be explained in any other fashion, for there was obviously no danger of meeting an enemy fleet in those parts, and heavy merchant ships would have been a more convenient means of transporting the colonists and their equipment. It is possible that, although they are not mentioned in the narrative, 'round ships' followed the spearhead of the expedition, and this would explain the evident discrepancy between the number of passengers and the number of ships.[56]

All this, however, is little more than conjecture. But there is absolutely indisputable proof of the Carthaginians' ability to cover distances considered quite out of the question by medieval mariners. Only about sixty miles or so to the west of Cape Juby are the heights of Fuerteventura, the easternmost of the Canary

Islands. Yet the Moroccans never landed there and when navigators from Spain and Dieppe landed there in the fourteenth century they found a virgin archipelago which still had its prehistoric inhabitants. The reason is that it is very difficult for a sailing-vessel to get there even from the nearest African shore on account of the opposing trade-winds and currents. But the Western Phoenicians from Gades and from Carthage had found a solution to this difficulty by a very skilful manœuvre which Pliny describes in detail, in his account of the expedition organized by King Juba.[57] The ships sailed boldly forward from Mogador heading west, and when they had passed the longitude of the islands, they allowed themselves to be brought back to them by the current.

Having dismissed this preliminary objection,[58] we may now come back to the thesis put forward in his book, *Le Maroc Antique*,[59] by Carcopino, who, revising and correcting Gsell's interpretation, seems to us to have arrived at the best interpretation so far available of the coastal voyage. Carcopino postulates as a first principle that Hanno in his narrative would have a twofold preoccupation—to give a convincing version of his voyage that would be acceptable to his companions, and at the same time to make sure that competitors—in particular the Greeks—could not make use of his narrative to reach markets which Carthage intended to reserve for herself.

The alterations were made, in all probability, not in the original text of the narrative, but in the Greek version which was produced at the request of the Carthaginian government to satisfy the curiosity of the Hellenes and to enhance the prestige of the Carthaginian navy. At the time when Hanno dedicated his stele the Greeks were for all practical purposes excluded from Carthage, and there was no need to fear a leakage. In particular, the passages which are spoiled in the inscription are precisely those dealing with distances and bearings. It is not necessary, therefore, to conclude, as some have done, that Carcopino's conclusions cast doubt on the truth of the story of the voyage. The account we have is certainly a mutilated one, but the untouched portions are perfectly valid, and contain no inventions. If Hanno had really wanted to make a systematic attempt to frighten his readers, he could, for example, have emphasized the supernatural side of what took place at the 'Horn of the West' and exaggerated the hostility of the natives, or the dangers of the volcanic eruption. But he gives 'a simple straightforward account of places visited and things seen, which brings conviction by its direct style and by its brevity'. This verdict of P. Charlesworth is especially true of the second part of the journey where, in describing the Negro territories, Hanno had no reason to lie about distant lands which no Greeks were ever likely to visit.

However, the first part, which we know as a continuous narrative, would appear to be a composite story derived from mutilated versions of three separate voyages. The Carthaginians sailed first from the Pillars of Hercules to Cape Cantin (Soloeis) and came back to Lixus, calling in turn at their colonies from south to north. Setting out again from Lixus they reached Cerne, in the Bay of Rio de Oro, and continued south as far as the estuary of the Chretes (the Senegal) and came back to their advance base at Cerne. Then a third expedition took them south for thirty-five days and then west to east for twenty-two days, following the enormous land mass of the African continent, noting on the way the lofty summit of Kakoulima, and as far as the volcano of the Cameroons, which the inhabitants still call the 'Mountain of Spirits'.

The interest and cogent reasoning of Carcopino's arguments must inevitably be lost in the attempt to summarize the pages in which he sets out his proofs, step by step, supporting them with an extraordinary wealth of evidence drawn from a great variety of sources, from ancient texts to medieval documents on navigation. The validity of his method inspires respect from the very beginning by its solution of the following enigma which had previously seemed insoluble: in the fourth paragraph of his account, Hanno states that after passing Cape Cantin, he headed east—which appears to be an impossibility unless one accepts Carcopino's interpretation, namely that Hanno turned about, as is suggested by the adverb *palin*; this would allow the Punic fleet to follow the Moroccan coast from West-South-West to East-North-East. By this interpretation, another difficulty is eliminated: the Lixites, who play the essential role of guides and interpreters throughout the voyage, are no longer seen as Libyan nomads encamped along the banks of the Draa *wadi*, whose linguistic and geographical competence, and their devotion to the Carthaginians seem equally incomprehensible, but instead the Tyrian colonists of that great and ancient city situated near the present-day Larache, which for centuries played a comparable part in Mauretania to that of Gades in Spain. This identification is all the more convincing since paragraph seven, which refers to the presence in the neighbourhood of Lixus of fierce Ethiopians and monstrous Troglodytes, seems to us to bear all the signs of an interpolation, in which some commentator, without much understanding of what he was doing, has collected together his reminiscences of Herodotus' description of the Sahara. This clumsy scholar was scarcely less perceptive than Pausanias,[60] who succeeded, in one single sentence, in mixing up the Lixites, whom he describes as Negroes, with the Atlantes of Herodotus, who lived in the Hoggar, and the Nasamones who came from Augila!

We disagree with Carcopino in only one minor detail: Hanno's 'Gorillas' were, according to him, and other scholars, hairy Pigmies. It would seem to us very unlikely that the Carthaginians would not have recognized Pigmies when they saw them, as all the peoples who crossed the Sahara would be well acquainted with them; in any case Pigmies are not hairy enough to give furs! The description does in fact fit anthropoid apes—not indeed those which nineteenth-century explorers called gorillas, precisely because of the passage in Hanno's narrative, but chimpanzees, which live together in fairly aggressive bands.

Finally Carcopino throws light on the reasons which sent the Carthaginians on such distant and perilous journeys. The granite of the Guinea massif contains gold-bearing seams which after being exploited for several thousand years are still not exhausted. Moreover, the Negroes do not attempt to work the seams themselves, but limit their efforts to collecting dust and nuggets from the streams which come down from this African watershed. To the Mediterranean peoples, athirst for the precious metal, which they needed so badly, these gold deposits in Senegal must have seemed a veritable Eldorado, all the more legendary because they were so far away.

The gold-dust and nuggets were brought to the coast down the

River Senegal, to which Hanno gives the name Chretes, but which Pliny calls Bambotus (Carcopino recalls the name Bambouk, which designates the gold-bearing mountains); or else they were carried by caravans across the Sahara. But however valuable the cargoes might be, the length of the journey and the exorbitant tolls extorted by the desert chiefs reduced very considerably the trade over these routes. The Carthaginians, therefore, tried to get nearer to the source of supply: Herodotus knew in his time that they were getting gold from a point on the coast beyond the Pillars of Hercules.[61] 'The Carthaginians', he writes, 'discharge their merchandise and spread it out on the shore for exhibition; they then return to their ships and send up smoke to attract the natives; the latter approach and place beside the merchandise, the gold they offer in exchange. They then retire. The Carthaginians come ashore again and examine what has been left. If they think enough gold has been left, they take it and depart. If not, they go back to their ships and wait. The natives then come back and add more gold until the Carthaginians are satisfied. Each side respects the other: the Carthaginians do not touch the gold until the amount left is sufficient for their goods; and the natives do not touch the goods until the Carthaginians have taken the gold.'

This passage has often been interpreted in too general a fashion; it must not be taken that such trading methods were used by the Carthaginians with all the Western Barbarians. It is probably a description of the most ancient methods of trading for gold before the Carthaginians established permanent bases in the great South. Later, transactions with the natives were conducted with greater confidence. However, a manuscript of the Arab geographer El Yacout,[62] who lived at the beginning of the thirteenth century A.D., describes a system of barter very similar to this, the only difference being that instead of smoke-signals, tom-toms were used. No doubt the development of the slave-trade and the fear of raids by corsairs disguised as merchant-men, caused the revival of a method of barter which was by then 1,500 years old.

The place where these transactions took place can be stated fairly confidently: it was in the Bay of Rio de Oro, a name which was given to it by fifteenth-century Castilian navigators who hoped to secure this outlet for the Guinea gold. In the centre of this gulf rises the island of Hern. Carcopino is confident that this name is a slightly altered form of Cerne; his conjecture does not seem to us to be in any way shaken by the suggestion of other authorities who say the name comes from the sea 'herons' which frequent the island, for the presence of large numbers of 'hawks' in Cerne had already been testified by Pliny the Elder.[63] And if modern sailors have given the name 'herons' to the cormorants which are in fact the only birds which nest in this ocean island, it is probably as a result of one of those frequent examples of a play on words, by which a place-name may preserve its phonetic identity in the languages of successive occupants, without preserving the same meaning.

Cerne was colonized for the first time by Hanno, and this should have deterred Mauny from identifying it with Mogador, for archaeological evidence shows that the Carthaginians were already there in the sixth century. It subsequently became the centre of an important trade with the natives along the neighbouring coast. A Greek geographical treatise dating from the fourth century B.C., *The Voyages*, by Scylax,[64] states that an Ethiopian town existed at that time opposite the island and that important fairs were regularly held there. The existence of a Negro settlement so far north would be enough to show that trade was carried on with the tropical regions of Africa, even if the arid climate of Mauretania were not enough to prove that the goods exchanged there must have come from much farther afield.

Scylax states that the Carthaginians left their ships off the island, where they disembarked in boats and camped in tents.

The Negroes, he says, brought skins and hides, ivory and even wine, although the latter seems unlikely.[65] In exchange the Carthaginians left them perfumes and pottery. The value of such a trade would scarcely merit such a long voyage in view of the fact that the Carthaginians could get skins and ivory much nearer home. The Greek author was probably inaccurately briefed by his informants who concealed from him the main purpose of the enterprise which was to get gold. But the main supply of gold had still to come overland by caravan across the Sahara. Hanno's narrative itself proves that he failed to get into direct contact with the gold-washers of Guinea. The Lixites, on whom he had counted to be his intermediaries, were of no help when once he got to tropical regions. The very conditions which made for the success of his exploit made it impossible to set up a regular and profitable trade: fifty-oared ships could hardly carry a useful cargo as well as food and water for their crews. Even in Scylax's time it was therefore considered impractical to go farther than Cerne. Similarly, it is very unlikely that another navigator, Euthymenes of Marseilles, ever reached Senegal.[66]

Political upheavals probably caused the decline of trade across the Sahara routes; Eratosthenes and Pliny maintain that the Phoenician colonies along the Atlantic coast were destroyed by the Pharusians.[67] These warlike horsemen, predecessors of the Moors, were probably tempted by the Ethiopian trading-station near Cerne, just as the fifteenth-century Moors were tempted by Timbuctoo. Finally, the steady drying-up of the Sahara made journeys across it more and more difficult in the west, and nobody resorted to camels, as the people of Leptis had done farther east. Archaeological research has established that although Carthage was reputed to be so rich in gold and silver, it was in fact not so. Scipio Emilianus decided that he would like definite information about Carthaginian resources in Western Africa: he therefore sent his master and his councillor, the historian Polybius, and the philosopher Panaitios, to go and find out. The two scholars had a squadron of seven ships at their disposal.

The narrative of their journey has not survived.[68] Nevertheless, it seems certain that they did not even reach Hanno's Cerne, though an island farther north in the region of the Anti-Atlas was named after Polybius. Carcopino thinks that the Lixites intentionally misdirected him in order to preserve their own profits from Guinea gold. But it is not very likely that there was any appreciable trade in gold at that time. Certainly it had completely vanished during the reign of King Jubal, whose fleet explored the Canaries, but was unable to get farther south than Mogador along the Moroccan coast. On the other hand, explorers he sent overland to reconnoitre the course of the Nile (which was thought to rise in the Atlas Mountains), followed the semi-dried-up *wadis* of the Sahara and probably reached the Niger.[69] Nevertheless, they made no contact with the Negro tribes and reported that the tropical forests were inhabited only by wild animals.

To sum up, therefore, it seems that both Hanno's and Nechao's expeditions did actually take place, but were not repeated, as they failed to produce the economic results their promoters had hoped for. The ancients were not in the habit of regarding exploration as a means of disinterested research; they abandoned it as soon as it became clear that there was little prospect of commercial or political advantages. However, thanks to the importation of camels by the people of Leptis, trade continued between the Mediterranean countries and the Sudan by overland routes across the Central Sahara; it greatly enriched the merchants of Garama and Cydamus, and enabled them to build showy mausoleums in the Roman manner. It explains how second-century lamps and Constantine coins were found as far afield as the Hoggar; it also accounts for the jewels found in the tomb of the legendary Tin Hinan and in the miniature fortress built to guard it.[70] But the great Sahara civilization which is revealed by the cave-paintings and the journeys described in Herodotus, faded away as the water-supplies dried up. In its place, a new kind of economy based on the cultivation of date palms[71] and on the breeding of camels, began to develop at the beginning of the Middle Ages.

HIMILCO AND THE TIN ROUTE

Paradoxically enough, we have less information about Carthaginian expeditions along the coasts of Europe than about their African voyages. Neither literary texts nor archaeological remains provide any direct evidence.

In the fourth century A.D., the Roman noble, Festus Rufus Avienus,[72] who was both scholar and poet, decided to give instruction in geography to a young relative of his named Probus. This boy was particularly interested in the *Palus Meotida*, or Sea of Azov. But before coming to that, Avienus thought his pupil should be saved from over-specialization by being given some preliminary general information about the shores of Europe.

This introduction, which took up no less than 709 lines of verse, is all that has come down to us. True to the tradition of his age, which had little use for direct observation, Avienus sought information in the oldest and most obscure texts he was able to find in the course of his long searches in ancient archives. Among these authors was the Carthaginian Himilco whom he quotes on three occasions; he also refers to the *Punic Annals*. We learn from Pliny[73] that the navigator Himilco was exploring the shores of Europe while Hanno was visiting those of Africa. Was his expedition the source of the information used by Avienus in his *Ora Maritima*?

In 1870, the German philologist Mullenhof put forward another theory, which is the one generally accepted today. According to this theory, Avienus was borrowing from an account of a voyage from Marseilles earlier than that of Himilco; his description of the ocean coasts could not have been based on Pliny's personal observations, for he had no access to them, but on information he picked up in Tartessus. Mullenhof thinks that Avienus inserted a few quotations from more recent works, in which Himilco is mentioned, but considers the Marseilles expedition to be completely hypothetical.

Berthelot, however, rejects this theory and maintains that Avienus had no intention of describing Europe at any particular period; instead, he collected all the information he could glean from a great variety of texts, about the earliest known condition of the countries he describes. In our opinion, the only complete description of the Atlantic countries before that of Pytheas, was that of Himilco. Avienus never used the work of Pytheas, the explorer from Marseilles, either because he thought it too recent, or because he shared Polybius' doubts as to its authenticity. We therefore think that the part of the *Ora Maritima* which deals with sea routes from Spain to the tin countries is a distorted image of the Carthaginian expedition.

This section of the poem occupies approximately the first half. But from line 145 onwards, Avienus deals exclusively with Spain; his description of the Atlantic occupies lines 80–145.

In twenty lines, the poem surveys the whole extent of what he calls the Atlantic Gulf, which corresponds with the Sea of Spain and the Bay of Biscay; he mentions only its two extremities: Gades, 'formerly called Tartessus', and the Pillars of Hercules, on the one hand, and the Promontory of Oestrymnis on the other. It is generally agreed that the latter is the Armorican Peninsula, and that the Oestrymnians were the Osismi who lived in Finistère at the time of Julius Caesar. Avienus describes the Oestrymnides as 'an island with long plains and rich mines of tin and lead. The people are proud, strong, brave-hearted, energetic and industrious, willing to trade in anything. Their vessels sail far and wide over the stormy channel and the ocean full of sea-monsters. They do not build their hulls of pine or maple, nor do they bend fir wood as is normally done; instead— a wonderful thing—they make their ships of skins sewn together, and thus often traverse the vast seas on leather.

'From their land to the sacred island, as the ancients called it, takes two days in a boat. This island covers a vast surface in the midst of the waters and is inhabited by the nation of the Hibernians. Near it, on the return voyage, stretches the Island of Albion. The people of Tartessus traded regularly with the Oestrymnides islands as did the settlers from Carthage. The peoples living round the Pillars of Hercules also visited these regions.

'The Carthaginian Himilco, who describes how he himself tried this voyage, says that it takes at least four months. There is no wind to blow the ship along, and the lazy waters of that ocean seem asleep. From them rise shoals of sea-weed, which often hold back the ship like a hedge; nevertheless, he says, the sea is not very deep—only a thin layer of water covering the land; marine animals swim hither and thither, and sea-monsters pass between the becalmed and motionless ships.' (From A. Berthelot's translation.)

The first impression from these passages is that Carthaginian expeditions north of Spain were rare and that there were no permanent Punic settlements in Gaul. Seams of tin do exist in the Morbihan and were exploited in the sixth century B.C. According to R. Dion,[74] the Isles of the Cassiterides were situated near these mines in a vast bay now filled in, at the mouth of the Loire. But as we have seen, the Osismi-Oestrymnians lived in Finistère, and Avienus makes no mention of the tribe of the Veneti from Vannes. Consequently it is very probable that the Carthaginians sailed straight across from Cape Finisterre in Spain to Cape Finistère in Armorica. This direct route may have given rise to the curious legend that the Osismi came from Spain, having been driven out of the Iberian peninsula by an invasion of serpents.[75]

Such a bold sea-crossing was obviously possible only in summer, when the anti-cyclone from the Azores comes up as far as the 45th parallel. Beyond that, there was always the risk of the ships running into a dead calm, and having to add several weeks to their voyage.[76] Information given about shallows, on the other hand, seems to indicate that these journeys were made by hugging the coast; the Mediterranean sailors were not used to tides and were always afraid of going aground on the beaches. Caesar noted that the Veneti used flat-bottomed boats to avoid this danger. However, we have just seen that the Carthaginians from Tartessus hardly ever visited the shores of Gaul. Moreover, playing on the Mediterranean fear of shallows was a device frequently used by the Carthaginians to frighten away their competitors from the seas where they wished to preserve their own trade monopolies. We know that they even went aground themselves when they knew they were being followed.[77]

Unlike Hanno, Himilco seems, therefore, to have emphasized in his narrative the difficulties and dangers of navigating in the seas he explored. Some of these dangers were certainly not imaginary; the Carthaginian mariners may even have got as far as the Sargasso Sea, which today extends from between 20° and 30° north and 30° and 50° west. Mariners in ancient times encountered banks of sea-weed nearer than this to the coasts of Europe.[78] As for the marine monsters, these were whales, which were common in the Bay of Biscay until the end of the Middle Ages.

Was this insistence on the perils of the ocean a real fear in the presence of seas new to them, or was it meant to conceal from possible future rivals the importance of a trade vital to the Carthaginians? It is unlikely that they ever envisaged the possibility of undertaking the shipment of tin from the Channel to the Pillars of Hercules in their own ships. No attempt was made to found colonies on the coasts of Portugal, Galicia, or Gaul. In order to sail the Atlantic regularly, it would have been necessary to build a new fleet on quite different principles from those used for Mediterranean traffic.

The strange vessels of the Armoricans always astonished the

Carthaginians and the Romans. According to Himilco, the Oestrymnians used large leather kayaks constructed on a wicker framework. This kind of craft was still used in Britain in the time of Pytheas,[79] but only for the short crossing between the Isle of Wight and England. What strange chance could have led the dwellers along the Channel coasts to choose a form of boat so ill-adapted to the ocean waves, and to the transport of heavy mineral ores? One would imagine that such craft would have been evolved in a land without timber, or for river journeys where the boats often had to be carried from one river to another. At all events, in Caesar's time the vessels used by the Armoricans were built of oak so tough that the spurs on the Roman galleys were unable to split them, and their high forecastles and poops gave them the appearance of medieval ships.[80]

If the Carthaginians wasted no time in Armorica it was probably because the tin-mines of Morbihan were not the main object of their journeys; in fact it appears that production from these mines declined in about 500 B.C., whilst that of the Cornish mines increased.[81] This shift of production may be one of the reasons for the Punic admiral's ambitious expedition—he may have been investigating in person the new conditions of supply. He certainly went to Ireland and England. Ireland is the land which Avienus calls the Sacred Island—as we have seen, it had traded with Spain in the Bronze Age, and therefore it is not surprising that the most northerly trace of Phoenician activity was found there. The Rev. O. Davies has recently published information[82] about a curious monument preserved in St Johnstown at the mouth of the River Foyle. It is an ovoid stone carved to suggest a human head, exactly like a well-known Carthaginian sacred stone in the Alaoui Museum. If it did come from Africa, it might be an ex-voto dedicated by Himilco or one of his immediate successors; in any case, it cannot be later than the fifth century.

Did Himilco or his successors venture still farther? The most northerly country mentioned by Avienus is the mysterious land of the Ligurians who had apparently been driven thence by the Celts before going to find a fresh home in the Alps. This passage has given rise to bitter controversy, and has been used to build up vast theories about a Ligurian empire prior to the Celts. However, these theories are now regarded as untenable. To our mind, the passage has never been explained and probably never will be.[83] In any case, there is nothing to prove that Himilco was responsible for this information. Gsell had pointed out that the Carthaginians never made any use of amber,[84] which proves that their ships never reached the Baltic beaches, where this 'Northern Gold' was gathered.

Himilco's voyage, like Hanno's, was undertaken for economic reasons. The results were by no means negligible: at the end of the fifth century an important bronze industry was developing in Carthage which must have needed 'Oestrymnian' tin.[85] The Carthaginians had recognized that it was out of the question to set up direct connexions with the remote British deposits, and instead had made useful contacts with the middlemen so as to ensure the continuation of this trade which had contributed so much to the fortune of Tartessus.

From time to time other merchants probably followed the route taken by Himilco, and may have gone farther still. Pytheas, who took only three days to cross the Bay of Biscay, went beyond the tin markets of Armorica and Cornwall. 'But unlike the Carthaginian envoy, he had a scholar's thirst for knowledge.'[85a] His English journey, his cruise in the Baltic and on to Norway, which he called Thule, seem to have been the first ever made by a Mediterranean navigator so far north.

The overseas tin routes had to stand the competition of the river routes through Gaul, which were safer and quicker. J. Carcopino has indeed shown that the information given by Diodorus and Strabo on the 'white lead' trade through the valleys of the Seine and the Loire, was obtained from much earlier sources. These two authors lived near the beginning of the Christian era and got much of their information from Pytheas himself.[86]

Already in the sixth century the Celtic princess who was buried in the tumulus at Vix controlled the porterage over the Burgundy pass by which the tin came from the Seine to the Saône. Whether these journeys were organized from Marseilles, as Carcopino thinks, or whether the Gauls themselves directed them in their own political and economic interests, towards Provence or the Alpine routes, they deprived the Punic industry of a considerable share of the British tin.

As we have seen, Hannibal tried to remedy this situation by using the route later taken by Caesar along the Aude and the Garonne, to save the long and dangerous voyage round Spain. If he had succeeded in thus reversing the normal trading currents, he would have ruined the Greek colonists in the West, to the advantage of the Carthaginians, and in addition would have secured for his allies the Gauls the valuable tolls which were shared with considerable bickering by the Aidui and the Sequani. Ruscino, which may have received its Phoenician name at about this time, was no doubt to have been the chief centre for this trade. In any case, it was at this time that Carthaginian trade carried as far afield as Switzerland the glass masks which provide the only archaeological evidence of trade relations between the Celts and the Carthaginians.

The Romans did not fail to draw the moral of Hannibal's plans. As early as 147 B.C., Scipio requested Polybius to investigate, in addition to the Moroccan gold route, the possibility of bringing tin across the Bay of Biscay. Carcopino has shown how the Marseillais, who had no desire to see a revival of this form of competition, managed to turn to account the unfavourable opinion of Pytheas held by this famous Achaean man of letters to persuade him to break off the expedition before it reached Armorica. It was no doubt too late in any case by this time, to resuscitate a trade route which had already received a fatal blow half a century earlier, when the Romans captured its Spanish outlet. The foundation of Narbonne in 121 B.C. was perhaps inspired by the memory of Hannibal's economic projects. But these were not effectively realized under the Roman aegis until 57 and 56 B.C. when Caesar and his legate Crassus managed to overcome all the obstacles which the Armorican sailors put in the way of a trade route, certainly very profitable for the shippers in Bordeaux and Narbonne, but which was ruinous for them.

ATLANTIC VOYAGES

There remains to be considered those aspects of Carthaginian navigation which suggest the most tempting possibilities to the modern mind. Did the Phoenicians, who were masters of the Pillars of Hercules and of the ports in Southern Spain from which Columbus sailed, ever venture farther out in the Atlantic

Ocean than the waters around the coasts of Europe? In line 380 and onwards of his poem, Avienus summarizes a passage from Himilco's narrative which deals with the perils of the ocean wastes.

'Towards the west, as far as the eye can see, stretches the boundless deep. No one has ever sailed upon these waters, none has ever risked his ships there, for not a single breath of wind from Heaven blows towards the open sea. The air is, as it were, clothed in a mantle of mist, a perpetual fog shrouds the deep, and the light of day is cut off by clouds.'

This passage revives the question of the reality of these ocean perils. In order to answer it, let us consider the few discoveries which may be attributed to the Carthaginians beyond the Pillars of Hercules.

Mention has already been made of a tradition culled by Diodorus of Sicily from the work of the historian Timeus of Taormina.[87] According to this story, a great island rose from the ocean, west of Libya, an enchanted spot, a dwelling-place fit for gods rather than for men. The mountains were covered with dense forests; all kinds of fruit-bearing trees grew wild beside plentiful and abundant springs of cool water. The wide plains were crossed by navigable rivers. The inhabitants led a life of plenty, tilling their gardens, fishing and hunting. In winter they lived in good solid houses, and in summer they moved to charming country-dwellings surrounded by gardens. Moreover, the climate was always temperate and the earth gave of its fruit all through the year. Some Phoenicians from Gades were one day driven there by a storm as they were sailing along the Libyan coast. When the Etruscans heard of this discovery from the people of Gades, they wanted to found a colony in this wonderful land. But the Carthaginians opposed the idea, and even refused to allow their own people to go there, lest Africa should be deserted in favour of such a very fertile country. However, they were anxious to keep it in reserve, in case any disaster should befall them in Africa.

A document wrongly attributed to Aristotle repeats this story almost word for word,[88] adding, however, that some Carthaginians did settle there. But the Carthaginian government forbade further emigration there, under pain of death, and even suppressed those who had already gone there, for fear lest a colony so greatly favoured by natural advantages, should become powerful enough to constitute a threat to Carthage itself.

There is obviously a good deal of legend about these stories. We have already mentioned the effects of an ancient prophecy concerning the destinies of Carthage which doubtless foretold a fresh emigration towards the West. If these hopes had any solid foundation, it would be most extraordinary if the Carthaginians never thought of fulfilling them when they saw themselves condemned to death by Rome. On the other hand, the belief that a marvellous land existed in the midst of the ocean was widely held by all the people of antiquity, and in particular by the Celtic tribes. There would have been nothing surprising if the Carthaginians had found such a haven in Spain. The reasons usually given why a people so eminently practical as the Carthaginians gave up any attempt to make use of this rich land, appear at first sight almost puerile. Yet one does get the impression that the Carthaginians had at their disposal more territories than they could find people to colonize them with. Hanno's great effort to establish Punic settlements along the Moroccan coast seems to have exhausted the human resources available to the Republic. As for the people of Gades, they were not sufficiently reliable allies to be entrusted with vast wealth. The policy of voluntary sterility which both Diodorus and Hanno attributed to the Carthaginian government was probably not without foundation.

Although the people of Gades were kept away from the Happy Isles, they did not forget how to reach them. In 80 B.C. when the exiled Sertorius sought refuge among them, they offered to take him there. It can therefore be assumed that they, and the Carthaginians, had visited the Madeira archipelago, whose situation agrees with that given by Diodorus.[89] But in any case they never settled there permanently.

The Canary Islands, which are farther south, but nearer Africa, were better known by the ancients, who called them the 'Fortunate Isles'.

One of the permanent mysteries of human history remains the prehistoric voyage to the Canaries by men of the African tribe of Mechta el Arbi, the ancestors of the Guanches.[90] We have seen that King Juba II's fleet reached the Canaries at the beginning of the Christian era.[91] They found the archipelago deserted. These Mauretanian sailors first visited the Rainy Island: they found no sign of habitation, but only a pool surrounded by mountains, and trees which looked like giant fennel, whose sap was drinkable. On the Island of Juno, probably so named in honour of Tanit, they found only a stone hut; another small island was also dedicated to this goddess. On the Isle of Goats, they found nothing but giant lizards.

Next they landed on Ninguaria, so named because of its high snow-capped mountain perpetually shrouded in cloud. And finally they reached the largest island, called Canaria, from the Latin *canis*, because the sailors captured enormous dogs there. Here they found ruined buildings. Although all the islands had fruit trees, this was the only one on which date palms grew. The forests were full of birds and bees. Sheat-fish swam in the streams where papyrus grew. The beaches were noisome with the stench of dead marine animals washed up by the waves.

These islands seem to correspond with the western part of the archipelago: the Rainy Island is what we call Lanzarota; the Isle of Goats is Fuerteventura, the island nearest Africa; Ninguaria with its high mountain is Teneriffe and Canaria the Canary Island. The three western islands remained undiscovered. The natives must have hidden at the approach of the boats which seem to have stayed there only for short periods.

As well as revealing the possibilities within the reach of the Punic navy, Juba II's account shows the precarious nature of the results it actually achieved. The ruins found on the Canary Island were doubtless those of the Punic settlement, but evidently what could have become a flourishing colony remained simply a chance port of call for sailors needing a rest, such as may still be found on the deserted islands of the Southern Hemisphere. If there had been a proper Carthaginian colony in the Canaries, it would have made its influence felt on the Guanches, but even as late as the fifteenth century A.D. this tribe had still not discovered the use of metal.

Madeira and the Canaries are the only ocean lands which we know with any certainty that the Carthaginians visited.[92] The Greeks often used their fertile imagination to romance about the mysterious Far West. Some of their efforts at first sight seem fairly convincing: thus a certain Marcellus[93] who lived before the fourth century A.D. wrote a book about Ethiopia in which he speaks of two ocean archipelagos, one consisting of three islands, the centre one dedicated to Poseidon. Its inhabitants cherished the memory of a vast island whose fleets had dominated the whole ocean for a very long time. The other archipelago had seven islands and may have been the Canaries. But it has not been possible to identify Poseidon's island, unless it was Madeira; but in any case it is most unlikely that Marcellus could have discovered the traditions of its inhabitants.

The most famous of all these Greek romances is Plato's *Atlantis*.

Although this is a much more serious work, it nevertheless belongs to the same category as Lucian's *True Story*. Lucian's heroes venture into the Atlantic and find a Cheese Island and an Island of·Human Vines; they are then swallowed like Jonah by a gigantic whale, within whose belly they wage epic battles with savages. This is far removed from the Carthaginians whose sea-dogs may have allowed themselves to spin a few bragging yarns to startle the land-lubbers, but whose admirals were quite capable, as we have seen, of drawing up serious restrained accounts in which there are fewer extraordinary incidents than are to be found, say, in the log of Christopher Columbus.

It would seem pointless to add that the Western Phoenicians, who never bothered to establish permanent colonies in Madeira and the Canaries, could not possibly have discovered America. But this hypothesis has been put forward by a number of publications which claim to popularize scientific discoveries for the benefit of the lay public. It is, of course, not entirely impossible for a boat to have set out into the Atlantic from Europe or Spain and to have been swept by the trade-winds as far as the Gulf of Mexico. However, it may be stated quite categorically that no expedition was ever organized to explore what lay on the far side of the Atlantic. It is also quite certain that if any luckless crew was driven on to the American coast, they must have perished without any hope of return, and certainly without any possibility of organizing a new life for themselves in the unknown world into which they had been cast.

To sum up, the achievements of the Carthaginian navigators

must be neither under-estimated, nor exaggerated. Overland, thanks to the unifying activities of the Libyans in the Sahara, they were able to cross practically the entire width of the African continent and to reach territories round the River Niger which Europeans reached with great difficulty only in the nineteenth century. On the high seas, the accounts of Hanno and of Juba's admirals, which confirm each other, prove that the Phoenician pilots in the West were quite capable of surmounting difficulties, which throughout the Middle Ages limited the Arab expeditions to Cape Bojador, and which in the fifteenth century took the Portuguese seventy years to overcome. But these adventurous voyages remained isolated exploits, which, at the most, were to secure some commercial advantages for the Republic. Especially in the West, Carthage seems to have suffered from the fact that she could not produce enough men capable of exploiting the newly discovered territories nor of converting them into bases from which to launch fresh enterprises. The main cause of this failure, as of so many others, was the narrow and selfish policy of its oligarchy which persistently refused to broaden the political and social system which had become too narrow for the tasks it was called upon to face, and because, in addition, they could not rely upon the co-operation of their allies whose interests, however legitimate, they subordinated to their own selfish greed.

REFERENCES

1. E. F. Gautier, *Le Passé de l'Afrique du Nord*, Ch. II.
2. J. Carcopino, *Le Maroc antique*, p. 18.
3. Cf. our *Castellum Dimmidi*, pp. 22 sqq.
4. 'La Tripolitaine et le Sahara au IIIe s.', *Mém Aca. des. insc.*, XLIII, 1.
5. *Le Sahara*, pp. 134 sqq.
6. Lastly, Ch. Courtois, *Les Vandales et l'Afrique*, pp. 98 sqq.
7. H. Lhote, 'Le cheval et le chameau dans les peintures et gravures rupestres du Sahara', *Bull. Hist. Fr. Afr. Nord*, XV, 1953.
8. R. Mauny, *Bull. Inst. Fr. Afr. Noire*, 1948, p. 176.
9. By far the most important are those of the Italian archaeologists, in Fezzan: B. Pace, S. Sergi, G. Caputo, 'Scavi Sahariani', *Mon. Antichi*, XLVI, 1951.

10. IV, 183.
11. Bibliography in the article of H. Lhote quoted *supra*, n. 7.
12. It must, however, be recognized that numerous Greek legends (Lotus-eaters, Gorgons, etc.) are localized in the region of Lake Triton, that is to say, at the end of the Gulf of Gabes, which has easy communications with the Fezzan. But the possibility of drawing any historical conclusions from such traditions remains extremely doubtful. F. Chamoux, *Cyrene*, who was the last to study the question, rejects the possibility of any Greeks coming to Libya before the foundation of Cyrene in 631.
13. They are, however, in a different style; R. Mauny, *op. cit.*, 1947, pp. 341 sqq.
14. XVII, 3, 7.
15. H. Lhote, *op. cit.*, p. 1225.
16. S. Gsell, HAAN, I, p. 301.
17. MC, pl. 3.
18. I Kings x, 22.
19. Strabo, *op. cit.*
20. Evidence collected by S. Gsell, HAAN, I, p. 109, n. 1.
21. X. Eliaenus, *Variae*, XIV, 90; Pliny, VIII, 35. The story of the tame lion is perhaps less absurd than Gsell says, II, p. 190. To hunt and keep wild beasts, especially lions, has always been a royal privilege in the East.
22. Especially that of Hippo, E. Marec, *Hippo*, fig. 12, which dates from the middle of the fourth century.
23. MC, pl. 40.
24. P. Cintas, *Céramique punique*, pl. LXIX, 235.
25. Reproduced by X. Eliaenus, *Nat. animalium*, Pliny, Plutarch, and others. Ref. in S. Gsell, HAAN, VIII, pp. 262–5.
26. *Banquet des Sophistes*, II, 44 d. Cf. J. Leclant, 'Per Africa Sitientia', *Bull. Inst. Fr. Arch., Or.*, XLIX, 1950, p. 208.
27. J. H. Reynolds and J. B. Ward Perkins, *Inscriptions of Roman Tripolitania*, p. 273.
27a. III, 256.
28. IV, 131. A much-annotated text, the latest version is by J. Leclant (p. 26) and Rhys Carpenter, *Am. Journ. Arch.*, LX, 3, 1956, pp. 231 sqq. We have used S. Gsell's translation, *Hérodote et l'Afrique*, pp. 18 sqq.
29. C. Levi-Strauss, *Tristes Tropiques*, p. 294.
30. H. Lhote, *op. cit.*, pp. 1167 sqq.
31. Pliny, V, 37.
32. Ptolemy, I, 8.

33. *Pun.*, III, 8–13.
34. VIII, 11, 11. On the validity of these proofs, denied by S. Gsell, cf. J. Leclant, *op. cit.*, p. 208, n. 1, and pp. 240–3.
35. S. Gsell, HAAN, IV, pp. 281 sqq.
36. We owe this information to M. J. Leclant, to whom we offer our sincere thanks.
37. The use of Garamant soldiers in the Carthaginian armies, especially by Hannibal, was invented by Silius Italicus, according to a procedure common in classical epics. M. H. Lhote, *op. cit.*, p. 1178, is therefore wrong in considering it to be historical.
38. B. Pace, S. Sergi, G. Caputo, *op. cit.* (*supra*, nn. 4, 9).
39. *Op. cit.*, fig. 12, no. 33.
40. Or rather the anthropomorphic signs of Tanit found on the neo-Punic stelae, the painting of which is doubtless contemporary.
41. Ptolemy, I, 8.
42. Livy, XXIV, 62–3 and the commentary of S. Gsell, HAAN, II, p. 319.
43. S. Aurigemma, *Mosaic di Zliten*. The date has been wrongly challenged.
44. G. Ch.-Picard, *Karthago*, II, p. 105.
45. Ammianus Marcellinus, XXVIII, 6. Cf. R. Bartoccini, *Quaderni di Arch. della Libia*, I, 1950, pp. 29–35.
46. S. Gsell, 'La Tripolitaine et le Sahara au IIIe s.', *Mém. Aca. des inscr.*, XLIII, 1. Many recent articles have been devoted to this question, the last by O. Brogan, 'The Camel in Roman Tripolitania', *Pap. Br. Sc. of Rome*, XXII, 1954, pp. 126 sqq. E.-W. Brill, 'The Camel and the Garamants', *Antiquity*, 1956, pp. 117–18. The camel seems to have been used in Tripolitania earlier than Gsell thought; he attributed its widespread use to Septimius Severus. The Tigi relief, published by Brogan, probably goes back to the first half of the second century. It bears a definite likeness to that of Henchir Beni Guedal (*Catalogue Mus. Alaoui, Suppl.* II, pl. IX). The technique of the incised line surrounding the relief is also found on monuments of the first century A.D. in the South of France (Arch in Orange): the ears of corn which figure on the short side of the sculptured block of stone resemble those of the reverse of Nerva's coinage (Mattingley-Sydenham, *Roman Imp. Coinage*, II). It is certain that the Hadrumetum figurines which represent camel-drivers, are the products of local industry. To the list of mosaics given by Brogan, we may add that of Thuburbo Majus (MC, pl. 41), interesting because the camel-drivers are Negroes, but it is not anterior to the second

half of the fourth century A.D. K. Johannenburg, 'Die Cameliden um Altertum', *Bonn. Jahrbuch*, 155–6, 1955–6, pp. 54 sqq. contribute nothing new concerning Africa.

47. J. Leclant, *op. cit.*

48. R. Mauny, *Rev. Et. Anc.*, LVIII, 1955, pp. 92 sqq.

49. P. Montet, *La vie quotidienne en Égypte*, pp. 180 sqq. Cf. S. Gsell, I, pp. 508–9.

50. IV, 40 sqq.

51. S. Gsell, HAAN, I, p. 509.

52. H. Breuil, CRAI, 1946, p. 203.

53. Herodotus, IV, 43.

54. Bibliography in Aubrey Diller, 'The traditions of the Minor Greek Geographers', *Phililog. Monographs*, XIV, 1952. Since then, beside the articles of R. Mauny, there have been published the following by J.-J. de Jarreguy, 'Las Islas de Canarias, y la carrera del oro y la porporo en el periplo de Hannon', *Actes du Ier Congrès Arch. du Maroc Espagnol*, which we have not been able to consult.

55. Article quoted above n. 46, and *Première Conf. des Afr. de l'Ouest*, II, 1951, pp. 109 sqq.

56. We cannot believe, with J. Carcopino, that each penteconter could have carried 500 men; this figure represents the maximum number which could be carried by a quinquereme. There must in fact be a definite ratio between the tonnage of the ships and the motive power, i.e. the rowers. A quinquireme with 275 rowers could not carry more than 200 passengers, and a penteconter could not have carried more than 40.

57. Pliny, VI, 202. Cf. Vidal de la Blache, *Mél. Perrot*, p. 328 and S. Gsell, HAAN, VIII, pp. 256–7.

58. Cf. with the same interpretation as ours, R. Thouvenot, *Rev. Et.Anc.*, XXXIV, 1956, p. 88.

59. Pp. 72–163.

60. I, 39, 5.

61. IV, 196.

62. Quoted by E. F. Gautier, 'L'Or du Soudan', *Ann. Hist. Écon. et Soc.*, 1935, pp. 118 sqq., from Monteil, *Bull. A.O.F.*, 1929, p. 336. J. Carcopino, *op. cit.*, p. 108.

63. Pliny, X, 22.

64. 69.

65. The Greek geographer has no doubt confused what the Phoenicians brought with what their customers brought.

66. As C. Jullian thinks, in *Hist. de la Gaule*, I, p. 245.

67. Pliny, V, 9–10.
68. We know about it from the fifth book of Pliny, who had made use of the lost twenty-fourth book of Polybius; cf. J. Carcopino, *op. cit.*, p. 159. For an opposite view, see R. Thouvenot, *Hesperis*, 1948, pp. 1 sqq. He thinks that Polybius reached Senegal. It is, however, difficult to believe that in the course of a single summer the fleet led by the historian could have visited in turn Senegal and the Loire.
69. Their report is the basis of Pliny's information, V, 51–3. For the interpretation of this text, cf. our *Castellum Dimmidi*, pp. 25 sqq.
70. M. Reygasse, *Monuments funéraires préislamiques de l'Afrique du Nord*, pp. 88 sqq.
71. E. F. Gautier, *Le Sahara*, p. 56, has insisted on the recent appearance of the palm groves of the Western Sahara. Those in Southern Tunisia, on the other hand, go back to farthest antiquity: cf. *supra*, pp. 90–1. The bas-relief of Béja, which depicts the Libyan gods on their thrones before an oasis (our *Les Religions de l'Afrique antique*, fig. 23), proves that for Africans, although they were settled in the middle of a fertile grain-growing region, the palm grove remained the symbol of a paradise of wealth and happiness.
72. We are using the annotated edition of A. Berthelot, Paris, 1934, in preference to that of A. Schulten, *Fontes Hispaniae Antiquae*, I; see the work of A. Berthelot, pp. 14–15, the relevant bibliography.
73. Pliny, II, 169.
74. R. Dion, *Latomus*, XI, 1952, p. 309. The Oestrymnides Islands are often identified with Ouessant or the Scilly Isles (S. Gsell, HAAN, I, p. 470, with bibliography; C. Jullian, *op. cit.*, p. 387). A.Berthelot thinks they are the whole of the British Isles. In any case the description of Avienus, *insulas . . . late jacentes*, cannot be applied to mere islets.
75. Unless we see in this (which seems very unlikely) a relic of an extension of Megalithic civilization beyond Portugal (cf. R. Thouvenot, *Essai sur la province romaine de Bétique*, 1940, pp. 34–5).
76. Himilco is said to have spent four months here. Pytheas, on the other hand, crossed the Bay of Biscay in three days (Strabo, I, 4, 5, as quoted by Eratosthenes).
77. Text of Strabo, XVII, 1, 19, often quoted.
78. S. Gsell, HAAN, I, p. 471, n. 8. According to the *De mirabilibus*

auscultationibus, 136, the masses of sea-weed were encountered four days west of Gades, which would correspond roughly to eight or nine hundred miles, and to between fifteen and twenty degrees of longitude.

79. On the attribution to Pytheas of the information transmitted, according to Timaeus, by Diodorus, V, 22, and Pliny, cf. J. Carcopino, *Promenades historiques au pays de la Dame de Vix*, Paris, 1957.

80. *Bel. Gal.*, III, 13.

81. R. J. Forbes, *Metallurgy in Antiquity*, pp. 241–3, according to M. Cary, 'The Greeks and the ancient trade with the Atlantic', *Journ. of Hell. Studies*, XLIII, 1923, p. 166.

82. *Journal of Royal Society of Antiquaries of Ireland*, LXXXIII, 2, 1953, p. 198.

83. Cf. J. M. de Navarro, *Camb. Anc. Hist.*, VIII, p. 52.

84. HAAN, IV, pp. 103–4.

85. *Supra*, p. 104.

85a.C. Jullian, *op. cit.*

86. *Promenades historiques au pays de la Dame de Vix*, pp. 35 sqq.

87. V, 19–20.

88. *De mirabilibus auscultationibus*, 84.

89. Mme de Boucher-Colozier suggests identifying this with Cerne, which is not in accordance with the information given in the text.

90. Cf. L. Balout, *Préhistoire de l'Afrique du Nord*, p. 482.

91. Pliny, VI, 202. Cf. S. Gsell, HAAN, VIII, pp. 256 sqq.

92. It is not absolutely impossible for them to have reached the Azores: the *De mirabilibus auscultationibus* speaks of a voyage four days west of Gades, which corresponds to a distance of eight to nine hundred miles and to just over three hundred miles west of the archipelago. The masses of sea-weed noticed by the Greek geographer doubtless correspond to the Sargasso Sea, which today begins at about thirty degrees of longitude West (but its limits have varied: cf. S. Gsell, HAAN, I, p. 471, n. 8). Cf. *supra*, p. 172.

93. *Frag. Hist. Graec.*, IV, 443; cf. S. Gsell, HAAN, I, p. 328, n. 2.

CHAPTER IX

CONCLUSION

As the reader closes this book, he may perhaps think somewhat wistfully of Salammbô. There, through Flaubert's eyes, he will have seen, with the vagueness of a dream, something of a magnificent, if barbarous, civilization. In place of this, we have offered the tangible, if sordid remains, of a prosaic city of shopkeepers. Even the impression of a strange remote world, which is so powerfully evoked in the novel, evaporates rapidly in the presence of a legacy of remains, which, apart from a few provincial peculiarities, are only distinguishable from Greek and Roman remains by their extreme mediocrity. A century of historical and archaeological research has cast a pitiless light into the empty void which Flaubert found in searching the records of the past for memories of Carthage, and which only his great talent succeeded in hiding.

However, we would ask the reader to overcome his feeling of disappointment and to consider dispassionately the balance-sheet of Carthage which we have tried to draw up. It is an austere one, but not so adverse as it seems at first sight. The sterility of Punic art is beyond question, and it is no use trying to excuse it by the catastrophe of 146 B.C. It springs, as we have shown, from the very character of the Phoenician people. If the visitor to the Louvre looks closely at the treasures brought back from Ras Shamra by C. Schaeffer, he will realize that they were the work of a nation obliged, from its earliest infancy, to subordinate the techniques of its craftsmen, who were often extremely skilled, to aesthetic conception borrowed haphazard, according to the current state of commercial relations, from the banks of the Nile, the Euphrates, or of the Aegean.

However, as soon as we turn from art to politics or religion, the impression of feebleness gives way to one of astonishing vitality. Even in this respect, Carthage obviously suffers from the lack of evidence available. If its sacred book had been written on tablets of clay which the flames would have made more durable, instead of on scrolls which they consumed; or if they had been fossilized in the sands like many papyri from Egypt or Palestine; or if they had been piously handed down like the Jewish Bible, through the miraculous escape from annihilation of some of the faithful, then we should certainly be able to experience again the nobility and creative imagination which we find in the Ugarit epic.

We can at least measure the strength of Carthage by the length of time her influence lasted in Africa, in spite of a most brutal catastrophe. The evidence of St Augustine proves that in the fifth century A.D. the peasants round Hippo Regius still spoke Phoenician and knew that they were distant heirs of Canaan; they were overjoyed to find in the Bible a reminder of their own ancestral traditions. Throughout the period of the Roman Empire, although Barbary was conquered by the Latin tongue and remained firmly loyal to Rome, it still remained spiritually an Oriental province. Baal and Tanit were still worshipped. When, towards the end of the second century A.D., the city-dwellers presented these deities in the likeness of Saturn and Heavenly Juno, the humblest of the devotees of Tanit and Baal still continued to crowd into the churches and synagogues. E. Renan, S. Gsell and E. F. Gautier have all put forward the view that the rapid spread of Islam in the Mahgreb in the seventh and eighth centuries was accomplished in so short a time, because the ancient Oriental traditions brought by Dido still lingered in the hearts of the people. Even if philologists have not succeeded in identifying any traces of Phoenician dialects in the Arabic spoken in the Mahgreb, it remains true that thanks to the Carthaginian tradition, Barbary feels more affinity with Asia than with Europe, in spite of the latter's geographical proximity. The influence of Carthage must therefore be counted as a contributory cause of one of the most dramatic problems still tormenting humanity today.

The intense vitality of the Punic race was displayed most of all in its individual citizens. In spite of the obscurity of its earliest traditions and the fanciful mythology which surrounds them, and in spite of the barren inadequacy of the meagre historical narratives which have been handed down by clumsy copiers, we can still form a clear picture of the men and women of Carthage, struggling and suffering, from the time the first humble trading-post was established there, to the long-drawn-out agony of the final siege. Poets and novelists have been more sensitive to this human aspect of Punic history than have historians. Long before Flaubert, Virgil was inspired by Dido's sacrifice, and Corneille by Sophonisba's devotion. Naturally enough, none of these writers was concerned with producing a historical work. For them reality provided only situations, and they created their characters in accordance with their own psychological and aesthetic principles. Nevertheless, the intensely dramatic history of the Western Phoenicians is a fact. Even the most insensitive person could scarcely read Gsell's restrained account of the Third Punic War, without sharing the anguish and the despairing reversals of hope suffered by the unfortunate citizens of Carthage condemned by the cold remorseless cruelty of the Roman Senate to an inevitable death. The pathos springs not from chance, nor from the particularly difficult situation of living in a city surrounded on all sides by enemies and Barbarians; but from the great contrast between the indomitable energy of the people of Carthage, which enabled their traders, explorers, and soldiers to display initiative, courage, and audacity, and the stifling hold of their despotic social system and their cruel inhuman religion.

The passionate intensity of feeling which characterized the Carthaginians compensates for their ineptitude in the plastic arts. It also explains why a civilization which is so unrewarding to the archaeologist, may yet capture the interest of the writer and provide the material from which his imagination can create an escapist world of fantasy. *Salammbô* is no manual of archaeology; but perhaps in evoking the spirit of Hamilcar's daughter, Flaubert was able to enter into some kind of communion with the soul of Carthage in a way which will always remain beyond the reach of the conscientious researches of the historian.

BIBLIOGRAPHY

We have given a critical bibliography of Carthage in our *Monde de Carthage* (referred to as MC).

The essential work is still the *Histoire ancienne de l'Afrique du Nord*, by STÉPHANE GSELL, Volumes I–IV, Hachette, Paris, 1912–29 (referred to as HAAN).

Extracts from the following works and periodicals are also quoted:

G. CONTENAU, *Manuel d'Archéologie orientale*, A. Picard, Paris, 1927–47: MAO.

Comptes Rendus de l'Académie des Inscriptions et Belles-Lettres: CRAI.

Bulletin archéologique du Comité des travaux historiques et scientifiques: BAC.

INDEX